CHURCHILL'S
FIRST WAR

CON COUGHLIN

CHURCHILL'S
FIRST WAR

Young Winston and the Fight Against the Taliban

MACMILLAN

First published 2013 by Macmillan
an imprint of Pan Macmillan, a division of Macmillan Publishers Limited
Pan Macmillan, 20 New Wharf Road, London N1 9RR
Basingstoke and Oxford
Associated companies throughout the world
www.panmacmillan.com

ISBN 978-0-230-75851-3 HB
ISBN 978-0-230-76888-8 TPB

Every effort has been made to contact the copyright holders of the material
reproduced in this book. If any have been inadvertently overlooked, the publishers
will be pleased to make restitution at the earliest opportunity.

Picture Acknowledgements
1, 2, 3: Mary Evans Picture Library. 4, 6, 7, 8, 9, 13, 14, 15: Getty Images.
5: Bridgeman Art Library. 10, 16, 25, 26, 27, 28, 29, 30: By courtesy of the author.
11, 12: By kind permission of the National Army Museum. 17: Topfoto.
18, 19, 20, 21, 22, 23, 24: By kind permission of H.S.L. Tottenham.
31: Churchill Archives Centre, Churchill College.

1 3 5 7 9 8 6 4 2

A CIP catalogue record for this book is available from the British Library.

Map artwork by ML Design
Typeset by SetSystems Ltd, Saffron Walden, Essex
Printed and bound by CPI Group (UK) Ltd, Croydon, CR0 4YY

Visit **www.panmacmillan.com** to read more about all our books
and to buy them. You will also find features, author interviews and
news of any author events, and you can sign up for e-newsletters
so that you're always first to hear about our new releases.

IN MEMORY OF

JOHN KEEGAN
(1934–2012)

FRIEND AND MENTOR

Contents

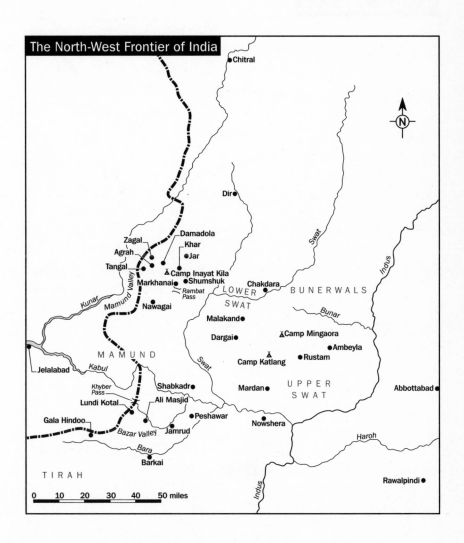

The North-West Frontier of India

Chitral

Dir

Damadola
Zagal
Khar
Agrah
Jar
Tangal
Camp Inayat Kila
Markhanai
Shumshuk
Chakdara
LOWER
SWAT
BUNERWALS
Rambat
Pass
Kunar
Mamund Valley
Nawagai
Bunar
Malakand
Swat
Indus
Dargai
Camp Mingaora
MAMUND
Camp Katlang
Ambeyla
Rustam
Jelalabad
Kabul
Khyber
Pass
Shabkadr
UPPER
SWAT
Abbottabad
Lundi Kotal
Ali Masjid
Mardan
Gala Hindoo
Peshawar
Bazar Valley
Jamrud
Nowshera
Bara
Haroh
Barkai
TIRAH
Indus
Rawalpindi

0   10   20   30   40   50 miles

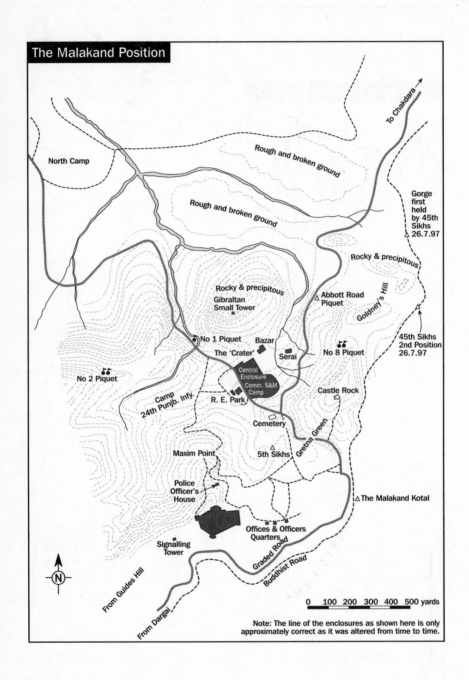

The Malakand Position

North Camp

Rough and broken ground

Rough and broken ground

To Chakdara

Gorge
first
held
by 45th
Sikhs
26.7.97

Rocky & precipitous

Rocky & precipitous
Gibraltan
Small Tower

Abbott Road
Piquet

Goldney's Hill

45th Sikhs
2nd Position
26.7.97

No 1 Piquet

Bazar

The 'Crater'

Serai

No 8 Piquet

No 2 Piquet

Central
Enclosure
Comm. S&M
Camp

Camp
24th Punjb. Infy.

R. E. Park

Castle Rock

Cemetery

Maxim Point

5th Sikhs

Gretna Green

Police
Officer's
House

△ The Malakand Kotal

Offices & Officers
Quarters

Signalling
Tower

Graded Road

Buddhist Road

From Guides Hill

From Dargai

N

0   100 200 300 400 500 yards

Note: The line of the enclosures as shown here is only
approximately correct as it was altered from time to time.

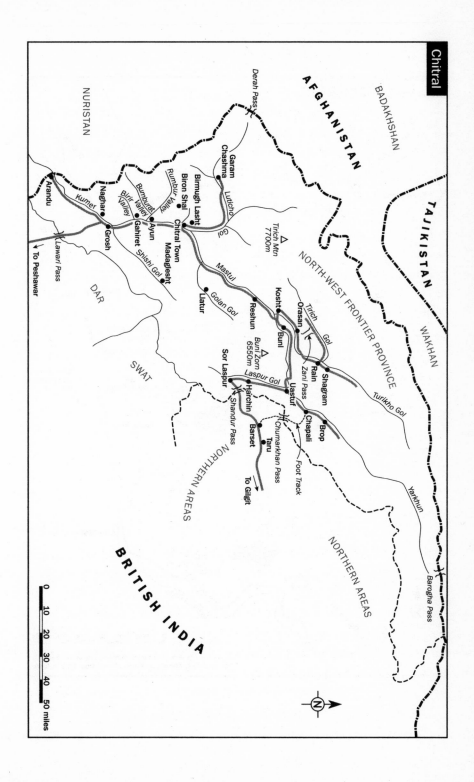

BADAKHSHAN

AFGHANISTAN

TAJIKISTAN

NURISTAN

WAKHAN

Derah Pass

Garam
Chashma

Lutkho Gol

Arandu

Naghar

Kun: r

Bumburet

Birir Valley

Rumbur Valley

Biron Shal

Birmugh Lasht

Chitral Town

Madaglasht

Ayun

Gahiret

Shishi Gol

Grosh

To Peshawar

Lawari Pass

DAR

SWAT

Liatur

Golan Gol

Mastuj

Reshun

Kosht

Buni

Tirich Mtn
7770m

Tirich Gol

NORTH-WEST FRONTIER PROVINCE

Orasan

Rain

Zani Pass

Shagram

Turikho Gol

Buni Zom
6550m

Laspur Gol

Sor Laspur

Harchin

Barset

Taru

Uastur

Chapali

Brop

Chumarkhan Pass

Foot Track

Yarkhun

Shandur Pass

NORTHERN AREAS

To Gilgit

NORTHERN AREAS

BRITISH INDIA

Barogha Pass

0

10

20

30

40

50 miles

N

Prologue

'Nothing in life is so exhilarating as to be shot at without result.'
Winston S. Churchill, *The Story of the Malakand Field Force*

On the outskirts of the old British fort at Malakand, there is a cemetery where the bodies of young officers who died fighting for Queen and Country in a hostile outpost of the British Empire were laid to rest. Throughout the course of the nineteenth century, thousands of British soldiers lost their lives fighting the warlike tribesmen who inhabited the forbidding mountain ranges that lay between Afghanistan and the North-West Frontier of the Indian Empire. And it was here, in 1897, that Winston Churchill, as a twenty-two-year-old subaltern in the British cavalry, fought in the first of the many wars he would experience throughout the course of his long and eventful life.

For nearly six weeks Churchill risked life and limb fighting against the frontier's rebellious Pashtun tribesmen, and on several occasions came close to being killed, or at the very least suffering serious injury. He was involved in at least three 'sharp skirmishes', and at times the fighting was so intense that the tribesmen were able to throw rocks at him when they ran out of bullets. In all, as Churchill later boasted to his mother, he came under fire '10 complete times', and received a mention in dispatches for his bravery. Despite putting himself at risk on several occasions, Churchill survived the ordeal, but many of the other young British officers who fought at his side were not so lucky, and their remains today lie in the old British cemetery beside the fort where Churchill was based.

Among the officers buried at Malakand is Second Lieutenant William Browne-Clayton of the Royal West Kent Regiment, who was killed on 30 September 1897. During his stay at Malakand Churchill became close friends with the Eton-educated Browne-Clayton, who was two years older than him and came from a prosperous family of Irish landowners. The two young officers were involved in an operation to clear hostile tribesmen from a village close to the Afghan border when Browne-Clayton was shot as he attempted to organize the withdrawal of his men, who were in danger of being overrun by the enemy. He died instantly when the bullet struck his heart, and his death had a profound effect on Churchill. *The Times* reported the skirmish in which Browne-Clayton died by printing a telegram sent by Lord Elgin, the Viceroy of India, to London, which reported matter-of-factly: 'Enemy made considerable resistance and troops, being hotly engaged at close quarters, suffered some loss.'[1]

As a young man, Churchill did not believe he was prone to overt displays of emotion, but Browne-Clayton's death hit him hard. In Churchill's later account of the campaign, he simply states the facts: 'Lieutenant Browne-Clayton remained till the last, to watch the withdrawal, and in so doing was shot dead, the bullet severing the blood-vessels near his heart.'[2] But in a letter home, written a few months after the fighting finished, he tells how he broke down in tears when he saw Browne-Clayton's body being removed from the battlefield on the back of a mule. 'I very rarely detect genuine emotion in myself,' he wrote. 'I must rank as a rare instance the fact that I cried when I met the Royal West Kents on the 30th Sept. and saw the men really unsteady under fire and tired of the game, and that poor young officer Browne-Clayton, literally cut to pieces on a stretcher – through his men not having stood by him.'[3] Had it not been for Churchill's own good fortune, he could easily have suffered a similar fate. At times during the fighting he said the tribesmen's bullets missed him by only a foot. Had they hit their target Churchill, like his friend Browne-Clayton, would lie today in some remote and forgotten grave, barely remembered. The world would have been denied one of its greatest wartime leaders, and the history of the twentieth century may well have taken a different course.

The Malakand campaign was the war that made Churchill's name. Before volunteering to join the punitive expedition of the Malakand Field Force on the North-West Frontier of India, Churchill was known as the impoverished son of a maverick British politician, though he traced his descent from the Duke of Marlborough, one of Britain's greatest warriors. An indifferent pupil at school who only narrowly managed – at the third attempt – to pass the entrance examination to the Royal Military College at Sandhurst, young Winston's prospects hardly looked promising. Nor were they improved when his father, Lord Randolph Churchill, died of syphilis shortly after Winston celebrated his twentieth birthday. Despite these disadvantages, Winston was determined from an early age to make a name for himself and pursue a career in politics. As a schoolboy, Winston had visited the Distinguished Strangers' Gallery at Westminster to hear Prime Minister William Gladstone, the 'Grand Old Man' of British politics, wind up the debate on the Home Rule Bill. The untimely death of Lord Randolph, which had cut short a political career that had once shown great promise, only strengthened his determination to succeed. No sooner had Churchill secured his commission to serve in the 4th (Queen's Own) Hussars, one of England's elite cavalry regiments, than he was thinking about how to secure the parliamentary seat that would launch his career in politics. Churchill believed that a distinguished military career was, for someone of his background and class, the perfect preparation for entering politics. Winning medals and decorations fighting for his country would enable him to 'beat my sword into an iron Despatch Box'. For Churchill, this was the perfect 'foundation for political life', after which he intended to 'devote my life to the preservation of this great Empire and to trying to maintain the progress of the English people'.[4]

Churchill's participation in the Malakand campaign laid the foundations for his future career in a number of ways. First and foremost, his decision to volunteer for duty on the Afghan border provided him with valuable combat experience. On various occasions he demonstrated courage under fire, winning the admiration of his commanding officers as well as an all-important mention in dispatches. General Sir Bindon Blood, the campaign commander, even suggested he might stand a chance of winning the much-coveted Victoria Cross. Churchill's successful campaign in Malakand resulted in him taking part in several more, including the Boer War, where his dramatic escape from captivity made him a household name, helping him to win his first seat as an MP for Oldham in 1900.

Apart from the military aspects, Churchill's brief interlude at Malakand was notable for other reasons. He wrote a series of articles on the conflict for the *Daily Telegraph*, which were well received in London, prompting the Prince of Wales to commend him for his 'great facility in writing'. The newspaper articles, moreover, resulted in Churchill receiving a commission to publish his first book, which appeared in March 1898 under the title *The Story of the Malakand Field Force: An Episode of Frontier War*. The critics reviewed the book favourably, with one describing it as an 'extremely interesting and well-written account'. Within weeks of publication, Churchill had received invitations to write biographies of his father and his great martial ancestor, the Duke of Marlborough, both of which he accomplished later in life. If all else failed, the future Nobel Prize-winning author believed he could 'supplement my income by writing'.[5] His experiences fighting on the North-West Frontier would feature prominently in his first autobiographical work, *My Early Life*, which was published more than thirty years later.

It was at Malakand that Churchill also discovered a lifelong fondness for whisky.

*

The Malakand campaign was a pivotal moment in Churchill's rise to greatness, which makes it all the more surprising that this period in his life tends to be overlooked. Churchill's exploits occupy a few pages of the major biographies, while Carl Foreman and Richard Attenborough's 1972 classic film, *Young Winston*, devotes only the opening frames to the young subaltern's hair-raising adventures fighting the 'fierce hill men' of the Afghan border, while the rest of the narrative concentrates on his more celebrated exploits in the Sudan and the Boer War. The film opens with a shot of Churchill astride a grey horse on a hilltop on the North-West Frontier.

'Who's that bloody fool on the grey?' asks the colonel.

'Someone who wants to be noticed, I imagine,' an officer replies.

'He'll be noticed – he'll get his bloody head blown off.'[6]

The neglect of this formative period in Churchill's life is partly because, compared with his later adventures in South Africa, Churchill was fighting for only a few weeks, and his role in the campaign was peripheral. Another consideration must be that the tale of his capture and subsequent escape from a prison camp in Pretoria is more compelling, especially in view of the effect it had on his political fortunes when Churchill, like Byron after publication of *Childe Harold's Pilgrimage*, awoke one morning to find himself famous. But Andrew Roberts, an eminent author on Churchill, believes the few weeks he spent on the North-West Frontier was the moment when his rise to greatness truly began. In Roberts's opinion, 'Churchill's participation in the Malakand Field Force is a neglected but fascinating period of his life, which formed his approach to war and laid the foundations of his path to political glory.'[7]

The revival of interest in Churchill's involvement with the Malakand Field Force began in the aftermath of the September 11 attacks of 2001, when a new generation of foreign soldiers found themselves returning to do battle in the daunting terrain of the Hindu Kush. The arrival of an American-led military coalition in Afghanistan in the autumn of 2001 followed the refusal of the Taliban government in Kabul to hand over Osama bin Laden, the head of the al-Qaeda network which was behind the September 11 attacks. The Taliban, led by Mullah Moham-med Omar, a radical cleric from the southern Afghan city of Kandahar, is an Islamic religious movement that originated among the Pashtun tribes that inhabit the mountainous border region between Afghanistan and Pakistan and which has con-trolled the North-West Frontier Province since the creation of Pakistan in 1947. Today the tribal areas where Churchill fought enjoy semi-autonomous status from the Pakistan government and are known as the Federally Administered Tribal Areas, or FATA. Mullah Omar's refusal to hand over bin Laden, who had been offered sanctuary in the Taliban's stronghold in southern Afghanistan, led to the coalition forces overthrowing the Taliban government and forcing Mullah Omar and his al-Qaeda allies to flee across the border to the tribal areas of Pakistan, where many of them sought refuge among the fiercely independent Pashtun tribes. Before long the Americans and their allies found themselves involved in a brutal conflict against the very same tribes that Winston Churchill had fought in the 1890s.

For the British army, which deployed to southern Afghan-istan in the summer of 2006, the feeling of déjà vu was even more intense, as soldiers arrived to fight in the same area where, more than a century before, their forebears had suffered one of their bloodiest defeats at the Battle of Maiwand in July 1880. Maiwand is situated fifty miles from Kandahar, Afghanistan's second city, and for many years the Taliban's headquarters. When the first British troops arrived as part of the NATO mission, they were pitched into some of the fiercest fighting experienced since the Second World War as the descendants of the tribesmen who had fought against Lord Roberts of Kandahar's troops in the nineteenth century attempted to inflict a similarly humiliating defeat. In the summer of 2009 General Sir David Richards, the newly appointed head of the British army, warned that the conflict in Afghanistan could last up to forty years.[8]

Like the British in the nineteenth century, America has acquired the unwelcome role of the world's policeman, and in that capacity it has been obliged to take the lead in the NATO operation to defeat the Taliban, eradicate al-Qaeda and bring peace and stability to Afghanistan, a country that has been involved in some form of conflict since the Soviet invasion of 1979. The technology available to American forces, particularly the introduction of unmanned aerial vehicles, or drones, is radically different from the more basic soldiering techniques employed by the Malakand Field Force, but the terrain and the targets remain much the same. If the Central Intelligence Agency, which directs many of the drone operations, were to draw up a map of the hundreds of drone strikes that have been launched against insurgent groups in the tribal areas, it would find that they were targeting virtually the same villages and valleys in the FATA area where Churchill and his colleagues fought more than one hundred years earlier. One of the most controversial American cross-border raids into Pakistan on 26 November 2011, when US aircraft killed twenty-four Pakistani soldiers during an attack on the border post of Salala, took place in exactly the same valley where William Browne-Clayton died in 1897.

Before 2001, *The Story of the Malakand Field Force* was out of print and largely forgotten, except by dedicated Churchill bibliophiles who were prepared to pay considerable sums for rare copies of Winston's first literary endeavour. But with the arrival of more than 100,000 foreign soldiers in Afghanistan, new editions were published as the finest military minds struggled to fathom the dynamics of the highly complex tribal revolt that confronted them. General Stanley McChrystal, the commander of US and NATO forces in Afghanistan until the summer of 2010, was said to listen to Churchill's account on his iPod during his daily eight-mile jog around the military base in Kabul. And General David Petraeus, who devised America's post-September 11 strategy for fighting counter-insurgency campaigns, said he drew on Churchill's account when writing the US army's new field manual which was published in December 2006.[9] A lifelong fan of Churchill, Petraeus, who became the CIA's director when he finished commanding NATO troops in Afghanistan in 2011, often took time out during trips to Britain to visit Churchill museums. He was keen, therefore, to learn from Churchill's experience when he devised his strategy for dealing with the Taliban. 'We captured the lessons of the British in the late nineteenth century in the field manual,' he explained. 'I am a great admirer of Winston Churchill, although what the British did in his book is not something you could do today.'[10]

Petraeus was referring to the British policy of burning villages to punish the tribes for rebelling against imperial rule, although there will be many who argue that the US drone strikes have inflicted just as much misery and hardship on the Pashtun communities. The different dynamics between the modern conflict and Churchill's experience were evident when I travelled to Pakistan in the autumn of 2012 to visit the area where operations of the Malakand Field Force took place. My first task was to persuade Pakistan's Inter-Service Intelligence (ISI) agency, which helped to create the Taliban movement and is said by many still to control it, to allow me to visit the area, and once I arrived I had to take care that its rival intelligence service, the CIA, was not planning to carry out one of its drone strikes.

At Malakand Fort I received a formal welcome from a young Pakistani army captain of 1st Battalion, the Azad Kashmir Regiment (*azad* means 'free' in Urdu), who agreed to show me to the room where Churchill stayed during his service with the Malakand Field Force, and where he wrote some of his articles for the *Daily Telegraph*. As he showed me round the fort, which was under construction at the time of the 1897 revolt, I was intrigued to find a large tracking device located in the centre of the main compound. The officer explained that it was an early warning system used to detect the movement of low-flying aircraft coming across the border from Afghanistan. The previous year a team of US Navy SEALs had flown from Afghanistan to attack bin Laden's compound in Abbottabad, a Pakistani military training academy about a hundred miles to the east of Malakand. Rather than fighting the Taliban, it seemed the priority of the Pakistani force at Malakand was to prevent the Americans carrying out any further 'kill or capture' missions on their territory.

In many respects, though, the challenges faced by the latest generation of soldiers fighting in this inhospitable mountain region of the Afghan border are strikingly similar to those encountered by the British at the end of the nineteenth century. They are fighting the same Pashtun tribesmen who are determined to maintain their independence from foreign interference, and who have been inspired by a particularly uncompromising brand of Islamist ideology to resist the occupiers. The cost of maintaining a campaign that has lasted longer than anyone imagined has become prohibitive, while Kabul is controlled by an Afghan ruler who is neither trusted nor respected. And the longer the conflict continues, the harder it becomes for Western politicians to decide whether they should stay the course, or leave and abandon the Afghans to their fate. The conclusions Churchill reached about the Malakand campaign were equally bleak. 'Financially it is ruinous. Morally it is wicked. Militarily it is an open question, and politically it is a blunder,' he wrote.[11] Churchill's views on waging war against the 'wild rifle-armed clansmen' on the Afghan border are as true today as they were when the young cavalryman set off to fight in his first war.

CHAPTER ONE

PASSING OUT

'No hour of life is lost that is spent in the saddle.'
Winston S. Churchill, *My Early Life*

When the young Winston Churchill arrived at the North-West Frontier of the Indian Empire in the early autumn of 1897 he very quickly formed a low opinion of the Taliban. In Churchill's day, the great-great-grandfathers of those who created the modern Taliban movement were known as the Talib-ul-ilms, a motley collection of indigent holy men who lived off the goodwill and hospitality of the local Afghan tribes and preached insurrection against the British Empire. To Churchill's mind, these Talibs were, together with other local priestly figures such as the mullahs and fakirs, primarily responsible for the wretched condition of the local Afghan tribesfolk and their violent indisposition to foreign rule. In Churchill's view they were 'as degraded a race as any on the fringe of humanity: fierce as a tiger, but less cleanly; as dangerous, not so graceful'.[1] He blamed the Talibs for the Afghans' lamentable absence of civilized development, keeping them in the 'grip of miserable superstition'. Churchill was particularly repelled by the Talibs' loose moral conduct. They lived free at the expense of the people and, 'more than this, they enjoy a sort of "droit de seigneur", and no man's wife or daughter is safe from them. Of some of their manners and morals it is impossible to write.'[2]

Churchill saw the conflict in even more apocalyptic terms when he published his first newspaper article on his experiences as a young British soldier locked in mortal combat with these fearsome Afghan tribesmen. 'Civilisation is face to face with militant Mohammedism,' he wrote. He entertained no doubts as to the conflict's ultimate outcome for, given the 'moral and material forces arrayed against each other, there need be no fear of the ultimate issue'.[3] Even so, he lamented the warlike nature of the tribes who inhabited the mountainous no-man's land between Afghanistan to the north and British India to the south. Many tribes, the majority of them Pashtuns, lived in the wild but wealthy valleys that led from Afghanistan to India, but they were all of similar character and condition. Except when they were sowing or harvesting their crops, Churchill observed that a continual state of feud and strife prevailed throughout the land. 'Tribe wars with tribe. The people of one valley fight with those of the next. To the quarrels of communities are added the combats of individuals. Khan assails khan, each supported by his retainers. Every tribesman has a blood feud against his neighbour. Every man's hand is against the other, and all are against the stranger.'[4] More than a hundred years later, when a new generation of Western soldiers deployed to Central Asia, they found that little had changed in the way the tribes of the Afghan frontier conducted themselves.

In criticizing some of the Talibs' more depraved practices, Churchill conveniently overlooked the conduct of his own social milieu back in London, which could hardly be described as a cradle of virtuous rectitude. The loose moral values observed in certain upper-class circles of late-Victorian England were most famously embodied by the louche conduct of the Prince of Wales, the future King Edward VII. A close family friend of the Churchills, 'Bertie' entertained a string of mistresses; one of his conquests was said to be Winston's mother Jennie, the wife of the Tory peer Lord Randolph Churchill and a notable society beauty. The American-born Jennie is credited with having had more than two hundred lovers of her own and was susceptible to the charms of young Guards officers who were barely older than Winston.

But Churchill was not much interested in comparing the social and religious codes of Victorian Britain with those practised among the mountain fastnesses of Afghanistan. Even at this early stage in his life his sole concern was to make his name, and in this regard his mother's high social connections worked to his advantage. One of her many admirers was General Sir Bindon Blood, who had been appointed to lead a punitive expedition against the Pashtuns, the dominant tribe on the Afghan border, after they had launched an unprovoked attack on the strategically important fort of Malakand on the North-West Frontier. One of the most accomplished soldiers of his day, Blood had fought in every British campaign since the Zulu wars of the 1870s. In 1895 he had been a senior commander of the British military incursion into Pashtun territory to liberate the British garrison at Chitral, the northernmost outpost of the Indian Empire, making him the ideal choice to lead the new expedition.

Blood had met and befriended Lady Churchill at country-house parties hosted by Winston's favourite aunt, Duchess Lily, at her home in Deepdene, Surrey. Winston met him at Deepdene, too, and had managed to make an impression on the old warrior, extracting a promise from him that if ever Blood commanded another expedition on the Indian frontier, he would allow Churchill to accompany him.[5] The moment his appointment to lead the campaign against the Afghans was confirmed, Jennie was able to intercede on her son's behalf and persuade Blood to allow the eager young officer to join what he called his 'pheasant shoot'.

A number of factors contributed to Churchill's desperation to join the thick of the action on the Afghan border, the most pressing of which was his unrelenting determination to further his personal reputation. As he wrote to his mother shortly after he had arrived at Blood's headquarters, 'I have faith in my star – that I am intended to do something in this world. If I am mistaken – what does it matter? My life has been a pleasant one and though I should regret to leave it, it would be a regret that perhaps I should never know.'⁶ The prevailing sense of fatalism expressed in this letter is perhaps surprising in a young man embarking on adult life, but then Churchill was no ordinary young man.

*

By a stroke of good fortune, Winston Leonard Spencer Churchill was born on 30 November 1874 at Blenheim Palace, which was given by a grateful nation to John Churchill, the 1st Duke of Marlborough as a reward for the stunning string of victories he won against the French during the War of the Spanish Succession in the early eighteenth century. Lord and Lady Randolph had planned for their baby to be born in London, but a heavy fall sustained by Jennie while accompanying a shooting party on the Blenheim estate caused her to go into labour early, thereby ensuring that the infant was delivered in a modest ground-floor room with a view of Blenheim's beautifully landscaped grounds. The baby was named Winston after the father of the 1st Duke and immediately became heir presumptive to the Marlborough dukedom, and would remain so until the birth of his cousin John. The significance of being born in a palace was never lost on young Winston, as it anchored him firmly to one of the greatest aristocratic families of the age. In later life he would remark, 'At Blenheim I took two very important decisions; to be born and to marry, and I am content with the decision I took on both occasions.' Throughout his life Churchill drew inspiration from his aristocratic lineage and descent from the warrior duke, which laid the foundations for his own success.

Indeed, the realization that he was unlikely to accede to the dukedom was one of the factors that spurred him on, not only to make his reputation, but to make his fortune too. For while Churchill could lay claim to membership of one of Britain's most famous families, by the time he volunteered to fight in India, his immediate family's position was dire. Lord Randolph had died in January 1895 at the age of forty-six and had, according to Lord Rosebery, the future British prime minister, spent the last six years of his life 'dying by inches in public'. His father's last months were particularly traumatic for Winston, who had to watch as Lord Randolph succumbed to tertiary syphilis, his appearance ruined and his speech incoherent.[7]

It was a miserable end for a man who, at one point in his short career, was hailed as a saviour of the Conservative Party and a serious contender to become a Tory prime minister. He was certainly unrecognizable from the dashing and brilliant young man who had won the heart of the young Jennie Jerome at a yachting regatta on the Isle of Wight in August 1873. Jennie was the latest in a long line of wealthy young American women – the dollar princesses, as they were known – to have married into the Churchill family. Winston's uncle, the 8th Duke of Marlborough, had married a member of the Hammersley family who had made millions out of New York real estate, and his cousin 'Sunny', who became the 9th Duke in 1892, married the railroad heiress Consuelo Vanderbilt in New York's St Thomas Church in 1895.

The Jerome family had originally settled in upstate New York after sailing to America from the Isle of Wight in 1710 in search of religious freedom. Jennie's father, Leonard, was a Wall Street buccaneer whose own family could lay claim to a modest military pedigree. At least two of his forebears had fought against the British in the American War of Independence while another had marched and fought with George Washington's army at Valley Forge. Leonard's experience of conflict, on the other hand, was as a speculator who made a vast fortune trading stocks during the American Civil War, which enabled him to build a six-storey mansion at the corner of Madison Avenue and 26th Street. The building was so vast it contained a theatre, which Leonard used to stage his own entertainments. His newly acquired wealth enabled him to buy a stake in the *New York Times*, which was then a strongly Republican newspaper, where he became a consulting editor. When, in 1863, violent draft riots erupted in New York, the paper's editorial board thought it prudent to fortify itself with two Gatling guns, which were mounted in the business office under Leonard's command to protect the building from being burnt and looted by the mob.[8] In the event, they were never used.

Although wealthy, Leonard Jerome was not in the same league as the Vanderbilts, and had suffered serious reverses on the stock market. He therefore settled on his daughter a relatively modest dowry of £50,000 (around £3 million in today's values). Even so, such a sum would have been sufficient for most young couples embarking on married life – Lord Randolph was twenty-five, and his wife just twenty. But the Churchills' social and political aspirations were such that they were forever living beyond their means. Lord Randolph had just become the Conservative MP for Woodstock, the local parliamentary constituency for Blenheim. Jennie, meanwhile, threw herself wholeheartedly into high-society life in London. As Lord Randolph's biographer R. F. Foster has remarked, 'If he and his wife were remarkable for anything in the first three years of his parliamentary career, it was for a life-style of conspicuous and frivolous consumption.'[9] This set the pattern for most of their marriage, which meant that Lord Randolph, who was also an inveterate gambler, was invariably in debt, a state of affairs that continued even when he was, for a brief period in the 1880s, appointed Secretary of State for India and then Chancellor of the Exchequer, both positions that provided reasonable salaries.

At this stage in Winston's childhood, when Lord Randolph's fortunes were very much in the ascendant and he was a prominent figure in the Fourth Party, a group of well-connected Tory modernizers, Jennie hosted one of the most sought-after *salons* in London, where an eclectic mix of politicians, artists and journalists would collect to discuss the pressing issues of the day. Early in their marriage she hosted a dinner party where the guests included both the Conservative leader Benjamin Disraeli and the Prince of Wales, and she maintained the same calibre of social connections throughout her life. One of her adoring male admirers, Lord D'Abernon, who in his youth was known as the 'Piccadilly stallion' because of his many extra-marital affairs, recounted meeting Jennie early in her marriage: 'A diamond star in her hair, her favourite ornament – its lustre dimmed by the flashing glory of her eyes. More of the panther than of the woman in her look, but with a cultivated intelligence unknown to the jungle.'[10] Jennie was entrancing to her young son too, who later recalled that she was 'a fairy princess: a radiant being possessed of limitless power and riches'.[11] But, as is the case with fairy princesses, he did not see very much of her.

For much of Churchill's upbringing his parents were far too concerned with their political and social activities to devote much energy to caring for their son and heir. Lord Randolph, until his health deteriorated, spent up to nine months of the year travelling for business and pleasure. Jennie, meanwhile, was juggling the attentions of her various suitors. Mary Soames, Churchill's youngest daughter, recalls an elderly relative who had known Jennie when Winston was a boy telling her, when asked whether Lord and Lady Randolph were really such bad parents, 'I think that even by the standards of their gener-ation . . . they were pretty awful.'[12] The woeful neglect of Churchill's upbringing by his parents had a potentially disastrous impact on his childhood, particularly when it came to his schooling. But it also had a profound influence on his develop-ment in later life, not least because, from an early age, Winston was accustomed to his family moving in the highest social circles, in which his parents mixed easily with royalty, politicians and newspaper barons, contacts that would prove invaluable when the time came for Churchill to make his own way in the world. Less helpful was his exposure to his parents' extravagant and spendthrift ways for, like them, Churchill would spend most of his life desperately seeking ways to escape the burden of his many debts.

In his parents' absence, Churchill and his brother Jack, who was six years younger than Winston, became devoted to their nanny, Mrs Everest, a middle-aged widow from Kent who had been hired soon after Winston's birth. 'Woomy', as the boys called her, became Churchill's emotional bedrock, especially after, at the age of seven, he was sent to board at a preparatory school in Ascot where the headmaster took a sadistic delight in administering regular floggings to his charges. It was mainly thanks to Mrs Everest, who noticed the tell-tale scars when Winston returned for the school holidays, that he was removed and sent to a more agreeable establishment in Brighton. By the time he reached his ninth birthday Winston was a sickly child, and the family physician believed the sea air would lead to a radical improvement in his health. The change of school resulted in a modest advance in his academic performance, particularly in Classics and French, although his boisterous behaviour meant that he invariably found himself bottom of the class for Conduct. His parents visited rarely, and it was only when, aged eleven, Winston contracted pneumonia and was close to death for two days that Lord Randolph could be persuaded to visit his son, even though he was often in Brighton to address political rallies. This was the period when Lord Randolph's political career was at its peak and, soon after Winston had made a full recovery, he was appointed Chancellor of the Exchequer in Lord Salisbury's second administration. Aged only thirty-seven, Lord Randolph had every reason to believe that he might ultimately become prime minister, although even at this juncture he had acquired many detractors. When a retired naval officer suggested Lord Randolph's name as a future Tory leader to Gladstone, he is said to have retorted: '*Never*. God forbid that any great English party should be led by a Churchill! There never was a Churchill

from John of Marlborough down that had either morals or principles.'[13] Queen Victoria expressed doubts of her own about
Lord Randolph's suitability for high office. She wrote in her
journal on 25 July 1886 that Lord Salisbury had informed
her that 'Randolph Churchill must be Chancellor of the
Exchequer and Leader, which I did not like. He is so mad and
odd and has also bad health.'[14]

Lord Randolph's health was certainly an issue, resulting in
frequent absences from front-bench politics and increasingly
erratic conduct when he was in attendance. His critics accused
him of contradicting himself, and of 'personal flightiness' in his
dealings with fellow politicians. His unconventional behaviour
led to his ignominious departure from the Treasury just six
months after his appointment as Chancellor. In an ill-considered
attempt to outmanoeuvre Lord Salisbury over a budget pro-
posal, Lord Randolph tendered his resignation in the hope of
forcing the prime minister to accept his plan to cut defence
spending. Rather than be bullied, Salisbury confounded Lord
Randolph by accepting his resignation, thereby bringing his
political career to an abrupt end. As the historian A. J. P. Taylor
once remarked, Lord Randolph 'might have been a great leader.
In retrospect he appears a great nuisance.'

The implosion of Lord Randolph's career had a profound
bearing on Churchill's own prospects. It had the immediate
effect of further weakening the family's financial standing, as well
as causing the Churchills to suffer social ostracism. Not only had
Lord Randolph made himself look foolish by his resignation
ploy, he had also managed to offend the monarch. He had written his resignation letter while staying as a guest of Queen Victoria at Windsor Castle on the assumption that it would never
be accepted. The Queen was dismayed that she only learned
about the resignation of one of her senior ministers through the
editorial pages of *The Times*. And her irritation was intensified
further when she discovered the letter had been written on royal
notepaper, an unforgivable breach of royal etiquette. Jennie was

so upset by her husband's conduct that she gave serious consideration to seeking a divorce. To add to his woes, Lord Randolph had managed to offend his long-standing friend George Buckle, the editor of *The Times*, who refused to take his side in his dispute with Lord Salisbury. The strained relationship between the Churchill family and Buckle would later hinder Winston's attempts to break into British journalism, when *The Times* declined his offer to file war dispatches to the newspaper, which led him to offer his services to the *Daily Telegraph*.

As a twelve-year-old schoolboy in Brighton, Winston was not aware of the enormity of his father's folly. But he soon felt the full force of the public's contempt for Lord Randolph when he was taken to a pantomime in Brighton in early 1887, where the crowd started to hiss when an actor portrayed his father in a sketch. Winston burst into tears, and then turned furiously on a man who was hissing behind him and cried, 'Stop that now, you snub-nosed radical.'[15] Despite the fact that his father still neglected to visit him, Winston remained fiercely loyal. The need for parental approval is a common enough trait in most children; all the more so in those who have absentee parents. For the rest of his life Winston was suffused with the desire to avenge the premature end to his father's career, even if Lord Randolph was undeserving of such filial loyalty. Churchill's ambition to pursue a career in politics and achieve high office, which was evident in him from a young age, was inspired to an extent by his belief that his father had been unfairly treated, a theme he later explored in his biography of Lord Randolph. Twenty years later, when he published an account of his father's resignation, Churchill said Lord Randolph's mistake in submitting his resignation letter had been to overlook 'the anger and jealousy that his sudden rise to power had excited'.[16]

Although not an impressive pupil, Churchill nevertheless applied himself sufficiently to pass the entrance examination to Harrow, where he immediately joined the school cadet force. As a child Churchill had taken a keen interest in the military and acquired an impressive collection of toy soldiers. It seemed as though he was obsessed with emulating the achievements of his great ancestors, while clinging to the old-fashioned view that proving personal courage on the field of battle was a prerequisite for the pursuit of a career in politics. At Harrow he was soon taking part in mock battles against local schools. He was taught to shoot the Martini-Henry rifle, the same weapon being used by the British army to fight the Pashtun tribesmen on the Afghan border. During normal school hours he showed promise in subjects he liked, such as English History and English Language. Although he languished in the school's lowest form, he nevertheless impressed the school's headmaster, Dr J. E. C. Welldon, by faultlessly reciting 1,200 lines from Macaulay's *Lays of Ancient Rome*, for which he won a prize open to the whole school. But his personal conduct left much to be desired, particularly his lateness and the frequency with which he lost his books and papers. He was accused of 'forgetfulness, carelessness, unpunctuality and irregularity in every way' by one of his exasperated masters, who wrote to his mother, 'He is so regular in his irregularity that I really don't know what to do.'[17]

*

At an early stage in Winston's school career at Harrow, Lord Randolph decided that his son should go into the army, and arranged for him to be placed in Harrow's Army Class, which provided special tutoring for pupils who opted for a military career. Churchill recollected that Lord Randolph took the decision after inspecting his son's collection of 1,500 toy soldiers, which were all lined up in the correct formation of attack. 'He spent twenty minutes studying the scene – which was really impressive – with a keen and captivating smile. At the end he asked me if I would like to go into the army. I thought it would be splendid to command an army, so I said "Yes" at once: and immediately I was taken at my word.' Years later Churchill discovered that his father had made his decision because he

decided his son was not clever enough to study law. 'The toy
soldiers turned the current of my life,' Churchill wrote. 'Hence-
forward all my education was directed to passing into Sandhurst,
and afterwards to the technical details of the profession of arms.
Anything else I had to pick up for myself.'[18]

The decision to place Winston in the Army Class effectively
removed him from the mainstream of the school, as he now
found himself in a segregated mixed-age group containing many
of the school's duller boys. Winston had demonstrated that he
had formidable powers of memory, and an aptitude for the use
of the English language. But he was hopeless at mastering the
complexities of Greek, Latin and Mathematics, which were the
mainstays of a traditional English education at that time. Welldon, though, thought Winston had some academic potential, as
he provided him with extra private tuition in Latin and Greek
in the hope that he might improve, but it was to no avail.
Welldon would maintain his personal attachment to Winston
long after he had left Harrow, and corresponded with him
regularly during his years as a young soldier fighting for the
British Empire in India. Of the four and a half years Winston
spent at Harrow, three were in the Army Class, and he made
steady progress, eventually being made a lance corporal in the
school cadet force. By the age of seventeen, despite the constant
episodes of ill health Winston suffered as a schoolboy, he
demonstrated that he was not totally without athletic ability by
winning the Public Schools Fencing Championship – a useful
attribute for someone who would soon be engaged in the
primitive form of warfare practised by Afghan warriors. 'His
success', we learn in the *Harrovian*, the school magazine, 'was
chiefly due to his quick and dashing attack, which quite took his
opponents by surprise.'[19]

So far as Churchill's academic potential was concerned, his
father's misgivings about his ability were proved correct. In the
later Victorian period official England demanded success in the
aforementioned Latin, Greek and Mathematics, and proficiency

in such subjects was the benchmark for entry into the foreign and civil services. The army's entrance requirements were lower. Winston's poor performance in Mathematics meant that he could not even contemplate going on to Woolwich, the academy for cadets seeking commissions in the Royal Artillery or Royal Engineers. Instead he had to settle for the Royal Military Academy at Sandhurst, the military institution for would-be infantry and cavalry officers. Despite working ten hours a day to prepare himself for Sandhurst, he failed miserably to pass the entrance examination in the summer of 1892, not even achieving sufficient marks to enter the cavalry, which set the lowest standard. He came 390th out of 693 candidates, although he did come 18th out of the 400 who took the English History paper. Nor did he fare much better when he retook the Sandhurst exam in November, even though Welldon, who had come to admire his pupil's dogged persistence, noted prior to the examination, 'he has done all that could be asked of him'.[20]

Winston failed again, but there was a significant improvement in his overall score. He had just celebrated his eighteenth birthday and, in his desperation to pursue a military career, left Harrow and enrolled at a crammer in West London specializing in getting dim young men into Sandhurst. The crammer prided itself on its 'renowned system of intensive poultry farming' – learning by rote. But it worked, and Winston finally passed at the third attempt in June 1893. Even then he just scraped through the examination, and did not receive sufficient marks to join the infantry, so had to settle for the cavalry. Winston was nonetheless triumphant, and wrote to his father that he was 'glad to be able to send you good news'. But in return he received a coruscating rebuke from Lord Randolph, whose infirmity had reached the point where he could no longer finish his speeches in the Commons. Lord Randolph had set his heart on Winston joining the infantry, and was keen that he be commissioned into the 60th Rifles, for which Prince George, the Duke of Cambridge, the Queen's first cousin and commander-in-chief of the British army, had recommended him. 'I am rather surprised at your tone of exultation over your inclusion in the Sandhurst list,' he wrote from the German spa resort of Kissingen. 'There are two ways of winning an examination, one creditable, the other the reverse. You have unfortunately chosen the latter method, and appear to be much pleased by your success.' By failing to get into the infantry Winston had 'demonstrated beyond refutation your slovenly, happy-go-lucky harum scarum style of work for which you have always been distinguished at your various schools'. Lord Randolph was concerned about the family's ability to pay the extra costs incurred by joining the cavalry, which included the purchase and maintenance of at least one horse. 'By accomplishing the prodigious effort of getting into the Cavalry, you imposed on me an extra charge of some £200 a year,' he sarcastically remarked.[21] To placate his father, Winston managed to secure an infantry cadetship after one of the other applicants dropped out, but this still failed to mollify his father's anger.

On enrolment at Sandhurst in September 1893, Churchill was told that he would need to overcome his physical shortcomings if he were to qualify for graduation. At a little over five feet six inches tall and with a chest measurement of just thirty-one inches, his physique was more akin to that of a racing jockey than a potential cavalry officer. Indeed, the one-piece 'siren suit' that the Jermyn Street tailor Turnbull and Asser made for him during the Second World War, one of which today is displayed at Blenheim Palace, looks more like a romper suit for a large child that the attire of Britain's greatest wartime prime minister.

Lord Randolph's rebuke certainly made an impression on Churchill, and he endeavoured to make the best of his new career at Sandhurst. Rather than being late for everything, which had been his custom at school, Churchill made it his habit to arrive at least five minutes early. He immersed himself in his studies, and wrote to his parents 'The work is very

interesting and extremely practical', although he was scathing of
the academy's 'dilapidated and tobacco-smelling rooms'. He
learned to shoot both rifle and revolver, and was among a group
of cadets who were allowed to fire the army's new 12-pounder
gun. At the start of the eighteen-month course he was still
dogged by ill health, and had to be helped off the parade ground
after he collapsed following a particularly demanding march,
prompting him to rue that 'I am cursed with so feeble a body.'[22]

But Winston thrived at Sandhurst, to the extent that he
passed the first set of examinations in all of the five compulsory
subjects: Fortification, Tactics, Topography, Military Law and
Military Administration. In later life Churchill remembered his
time at Sandhurst with fondness, saying it was a period of
learning and comradeship. 'In contrast with my schooldays I
had made many friends, three or four of whom still survive.' But
this was a generation of young British officers for whom living
to a ripe old age, as Churchill did, would be the exception,
rather than the norm. Some of Churchill's direct contemporaries
at Sandhurst were killed in the Boer War, but the majority
perished during the First World War when Churchill himself,
following his resignation from the government over the Darda-
nelles fiasco, volunteered to serve for a brief spell in the trenches.
'The few that have survived have been pierced through thigh or
breast or face by the bullets of the enemy. I salute them all.'[23]

Horses, though, were Churchill's greatest pleasure at Sandhurst, which was just as well as he needed to draw on all his
horsemanship skills when fighting on the North-West Frontier.
In addition to the time he spent at Sandhurst's riding school
he attended a specialist course at Knightsbridge Barracks with
the Royal Horse Guards. Afterwards, when he succeeded in
fulfilling his dream of joining a cavalry regiment, he undertook
another full five-month course, so that by the time he set off for
Afghanistan 'I was pretty well trained to sit and manage a
horse'.[24] He and his friends at Sandhurst spent all their money
hiring horses from the local livery stables, running up bills on

the strength of their future commissions. 'We organised point-to-points and even a steeplechase in the park of a friendly grandee, and bucketed gaily about the countryside,' he recalled. 'No hour of life is lost that is spent in the saddle. Young men have often been ruined through owning horses, or through backing horses, but never through riding them; unless of course they break their necks, which, taken at a gallop, is a very good death to die.'[25] Churchill's great enthusiasm for equestrian pursuits paid off when he took part in Sandhurst's end-of-course Riding examination and came second out of 127 cadets. The frequent horse riding, combined with Sandhurst's demanding regime of drill and physical training, had helped him to overcome his frail physique, and he passed out from Sandhurst a fit young man with an excellent cadet record. Although he had entered Sandhurst near the bottom of the class, a lowly 92nd out of an intake of 102, his place in the final order of merit was 8th out of a class of 150, and he did particularly well in the final exams for Tactics, Drill and Gymnastics, as well as Riding.[26]

Despite his indifferent performance in getting into Sandhurst, Churchill is the only one of his generation whose name today is commemorated with a building named in his honour. Churchill Hall, a modern 1,200-seat complex used for lectures and presentations, is one of the newer buildings on the Sandhurst estate. The cadets' mess in the Old College building, which was built in the early nineteenth century and where Winston dined in the 1890s, is now the Indian Army Memorial Room, dedicated to the exploits of British soldiers who served on the subcontinent. The display cabinets around the walls are filled with various cups and trophies from regimental polo competitions, while the stained-glass windows honour its most notable campaigns, including Afghanistan, Burma, Palestine and the First and Second World Wars. There is not much use for the Riding School at the back of the Old College, where Churchill learned his riding skills, as modern British cavalry officers are more likely to be found driving tanks on Salisbury Plain than honing their equestrian prowess. It is mainly used by the local pony club, while only a few of the cadets can afford to maintain the academy's distinguished polo-playing tradition.

Churchill's impressive performance at Sandhurst should have allayed his father's fears about his commitment to pursuing a military career, but by the time he had completed his military training Lord Randolph's health was in rapid decline. His father's illness cast a dark shadow over Churchill's time at Sandhurst, although it was not until the final months of his cadetship that he was informed of its seriousness. Churchill, still bruised by the intemperate letter he had received on gaining entry to Sandhurst, remained wary of his father, although in the last year of his life Lord Randolph confided his pride in the noticeable improvement he had detected in Winston's conduct once he had become a gentleman cadet. Shortly after Winston enrolled at Sandhurst Lord Randolph took his son to Tring in Hertfordshire to visit the country home of Nathaniel Rothschild, the renowned Victorian banker and socialite who, at the age of forty-four, had become Britain's first Jewish peer in 1885. 'Natty', as he was known among his circle of aristocratic friends, was a close acquaintance of the Churchills, and later took a personal interest in Winston's career. After the Tring visit Lord Randolph wrote of Winston, 'He has much smartened up. He holds himself quite upright and he has got steadier. The people at Tring took a great deal of notice of him but he was very quiet and nice-mannered.'[27]

As Churchill was passing out from Sandhurst it was evident that Lord Randolph's health was in terminal decline. A hastily arranged world tour designed to improve his strength had to be cut short when Lord Randolph became so disorientated while visiting Sri Lanka that he had to be put in a straitjacket. The two of them eventually returned to the family home in Grosvenor Square. Lord Randolph 'lingered pitifully' for another month, Winston recalled, as he battled against 'General Paralysis', the term used by the Prince of Wales's personal physician to describe the final manifestation of syphilis, which reduces the patient to a state of mental incapacitation. For the final month of his life Randolph could speak only with difficulty, slept fitfully and survived on occasional sips of coffee because he could hardly swallow. The agonizing pain he suffered was relieved by heavy doses of morphine. In early January there was a brief improvement in his physical condition, but his mental deterioration was so advanced that Jennie, who, in spite of the couple's strained relationship, nursed him attentively, wrote that 'even his own mother wishes now that he had died the other day'. At one point Randolph rallied briefly when Winston paid him a visit and asked how he had got on with his Sandhurst exams. 'That's all right,' he commented when Winston informed him of his commendable performance.[28]

Lord Randolph died quietly at 6.15 on the morning of 24 January 1895, three weeks before his forty-sixth birthday. Winston himself died on the very same day seventy years later. On the morning of his father's death Winston had been sleeping at a nearby house, and 'ran in the darkness across Grosvenor Square, then lapped in snow', when told that his father was dying.[29] By the time the first relatives arrived to comfort Jennie, Winston was already reading the sympathetic telegrams. The Prince of Wales wrote a formal letter of condolence, as did George Curzon, an up-and-coming Tory politician who, as Lord Curzon, was soon to be appointed Viceroy and Governor General of India, with responsibility for maintaining the peace on India's problematic border with Afghanistan. Curzon wrote to Jennie, 'Everyone says how tenderly and heroically you have behaved throughout . . . you did all that lay in your power.' The Duke of Cambridge, another close family friend and the head of Britain's armed forces, wrote from his holiday villa in the south of France of his 'deep sympathy and sorrow at the great loss you and your family have sustained in the death of poor Randolph, the chief consolation being that his sufferings were I

fear great and that the end was a consequent relief to himself
and even to those who constantly watched over and surrounded
him'.[30]

The family was understandably secretive about the cause of
Lord Randolph's death, though rumours abounded throughout
London society as to the true nature of his illness. A funeral was
swiftly arranged, and the service was held at Westminster Abbey
three days later. An indication of the Churchill family's continued ostracism from the highest rankings of the court was
reflected in the non-attendance of Queen Victoria and Gladstone, the two great national figures of the era. Lord Salisbury,
who was primarily responsible for ending Lord Randolph's
political career, did attend, and the coffin was taken from the
Abbey to the slow movement of the Dead March from Handel's
Saul. Lord Randolph was buried later that day in the churchyard
at Bladon, a small village just beyond the family estate at
Blenheim, where Winston is also buried. 'Over the landscape
brilliant with sunshine,' Churchill recalled of the funeral, 'snow
had spread a glittering pall.' Winston certainly approved of his
father's final resting place. When he visited the graveyard six
months after the burial service he wrote to his mother, 'The hot
sun of the last few days has dried up the grass a little – but the
rose bushes are in full bloom and make the churchyard very
bright. I was struck by the sense of quietness and peace as well
as the old world air of the place – that my sadness was not
unmixed with solace. It is the spot of all others he would have
chosen.'[31]

Lord Randolph's death had a profound impact on Churchill,
who, at the age of twenty, suddenly found himself the head of a
relatively impoverished family with a somewhat tarnished reputation. Lord Randolph's spectacular fall from high political
office resulted in the Churchill family acquiring a reputation
for mental instability. So far as Winston was concerned, his
father's premature death instilled in him the firm belief that
Churchills died young. He had no time to waste. Moreover, he

was determined to restore the Churchill name, which had suffered badly through the failure of his father's political career, to its rightful glory. And what better way to prove himself than to volunteer to fight on a remote and inhospitable frontier of the British Empire.

CHAPTER TWO

THE WILD FRONTIER

'That religion, which above all others was founded and
propagated by the sword . . . stimulates a wild and
merciless fanaticism.'

Winston S. Churchill, *The Story of the Malakand Field Force*

While Churchill mourned the loss of his father, 3,500 miles
away on the North-West Frontier of what was then India's
border with Afghanistan a group of young British soldiers were
engaged in a desperate fight for their lives. Trouble had been
brewing on the Afghan border since the turn of the year after a
tribal chief loyal to the British had been murdered while out
hawking with his companions. Rival tribal leaders deeply
resented the generous allowances that were paid to friendly
tribesmen by the British-controlled government in India, as well
as the protection they received in return for their loyalty. The
arrangement was part of Britain's highly effective 'divide and
rule' policy to keep the peace among the frontier tribesmen. But
the tribes that took the Queen's shilling were not popular with
those that chose to reject British advances and maintain their
independence, and the murder of one of Britain's most important tribal allies on 1 January 1895, was taken as a rallying cry
for a number of rebellious tribesmen to raise the banner of
revolt. Within weeks a sizeable rebel force had surrounded the
isolated British garrison at Chitral, the northernmost outpost of
imperial Britain's defences on the Afghan border.

The small British force made a valiant effort to get the
tribesmen to disperse by launching a pre-emptive attack, but

they were overwhelmed by the enemy's superior numbers, and the deadly accuracy of their snipers. The garrison, which comprised British officers commanding a detachment of predominantly Sikh sepoys – locally hired Indian soldiers – had to make a hasty retreat, with the loss of 25 killed and 30 wounded out of a fighting complement of just 150 men. By early March, the garrison at Chitral was being subjected to a full-scale siege, and a heavy and constant barrage of fire was directed against the fort's hastily arranged defences. For forty-seven days the garrison had to survive in extremely unpleasant circumstances in a confined area that was no more than eighty yards square. The survivors later recalled that their greatest sufferings were anxiety, confinement, bad sanitation, overcrowding and fetid smells. Food was scarce and, as the siege took hold, the British commanders decided to expel 'all unnecessary mouths', such as the prisoners, from the compound to preserve food stocks. Even so the garrison was reduced to desperate measures to keep the defenders alive and, towards the end of March, as the resident intelligence official later recalled, 'the British officers killed and salted their ponies, and commenced to eat horseflesh'.[1]

The siege of Chitral in early 1895 was another episode in the long and bloody history of skirmishes between the British and the tribes that inhabited the border area with Afghanistan, a conflict prompted by Britain's desire to protect India, its prize colonial possession. Originally the British had set the northernmost border of the Indian Empire at the Indus river, which stretches nearly 2,000 miles from the Tibetan plateau to the Arabian Sea and today forms the longest river in Pakistan. But at various moments from the start of the nineteenth century onwards the British felt it necessary to venture northwards from the Indus towards the imposing mountain ranges that separated the settled Indian plains from Afghanistan. Running southwards from the Hindu Kush, a western offshoot of the even mightier Himalayan chain, the mountains formed a formidable barrier between the two countries.

The Afghans have a saying that when Allah created the world, he had a pile of rocks left over, out of which he created Afghanistan. And since the dawn of history these rocks have formed a natural frontier between it and the Indian subcontinent. Consequently, any power that controlled the mountains controlled the gateway to India and its abundant riches. Successive generations of invaders from the steppes of Central Asia had traversed the remote mountain passes on their way to conquer the rich and fertile plains of India. Alexander the Great passed this way as he sought to establish the final frontier of his empire, while the Mongols took the same route on their mission of pillage and murder. Over the centuries Afghans, Turks and Pashtuns penetrated the mountains in their various attempts to conquer northern India until, in the early sixteenth century, the Mughals, another dynasty of Central Asian stock, established themselves as the undisputed power in Delhi.

The state we would today recognize as Afghanistan began to take shape in the eighteenth century under the guidance of Ahmad Shah Durrani, a powerful Pashtun tribal leader who made his name fighting on behalf of the Iranian emperor during Iran's brutal conquest of the Mughal Empire in 1737. The Pashtuns are the most numerous of the Afghan tribes, and dominate the border region. Historically the country's amirs, or kings, have been drawn from the Pashtuns, a tradition that exists to this day. President Hamid Karzai, who took power after the September 11 attacks in 2001, is a Pashtun, as is Mullah Omar, the founder of the Taliban movement. In the early eighteenth century the Pashtuns came to prominence under Ahmad Shah, who commanded a detachment of Pashtun bodyguards charged with protecting the Iranian monarch. When the Shah of Iran was murdered in a palace coup, Ahmad Shah fled with his entourage to Afghanistan, where he soon established himself in Kabul. Within a few years he had seized control of the territory between the mountains of the Hindu Kush in the south and the northern border he established at the Oxus, another of the great

rivers that define the geographical landscape of Central Asia.
This kingdom also included a large swathe of land to the north
of the Indus, territory which today forms part of Pakistan. By
governing the Indian provinces of Sind and West Punjab,
Ahmad Shah was able to enjoy undisputed control of the major
mountain passes that lie between India and Afghanistan. So
integrated were these provinces into the Afghan kingdom that,
for many years, the Afghan amir of the day acquired the habit
of spending the summer in Kabul and the winter on the other
side of the mountains in Peshawar, the border town which today
is located in northern Pakistan and takes its name from the
Mughal for 'advanced post'. At the onset of the summer heat
the amirs swapped the aridity of the Afghan plains for the cooler
climes of the hills, a tradition that was later adopted by the
British at the height of the Raj.

    Britain's initial interest in Afghanistan arose purely out of a
desire to protect the overland route to India, rather than from
any pressing interest in the Afghans themselves. Until the
nineteenth century, the British had no great desire to involve
themselves in the Afghans' affairs. Up to that point their primary
focus was on commerce, exploiting the riches of India to sustain
the wealth, prosperity and glory of the British Empire. Their
entrepreneurial enthusiasm for exploring new and profitable
markets, which led them to establish footholds in such far-flung
places as Burma, did not extend north beyond the Indus. British
administrators generally shared the view of their regional neighbours, such as Iran, that the Afghans were nothing more than a
race of wild, savage hillmen, uncouth barbarians, ever ready to
prey on each other, to rob and harass travellers passing through
their country or even to sweep down upon the more fortunate
and richer countries outside their borders. In 1908 the *Imperial
Gazetteer* of India summed up the view of the overwhelming
majority of British soldiers and officials who had been obliged
to engage with the Afghan tribesmen for a century or more.
'Their step is full of resolution, their bearing proud and apt to

be rough. Inured to bloodshed from childhood, they are familiar with death, audacious in attack, but easily discouraged by failure. They are treacherous and passionate in revenge ... They are much under the influence of their Mullas, especially for evil.'[2] Churchill reached much the same conclusion when he fought the tribesmen at the end of the nineteenth century.

Initial British reluctance to become involved with Afghanistan was overtaken by concerns that their European rivals, who were deeply jealous of Britain's exclusive access to India's riches, might use the country to launch an invasion. By the early nineteenth century, for example, British administrators had convinced themselves that imperial Russia's growing influence in Central Asia might lead to a land-based assault on India from Afghanistan. To counter such a possibility the British made it their priority to acquire control of the mountain passes that provided the main crossing points between the two countries. Britain's first serious attempt to engage with the Afghans was undertaken in 1808 by Mountstuart Elphinstone, a twenty-nine-year-old British political officer, who set off from Delhi on a mission of 'great magnificence' to Peshawar to negotiate a defence pact with the Afghan amir. Although Elphinstone himself was a respected classical scholar and linguist, his mission was not motivated by any interest in the Afghans per se. It was born entirely of London's anxiety that Russia, with French backing, was planning to invade India by sending a 70,000-strong army through the Khyber Pass, the treacherous mountain track that forms one of the major access points between Afghanistan and the North-West Frontier. Elphinstone's retinue included 600 camels and a dozen elephants laden with presents. Up to this point, Britain's general neglect of Afghanistan was so profound that Elphinstone, who spoke fluent Persian and Hindi, had to draw on accounts left by Alexander the Great, and written 2,000 years before, to help him plan his expedition across the Indus.

When Elphinstone arrived in Peshawar he was greeted by

the amir, Shuja Shah Durrani, who received him perched on a
gold-coloured throne, elevated above the heads of his eunuchs.
The British were given a cautious welcome by the Afghans, who
accepted the generous gifts that Elphinstone had brought with
him, while at the same time entertaining serious doubts about
the nature of the British expedition. The meeting between
Elphinstone and the amir set the tone for Britain's dealings with
the Afghans for many years to come. Shuja, who had recently
taken the strategically important cities of Kandahar and Herat
in southern Afghanistan, was looking for British support to shore
up his precarious hold on power. The amir's brother, Mahmud
Shah, the former Afghan ruler who had been deposed following
a violent quarrel between rival Pashtun tribes, had fled into exile
in British-controlled India, but not before his enemies had
gouged his eyes out. Shuja was keen to avoid suffering a similar
fate, but the British were not interested in becoming embroiled
in internal Afghan politics. The primary purpose of Elphinstone's mission was to secure a defence pact with the Afghans to
counter the threat of a Russian invasion. At this stage in Anglo-
Afghan relations the British showed little interest in maintaining
a pro-British ruler in power in Kabul. No support for Shuja
Shah was forthcoming with the result that, only a few years
later, the Afghan amir was forced from the throne by his
political rivals and obliged to join his brother in exile in India.
As future generations of Afghans have learned to their cost, the
intervention of foreign powers in their affairs is principally
motivated by self-interest, whether it relates to tsarist Russia's
territorial ambitions in the nineteenth century or the West's
attempt to purge the country of Islamist militants in the twenty-
first.

    Elphinstone returned to India, where he provided his British
colleagues with their first detailed account of the Afghan way of
life. Elphinstone's description was limited by the fact that he did
not succeed in visiting the country itself. His meetings with the

amir and his entourage took place in Peshawar, and he based his account on lengthy conversations with members of the amir's court. Indeed, most of the British maps of Afghanistan at this time were drawn on the basis of interviews conducted with local Afghans, rather than first-hand surveys. Elphinstone's depiction of the Afghans nonetheless helped to inform British understanding of their unruly neighbours to the north. Elphinstone compared the tribes to the clans of the old Scottish Highlands, and noted that the Afghans engaged in continual inter-tribal warfare, and bitterly resented any attempt by the government in Kabul to intervene in their affairs. As one old tribesman remarked to Elphinstone, 'We are content with discord, we are content with alarms, we are content with blood . . . but we will never be content with a master.'[3] Elphinstone perceived flaws in the Afghan character such as 'revenge, envy, avarice, rapacity and obstinacy; on the other hand they are fond of liberty, faithful to their friends, kind to their dependants, hospitable, brave, hardy, frugal, laborious and prudent'. He observed that they lived in neat houses, tended to be taller than Indians and had fairer skins. And he preferred the Afghans' Islamic faith to the superstitious Hinduism practised by the Indians with whose customs he was more familiar. 'They have also a degree of curiosity which is a relief to a person habituated to the apathy of the Indian.' Overall the Afghans made a good impression, and Elphinstone concluded, 'I know no people in Asia who have fewer vices, or are less voluptuous or debauched.'[4]

Ninety years later the subtleties Elphinstone detected in the Afghan temperament were overlooked by Churchill, who, rather than comparing the Afghans to noble Scottish Highlanders, regarded them as being more akin to Corsican cut-throats. 'Every influence, every motive, that provokes the spirit of murder among men, impels these mountaineers to deeds of treachery and violence,' Churchill wrote. 'The strong aboriginal propensity to kill, inherent in all human beings, has in these valleys been preserved in unexampled strength and vigour . . . A code of honour not less punctilious than that of old Spain, is supported by vendettas as implacable as those of Corsica.'[5]

*

In the 1830s, Britain's disinclination to involve itself in the affairs of the Afghans ended when London again became convinced that the Russians were reviving their interest in India. Napoleon's defeat at Waterloo had led to the emergence of Britain and Russia as the two most dominant powers in Europe, and Lord Palmerston, Britain's combative Foreign Secretary, concluded the most likely location for any clash between the two powers was in Central Asia. While the main focus of the British was to consolidate their maritime empire, the Russians were reviving Peter the Great's dream of expansion to the south. The more the Russians extended their territorial influence southwards through the Caucasus into the primitive Central Asian states that bordered the northern banks of the Oxus, the more concerned Britain's master strategist became that Moscow's ultimate objective was India, the jewel in Britain's imperial crown.

Palmerston's suspicions deepened further as Russia replaced Britain in the affections of the Shah of Persia, to the extent that, in November 1837, a Russian regiment was dispatched to support a 30,000-strong Persian army that had marched into eastern Afghanistan with the intention of capturing Herat, the region's ancient capital. If Persia, with Russia's backing, captured this strategically important city, then India would be at risk of a Russian invasion. The siege of Herat was eventually lifted after the Royal Navy deposited a force of Royal Marines on Kharg Island in the Gulf (which today is one of Iran's main oil terminals) as a warning to the Shah not to pursue his Russian-backed adventure in Afghanistan. This decisive British intervention in the Gulf forced the Shah's hand, and the siege ended with the Persian troops returning home. But Russia's support for the Persian advance on Herat, together with the arrival in Kabul of a personal emissary bearing letters of introduction from Tsar Alexander II to the Afghan amir, was enough to convince Lord Palmerston that Britain could no longer afford to leave the Afghans to their own devices. Had Herat fallen to the Persians, Russia would have been presented with an open road to India. The prospect appalled Palmerston. So far as he was concerned Afghanistan's mountainous border region provided 'the best rampart India could have'.[6] He was not prepared to tolerate a situation in which the Russians seized control of these ramparts and, eschewing diplomatic niceties, he resolved in Churchill's famous phrase, 'to use a sledgehammer to crack a nut'. Britain decided to mount its first invasion of Afghanistan, thereby firing the first salvoes in the Great Game, the century-long feud between Britain and Russia in Central Asia.

To conquer Afghanistan the British formed the Grand Army of the Indus, a 39,000-strong force comprising an exotic mix of British and Indian regiments. It was by far the most grandiose expedition the British military had ever undertaken, a profligate example of Britain's claim to be the world's pre-eminent imperial power. Seasoned British regiments such as the Coldstream Guards, 4th Dragoons and 16th Lancers, which had fought with distinction at Waterloo, joined forces with locally raised regiments such as Poona Horse and Skinner's Horse, which were commanded by British officers but drawn from the native Indian population. In addition to the 30,000 camels requisitioned to transport the equipment and supplies, British officers took along a pack of foxhounds, in anticipation of the sporting opportunities they hoped to enjoy. Two camels were designated solely to carry the regimental cigars, suggesting that the majority of young British officers taking part in the expedition had not the slightest clue as to the hazards that lay ahead.[7]

The primary objective of the Army of the Indus was to

restore to power Shuja Shah Durrani, the Afghan ruler who had fled into exile in British-controlled India twenty years previously because the British would not back him. This unexpected revival in Shuja's fortunes came about because the British decided they needed a suitable candidate to replace Dost Mohammed, the ruler known today by Afghans as the 'Great Amir'. Dost Mohammed was seen as being far too cosy with the Russians for British tastes, and re-establishing Shuja in power in Kabul seemed a good way of solving the problem. In fact Dost Mohammed was not really anti-British. His main grievance was that he wanted London to support his campaign to secure the return of the strategically important border town of Peshawar, which had recently been seized by the powerful Sikh nation that ruled in the Punjab region of northern India. Most Afghans saw Peshawar as being an integral part of their own country, a view Dost Mohammed made clear to Alexander Burnes, another indomitable young British adventurer who, like Elphinstone before him, had travelled to Kabul to persuade the amir to abandon his new-found Russian friends in favour of an alliance with Britain. Dost Mohammed informed Burnes that he would reject the Russian advances, but only if the British first helped him to retrieve Peshawar from the Sikhs. This they were not prepared to do because the Sikhs were seen as valuable British allies, whose support was deemed vital to preserving the security of India's northern border. There was clearly little appetite in London for addressing Dost Mohammed's concerns, and his frustration with the British led him to be more responsive towards his Russian suitors.

The removal of Dost Mohammed, and his replacement with Shuja Shah, therefore became the principal objective of the Army of the Indus when it set off for Afghanistan in early 1839. The Sikhs may have been regarded as valued allies of the British, but they were not prepared to allow them to use Sikh-controlled territory in the Punjab to mount their Afghan adventure. The Sikhs knew better than to meddle with the fiercely independent Afghan tribesmen. The British were obliged to take the more circuitous and challenging route, crossing into Afghanistan further south from Sind Province through the Bolan Pass, a narrow, fifty-five-mile-long defile. By the time the Army of the Indus arrived in the village of Quetta, the capital of Baluchistan, a few weeks later, it resembled not so much a dazzling spectacle as a bedraggled rabble. The route from India was lined with dead camels and abandoned baggage, and food supplies were so low that the entire army was placed on short rations the moment it arrived. A crisis was averted only when the enterprising Burnes managed to procure emergency supplies of 10,000 sheep from a local chieftain.

Fully replenished, the army pressed on through the Khojak Pass, the precipitous gorge that bisects the border of modern Afghanistan, until it reached Kandahar in late April. Shuja was afforded the privilege of entering the city first, hoping to persuade the Afghan people that this was entirely an internal affair, as opposed to a British-controlled imperial adventure. At first Shuja received a hero's welcome, with women tossing flowers into his path from their windows and rooftop perches. But after a few days the mood changed, as the Afghans realized Shuja's army mainly consisted of Indian mercenaries, who were themselves heavily dependent on the backing of the well-drilled regiments of British troops. When, a couple of weeks after their arrival, the British staged a grand ceremonial parade in Shuja's honour in Kandahar, fewer than a hundred Afghans turned up to watch.

Unperturbed by the Afghans' lack of interest, the British advanced regardless, leaving a small garrison behind in Kandahar as they proceeded north-east towards Kabul 320 miles away. But before reaching the capital the British first had to overcome the imposing walled fortress at Ghazni, one of the most famous fortifications in all of Central Asia, which was controlled by one of Dost Mohammed's sons. Built along a mountain slope, the citadel and its two towers stood 150 feet high, while the surrounding walls were sixty feet thick, causing the British commanders to regret their decision to leave their heaviest guns behind at Kandahar. Ghazni's defences were breached after a young British engineer, Lieutenant Henry Durand, led a team of sappers to blow up one of the fortress's principal gates, thereby allowing the British force to storm the citadel and overwhelm the defenders in brutal hand-to-hand combat. The discrepancy in the respective casualty rates, with British losses totalling 17 killed and 165 wounded compared with more than 500 Afghan dead, pointed to the superiority of British weapons and tactics.

So far as the Western powers' more recent military involvement in Afghanistan is concerned, the assault on Ghazni was notable for two reasons. Firstly, the British, when they engaged with the Afghans, discovered that these so-called primitive Afghan fighters were a formidable foe for even the best prepared military force. In the nineteenth century the Afghan's weapon of choice was the *jezail*, a long-barrelled matchlock rifle, which proved far more effective in the craggy terrain than the British army's standard-issue Brown Bess muskets. In conventional military terms, the Afghan fighters should have been no match for the British. But they proved themselves to be highly skilled in the art of guerrilla warfare, and the *jezail*, with its greater range and accuracy, was ideally suited to their purpose. This enabled the Afghans to indulge in their traditional hit-and-run tactic of sniping at the enemy from well-protected positions in the hills, or attacking vulnerable targets such as camps or formed bodies of men, before disappearing back into the mountains. These tactics were as familiar to Western soldiers fighting in Afghanistan in the modern conflict as they were to the British in the nineteenth century.

The other unwelcome discovery the British made at Ghazni was the existence of the Ghazis, groups of fanatical Muslim fighters who were prepared to sacrifice their lives to evict infidels from Afghan soil. The Ghazis – religious warriors – can be seen as the forerunners of the suicide bombers who have become a grisly feature of life in modern-day Afghanistan. They drew their inspiration from the fundamentalist strain of Islam founded by Mohammed ibn Abd al-Wahhab, a deeply conservative preacher who colonized the desert wastes of the Arabian peninsula in the early eighteenth century. Wahhabism, as this uncompromising strain of Islam became known, insists on a strict interpretation of the Koran. It is intolerant of non-Islamic faiths, such as Judaism, Christianity and Hinduism, then the dominant faith in northern India, and has inspired generations of Muslims to sacrifice their lives in the name of the Prophet.

Apart from being the official faith of modern Saudi Arabia, Wahhabism has been the inspiration for the formation of radical Islamic groups such as the Taliban and al-Qaeda. Osama bin Laden, the founder of al-Qaeda, observed the Wahhabi faith, as do the majority of his followers. The growth of Saudi influence in Pakistan has had a profound effect on the country's recent development. The Saudis paid $120 million to build the impressive Faisal Mosque in the centre of Islamabad, and have spent millions more funding Wahhabi madrasas throughout the country, with the result that the country has become more fundamentalist – and anti-Western – in its outlook. In Afghanistan, meanwhile, Wahhabi influence has led to Taliban supporters pursuing a social and religious agenda that is almost indistinguishable from that of the Afghan fanatics Churchill came across in the nineteenth century. When Winston fought against them he was particularly appalled at their conduct, describing them 'as dangerous and as sensible as mad dogs: fit only to be treated as such'.[8]

British soldiers fighting in Afghanistan in 1839 made their first acquaintance with the Ghazis at Ghazni as they finalized their plans to storm the fort. Hoping to rally the support of the Afghan tribes against the British, the amir had declared a jihad, or holy war, against the infidel invaders. Dost Mohammed was the first Afghan leader to appreciate fully the power of jihad.

To this end he even went so far as to declare himself Amir al-Mu'minin – not only Afghanistan's spiritual leader, but the king of all Muslims. He did this following a rare public display of Afghanistan's most precious object, a cloak said to have been worn by the Prophet himself. Mullah Omar, the founder of the modern-day Taliban, was the next person to repeat the ceremony when, in 1996, he donned the cloak and declared himself to be Amir al-Mu'minin.

Dost Mohammed's call to jihad succeeded in inspiring thousands of Ghazis to join his cause – for the most part backward villagers who had been converted to the Wahhabi faith. As a result, when the British reached Ghazni they found that a sizeable force of black-shirted warriors bearing the green banner of Islam had appeared on a nearby ridge. Mounted on horseback, they swept down on the British camp and, supported by cannon fire from the fort, they fought with a suicidal intensity that future generations of Western soldiers would come to know so well in Afghanistan. They were no match, though, for the well-drilled British infantry and cavalry, which forced them off and managed to capture about fifty, who were then handed over to Shuja to be dealt with. Such was their fanaticism, though, that as the Afghan king approached them, one Ghazi drew a dagger and thrust it into one of the king's attendants. The king responded by giving the order for them all to be killed immediately. The butchery took place behind Shuja's tent. A British officer who happened to be passing by the royal camp was horrified to discover the amir's men 'amusing themselves (for actually they were laughing and joking, and seemed to look upon the work as good fun) with hacking and maiming the poor wretches indiscriminately with their long swords and knives'.[9]

After the British success at Ghazni, the estimated 5,000 fighters that Dost Mohammed had summoned to repulse the invaders simply observed the long-held Afghan practice that had served them so well over many centuries of confronting invaders. They melted away to their homes and villages as quickly as they had heeded the call to jihad, preserving their freedom and energy for the day that would most certainly come when circumstances were more propitious to their cause. Realizing that all further resistance was futile, the amir and his family also fled the city, and on 7 August the Army of the Indus made its triumphant entry into Kabul, thereby completing its mission to restore Shuja to the throne. In military terms the campaign had been a great success, the first triumph of British arms in the reign of Queen Victoria who, at the age of eighteen, had ascended the throne just two years previously. But, as is so often the way in Afghanistan, the triumph was short lived, and it was not long before the British government faced its worst military catastrophe since the American War of Independence.

*

The disastrous fate that befell the first military force to be deployed by a Western power to Afghanistan can be attributed to two principal factors. To start with, for a nation that had many years of experience in governing native peoples, the British, once they had established themselves in Kabul, displayed a woeful disregard for the feelings of the ordinary Afghans they claimed to have liberated. The Afghans had never been terribly enthusiastic about Shuja in the first place. Before his surprise restoration to power he had been living in exile in India for so long that they barely remembered him. They remained sceptical about their new ruler and his British supporters who constructed a massive military base, or cantonment, on the outskirts of Kabul, which soon took on the appearance of a parallel city. (The NATO coalition did much the same when it took up residence in the Afghan capital many decades later.)

And while the Afghans were prepared to indulge the British soldiers' sporting pursuits, such as horse-racing and polo, they were less tolerant of their immorality. The British rank-and-file, whose families were left behind in India, resorted to Indian prostitutes who had accompanied the army to Kabul. Bachelor

British officers, meanwhile, had illicit liaisons with the wives of local Afghan men. Some Afghan women went so far as to leave their husbands and move in with their wealthier and more generous British lovers. Murderous feelings of revenge soon took root in the hearts of those proud Afghan tribesmen who had been cuckolded, many of whom exercised considerable influence in the city. 'The Afghans', commented the Victorian historian Sir John Kaye in his history of the conflict, 'are very jealous of the honour of their women, and there are things done in Caubul which covered them with shame and roused them to revenge . . . it went on until it became intolerable, and the injured then began to see that the only remedy was in their own hands.'[10] Add to this the brutality with which the British dealt with 'irreconcilable' tribal leaders – in Kandahar one particularly rebellious Afghan leader 'was executed, being blown from a gun', as one British officer later recounted[11] – and it was clear the British were overstaying their welcome.

The other great miscalculation was their failure to grasp the venality of the Afghan tribes, particularly those that controlled the highly profitable trade routes between their country and the outside world. The old adage 'You can rent an Afghan, but you can't buy him' is as true today as it was then. In *The Story of the Malakand Field Force*, Churchill concluded that 'silver makes a better weapon than steel' in keeping the Afghan tribes in check.[12] But that only worked so long as the British continued to pay the tribes a handsome remittance in return for their loyalty, in which case the Afghans were prepared to tolerate their presence in Kabul, even if they did not approve of it. But once the funds started to dry up, as happened after cost-conscious British officials insisted on reducing the budget, the Afghan tribes that supported Shuja's British-backed regime abandoned their erstwhile benefactors, with disastrous consequences for the British. The final straw came in September 1841 when the British announced they were implementing a 50 per cent reduction in the annual stipend paid to the tribes. As Major

Henry Rawlinson, an experienced political officer with the Indian government, observed, 'The feeling against us is daily on the increase and I apprehend a succession of disturbances . . . Their mullahs are preaching against us from one end of the country to the other.'[13]

The storm broke in November when a mob attacked the British Residency in Kabul and massacred the British inhabitants, including the British adventurer Alexander Burnes, who had been openly cohabiting with his Kashmiri mistress. Burnes, who described himself as a 'highly paid idler', was supposed to be monitoring the Afghans, but so distracted was he by his other activities that he completely misjudged their seething anger. Within days the reduced British garrison – half the force had already been sent back to India because the country was deemed to have been pacified – was besieged and fighting for their lives. Dost Mohammed had surrendered to the British the previous year, and gone into exile in India. But his son, Akbar Khan, had remained at large in the Hindu Kush, and now raised a sizeable army to drive out the infidel British. After several days of skirmishing, the garrison, numbering around 4,500 fighting men together with 12,000 non-combatant camp followers, were allowed to leave Kabul to march to Jalalabad. But, with the exception of a British doctor, none of them completed the treacherous 100-mile journey, undertaken in the depths of an Afghan winter when heavy snow blocked most of the passes. At first only the stragglers were picked off by the vengeful Afghans, but as each day passed and the column grew more extended, the attacks became bolder. The column was eventually broken up into a series of isolated groups, each pinned down by Afghan marksmen equipped with their deadly *jezails* or surrounded by large bodies of horsemen. After six days of carnage only one survivor reached Jalalabad, an army doctor by the name of Dr Brydon, thereby proving Akbar Khan's boast that he would 'annihilate the whole army except one man, who would reach Jalalabad to tell the tale'.[14]

The humiliation visited upon the British had a salutary effect on their future involvement in Afghanistan. From now on the British administrators of the Indian Empire regarded Afghanistan as a poisoned chalice best left untouched, while in London the name became synonymous with military disaster. The barbarous tribes of Afghanistan were regarded as entirely unsuited for the introduction of the type of civilized government the British had brought to India. John Nicholson, one of the few survivors of the British expedition who later became a legendary political officer in the frontier provinces, wrote that the Afghans were 'the most vicious and bloodthirsty race in existence, who fight merely for the love of bloodshed and plunder. I cannot describe their character in language sufficiently strong . . . From the highest to the lowest, every man of them would sell both country and relations.'[15]

Before the British abandoned Afghanistan, the small matter of retribution first had to be addressed. In London, where the sheer scale of the disaster had left most Victorians speechless, Queen Victoria made it plain that the deaths of the butchered English soldiers must be avenged, while the Duke of Wellington, who had himself fought with distinction in India, sent a blistering memo, with the Queen's blessing, to the British Governor General in Calcutta urging him to take immediate retaliatory action. 'It is impossible to impress upon you too strongly the notion of the importance of the Restoration of Reputation in the East. Our enemies in France, the United States, and wherever found [by which he meant Russia] are now rejoicing in Triumph upon our Disasters and Degradation. You will teach them that their triumph is premature.'[16] With the Iron Duke's rebuke ringing in their ears, a new army set off once more for the Khyber Pass in April 1842, and swiftly overcame Akbar Khan's forces, who had laid siege to the small British force that continued to hold Jalalabad. Having delayed their advance on Kabul to avoid the sweltering summer heat, the offensive was renewed in August, obliging the British to traverse the same passes where their comrades-in-arms had been massacred the previous winter. 'They lay in heaps of fifties and hundreds, our gun-wheels passing over and crushing the skulls and other bones of our late comrades at almost every yard, for three, four, or five miles,' one young British officer noted in his journal.[17] Another young officer, Neville Chamberlain, who became one of Britain's most distinguished soldiers in India, passed along the same route, noting, 'In some places the Affgans, to add insult to all the misery they inflicted, had placed the skeletons one in the arms of the other, or sometimes sitting or standing against the rocks as if they were holding a consultation!'[18]

In mid-September the British reached Kabul, where most of the Afghan fighters undertook their customary disappearing act into the north and west of the country. This did not discourage the British from exacting the most terrible retribution on the city. Initially they wanted to blow up the Bala Hissar fortress, the traditional residence of the Afghan kings, although this was overruled on the grounds that the British still hoped to have a working relationship with future rulers. Instead they blew up the central bazaar, one of the most famous structures in Central Asia, which prompted an orgy of looting, with troops and civilians indulging in plunder, rape and murder. These shameful scenes are still recalled to this day in Kabul, as a British officer discovered when he took up his posting in the Afghan capital in 2011. 'You blew up our market,' an Afghan official complained when they were discussing progress made by the NATO mission. Initially alarmed that his men had committed some unspeakable error, the officer was on the point of phoning his soldiers for clarification when the Afghan clarified he was speaking about the 1840s, not the present day.[19]

British honour having been restored, the Army of Retribution marched back to India through the Khyber Pass, vowing never to return. From now on they would rely on a policy of 'Butcher and Bolt', using one-off punitive expeditions to keep

the tribes in check, rather than launching costly military interventions. The whole sorry saga of British intervention was best
summed up by John Lawrence, a future Viceroy of India, who
concluded that 'to endeavour to hold such a country firmly, to
try to control such a people, is to court misfortune and calamity.
The Afghan will bear poverty, insecurity of life: but he will not
tolerate foreign rule. The moment he has a chance he will
rebel.'[20] Lawrence later became one of the most committed
adherents of the policy known as 'masterly inactivity', which
held that Britain should have nothing to do with Afghanistan,
but merely confine itself to guarding the border territory with
India while attempting to maintain a cordial relationship with
whomsoever held sway in Kabul. It was the total opposite of the
Forward Policy advocated by Lord Palmerston, who believed
the only way to steer Afghan policy in a direction favourable to
Britain was to subjugate the country.

For now, though, the priority was to disengage at the earliest
opportunity, and it was to this end that the British found
themselves in the invidious position of signing a treaty with
Dost Mohammed, the Afghan ruler they had originally sought
to depose. The amir had made his way back to Kabul as
the British retreated, and reinstated himself in power after the
hapless Shuja was murdered by an assassin as he stepped out
of the Bala Hissar fortress. At the very least the British had
hoped they might be able to maintain an embassy in Kabul,
so that they could keep a watchful eye on their Russian rivals.
But even this small concession was denied to them by Dost
Mohammed, who offered them the border city of Kandahar
instead. The British despaired of ever getting the Afghans to
enter into a proper agreement. As Lord Ellenborough, the Governor General of India, wryly observed in late 1842, he would
'leave it to the Affghans themselves to create a government
amidst the anarchy which is the consequence of their crimes'.[21]

The British had learned a harsh lesson, one that is as valid
today as it was in the 1840s: the Afghans do not take kindly to

being bullied by foreign powers. The other alarming discovery
they made during the course of the campaign was that, despite
their overwhelming superiority in terms of men, equipment and
firepower, the British were no match for the Afghans' guerrilla-
style tactics. Only rarely did the Afghans engage the British in
set-piece battles. For the rest of the time they played a clever
waiting game, watching for any sign of weakness in the British
dispositions before launching a deadly attack. As Churchill
found when he fought on the North-West Frontier, the British
were at a great disadvantage because they were fighting 'an
active enterprising enemy that can move faster and shoot better,
who knows the country and who knows the ranges . . . daring
riflemen, individually superior to the soldier, and able to support
the greatest fatigues, can always inflict loss'.[22] NATO soldiers
who have fought in the more recent conflict became familiar
with the same tactics.

*

The new policy of 'masterly inactivity' was pursued virtually
uninterrupted for the next thirty or so years as the British
concentrated their energies on consolidating their hold over
other areas of India. The annexation of Sind Province was
completed by 1843, and the Sikh province of Punjab fell under
British suzerainty in 1849. One consequence of the annexation
of these two vast provinces of northern India, which now form
a large part of Pakistan, was that the British acquired a lengthy
and uninterrupted border with Afghanistan stretching for hundreds of miles. But having acquired the border, the British had
no clear idea of how to police it.

British interest in Afghanistan did not revive until Benjamin
Disraeli's Conservative Party came to power in 1874, when the
great statesman's election victory restored to power once more
the champions of the policy that had led to the disastrous 1839
military intervention. The more hawkish Forward Policy advocates continued to argue in favour of the complete colonization

of Afghanistan, extending Britain's sphere of influence to the Hindu Kush and the Oxus itself, placing British soldiers menacingly on the frontier of the Russian Empire. Disraeli was not prepared to go that far, preferring to establish the most strategically advantageous frontier that could be maintained by the least possible interference in Afghan affairs. The Forward Policy debate was still very much a live issue in the 1890s, and the conclusion Churchill reached was more pragmatic than ideological. He rejected the Forward Policy advanced by the hawks on the grounds that 'we have neither the troops nor the money to carry it out' – an argument that is as true today for the Western powers as it was for the British government in the nineteenth century. Instead Churchill recommended 'a system of gradual advance, of political intrigue among the tribes, of subsidies and small expeditions'.[23] In other words sticking to the tried and tested imperial 'divide and rule' formula.

Like Palmerston before him, Disraeli, whose statue now stands beside Churchill's in Parliament Square, was not prepared to tolerate Russian meddling in Afghanistan's affairs. So, when the Russians sent yet another delegation to Kabul in 1877 to request Afghan support for an invasion of British India, the British government issued an ultimatum demanding that a permanent British mission be established in Kabul. Sher Ali, who had succeeded Dost Mohammed in 1863, was unable to provide the British with the assurances they sought. As a consequence, in November 1878 British soldiers found themselves launching another invasion of Afghanistan through the Khyber Pass. Although the British force of 45,000 men enjoyed, as they had in 1839, overwhelming military superiority, the fighting was every bit as intense, with neither side giving any quarter. British soldiers learned from bitter experience the fate envisioned for them in Rudyard Kipling's 'The Young British Soldier':

When you're wounded and left on Afghanistan's plains,
And the women come out to cut up what remains,
Jest roll to your rifle and blow out your brains,
An' go to your Gawd like a soldier.

The British adopted a policy of zero tolerance towards the Afghans as they advanced through the country, and the summary executions they conducted against captured Afghan tribesmen might today be categorized as war crimes. Sher Ali's makeshift army of 15,000 tribesmen was easily defeated by the better organized and disciplined force of General Frederick Roberts, and the survivors again disappeared to their homes to fight another day. This time, though, the British maintained their pursuit, taking little care to distinguish between combatants and civilians. Villages suspected of hiding Afghan fighters were razed to the ground, and the male inhabitants shot. In one assault against the Shinwari tribe close to the Khyber Pass, thirty-three tribesmen were executed after the British found the mutilated body of a Bengal Lancer nearby.[24]

The military campaign quickly concluded, and Sher Ali fled to the Hindu Kush, where he died a broken man after the Russians declined to support his doomed defiance of the British. The British retook Kabul, meeting only limited resistance, and on 26 May 1879 they finally got the agreement they had been seeking for decades when Mohammed Yaqub Khan, the new amir, signed the Treaty of Gandamak, in which the Afghans ceded control of large areas of the south and east of the country – including the all-important Khyber Pass – to British control. In addition Yaqub agreed to hand over Afghanistan's foreign policy to the British and to allow a permanent British mission in Kabul. The treaty stipulated that Afghanistan agreed to 'henceforth conduct all relations with foreign states in accordance with the advice and wishes of the British Government'. The British, by way of recompense, agreed to pay the new amir a handsome retainer of 600,000 rupees, as well as agreeing to support him against any foreign aggression. Never again would the Russians be allowed to engage in anti-British intrigues with the Afghans, as the British now enjoyed complete mastery of all the main mountain passes leading to India.

Or so they thought. Within months of signing the new Anglo-Afghan accord the British found themselves facing yet another disaster when thousands of disgruntled Afghan tribes-men converged on Kabul to protest against British interference in their affairs, and attacked the British Residency, which had been established within the Bala Hissar. In days the entire British mission, including the recently appointed Consul, lay dead. General Roberts, who had decamped his forces fifty miles south of the capital to avoid upsetting Afghan sensibilities, immediately set off for Kabul to restore order. During the advance on Kabul the British used their new Gatling guns for the first time. Firing rounds at a speed of two hundred a minute, they proved more than a match for the Afghan tribesmen and their primitive *jezails*. When he reached Kabul, Roberts adopted methods similar to those that had been employed by Judge Jeffreys in the West Country to suppress the Jacobite rebellion of the late seventeenth century. He set up a 'Black Assize', as it became known, outside the still-smouldering ruins of the British Residency to punish those responsible for massacring the British delegation, and eighty-seven Afghans were hanged on specially constructed gallows. The executions sparked a barrage of criticism in London, where Roberts's opponents accused him of engaging in 'judicial murders'. But Roberts, who rose to the rank of Field Marshal, contended that the accusations of foul play had been 'got up' by journalists with some unspecified grudge against him. Nevertheless, reports persisted of Afghan men being shot indiscriminately on Roberts's orders, which did little to endear the British to the Afghans. Anger over Britain's continued presence in the country, meanwhile, deepened as living costs in the capital soared when the military appropriated its share of the government crop to feed its troops.

Before long the cry of jihad once more echoed through Kabul's narrow alleyways. The mullah leading the call for revenge was Mushk-i-Alam, which means Perfume of the Universe. By December the British faced yet another nationwide uprising against their rule, only this time they were better prepared. When thousands of black-shirted Ghazis chanting 'Allahu Akbar' – God is the Greatest – attempted to storm the new British cantonment on the outskirts of Kabul, they were beaten back by the heavily armed British, with horrendous losses. Elsewhere in Afghanistan, though, an army of fanatical Ghazis came close to wiping out the entire British garrison at Kandahar. At the Battle of Maiwand, fought fifty miles to the east of Kandahar, the Ghazis killed 969 British soldiers – the worst British losses since the 1839 retreat from Kabul – as they launched wave after wave of suicidal attacks under the command of Malalai Ana, a young Pashtun woman who waved her veil as a standard before she was killed. Today she is remembered as an Afghan Joan of Arc for her defiant stand against the English occupiers. The Ghazis paid a high price for their victory, losing nearly 3,000 killed and 1,500 wounded against just 22 British dead, a graphic illustration of their suicidal tendencies. Even so, Malalai Ana's role in leading them to victory has entered into Afghan folklore, and is celebrated in verse by the Taliban to uphold the virtues of martyrdom. 'My lover if you are martyred in the Battle of Maiwand, I will make a coffin for you from the tresses of my hair.'[25] It was during this campaign that the British experienced their first recorded suicide attack by an Afghan. It took place in Kandahar, when a Talib-ul-ilm attempted to kill a British soldier with a knife after gaining entry to the citadel at Kandahar by posing as a delivery man with a load of wood.[26]

Kandahar was saved by General Roberts, who again rode

to the rescue and, at the Battle of Kandahar, inflicted a comprehensive defeat on the Afghans – a stunning feat of arms for which he is remembered today as Lord Roberts of Kandahar. 'Bobs', as he was known to his troops, became one of the greatest soldiers of the Victorian era, later making a vital contribution to the British effort in the Boer War. He died of pneumonia in France, during a visit to Indian troops at Saint-Omer in 1914, and was accorded the rare privilege of lying in state in Westminster Hall, one of only two non-royals to do so in the twentieth century – the other being Winston Churchill – before being given a state funeral.

*

By the time the British had subdued the Afghans, a change of government in London prompted yet another volte-face in British policy towards Afghanistan. The fall of Disraeli's government in May 1880 put an end to the Forward Policy whereby Britain sought to dominate Afghanistan. With Gladstone's return to office, London determined to cut its losses and undertake an immediate withdrawal of British forces, thereby undermining the valiant efforts made by General Roberts and his men to assert Britain's military superiority. Not for the first time would a sudden change of heart on the part of politicians living thousands of miles away from the rugged mountains of Afghanistan have a dramatic impact on the fortunes of the soldiers fighting there. Comparisons can certainly be drawn between Gladstone's reversal of British policy in 1880 and US President Barack Obama's decision in the summer of 2011 to bring America's combat operations against the Taliban to an early conclusion. In both cases, rather than pressing ahead with a military-led solution to the conflict, the priority was to negotiate a quick political fix with the Afghans, and to bring home the troops at the earliest opportunity.

In 1880 this meant trying to persuade Abdur Rahman, the new claimant to the Afghan throne, to accept a deal similar to the one previously agreed with Mohammed Yaqub Khan, who by this time had made the journey into exile in India common to deposed Afghan kings. Abdur Rahman, the deposed amir's cousin, was the grandson of the mighty Dost Mohammed and possessed many of his ancestor's ruthless qualities, later earning himself the title 'Iron Amir' for his uncompromising adminis- tration of his lawless country, which he ruled until 1901. From the outset of Abdur Rahman's negotiations with the British the amir was determined to assert his independence. He arrived for the conference in Kabul dressed in a Russian uniform, with a bagful of roubles and his entourage armed with Russian pistols. In the event the British had no cause for alarm over this clumsy exhibition of Russophilia: Abdur Rahman was no great fan of the Russians, having lived among them in exile for many years and gained first-hand knowledge of their territorial designs on his country. Indeed, once firmly established in power, the new amir became something of an Anglophile. He hired an English governess for his children, an English tailor, an Irish dentist and a cockney engineer who produced high-quality copies of Euro- pean guns at his Kabul factory.

This was just as well, for Britain's desire to expedite its with- drawal meant that it did not want to waste too much time on negotiations, and was prepared to take a gamble on Abdur Rah- man's bona fides. As General Donald Stewart, who had replaced Roberts as commander of the Kabul garrison, wrote to his wife when the British prepared to leave, 'Abdur Rahman seems sen- sible . . . I hope he will be a success. It is a regular lottery, though.'[27] In return for allowing Abdur Rahman to become the new amir, the British insisted that he accept the terms of the Treaty of Gandamak, thereby allowing the British to maintain control of the all-important passes as well as large tracts of land on the Afghan side of the border. Some British officials even wanted to annex Kandahar to India, but this was unacceptable to Gladstone, who wanted to put an end to Britain's imperial adventures in Central Asia. Even though the British government dropped some of its more outrageous demands, Abdur Rahman was not happy with the terms of the treaty that he signed with a heavy heart in April 1881. The amir, who became the dominant figure in Britain's relations with Afghanistan for the rest of the century, and whose double-dealing Churchill came to know well when he was fighting on the North-West Frontier, claimed the British had duped him into signing the agreement. He never accepted Britain's claims to control large areas of his territory, and he continued to regard the entire frontier region as 'the hereditary property of Afghan kings, being part of their country' all the way to the Indus river. When he learned that the British were planning to build a railway line to Kandahar – Afghanistan's second city – he wrote that Britain's move into southern Afghanistan was like 'pushing a knife into my vitals'.[28]

Abdur Rahman, like his grandfather, proved to be a shrewd and powerful leader who, in time, consolidated the Afghan state and accepted British diplomatic aid to secure his frontiers. He ruled his kingdom with a rod of iron. Criminals were impaled or stoned to death, robbers hung in cages and left to die at the scene of their crimes, while unjust tradesmen had their ears nailed to the entrance of their shops in the bazaar. The British were under no illusions about the new amir, who, 'like all his family, thinks the people are made for the sole purpose of supplying him with men and money', Stewart wrote before departing Kabul. 'They are a vile race, and we shall never make anything of them. The more I see of them, the more hateful does their character appear.'[29] But the British were prepared to tolerate Abdur Rahman, who received many glittering awards from Queen Victoria, on condition that he kept the peace on the border.

In 1893 Britain made one final effort to resolve the border issue once and for all when Sir Mortimer Durand began work on establishing an official frontier between India and Afghanistan. Durand, a career civil servant who regarded Abdur Rahman as a 'brutal savage', was determined to ensure that

Britain controlled all the land around the strategic passes into Afghanistan. To this end, he established an arbitrary border that cut through territory controlled by the local Pashtun tribes. The Durand Line, as it became known, ran through the middle of villages and grazing grounds, so that Pashtun farmers found themselves living on one side of the border while their fields and livestock were located on the other. Durand showed little sympathy for the Afghans' objections to his plan. 'The Amir is not the Emperor of Germany,' he declared when Abdur Rahman criticized the British envoy's high-handed approach. 'What they [the Afghans] understand and expect is action, not talk.'[30] The establishment of the Durand Line, which survives to this day marking Afghanistan's frontier with modern-day Pakistan, attempted to satisfy Britain's long-held desire to define the Afghan border, thereby discouraging imperial rivals such as Russia from casting covetous glances at the Indian Empire. But it did nothing to improve Britain's relations with the war-like tribes whose way of life had been so crudely disrupted. It left the Pashtun tribes in an almost constant state of agitation against the British.

*

The vexed issue of the border cast a dark shadow over Anglo-Afghan relations for many decades, and the persistent skirmishing gave the North-West Frontier the same reputation among the British as the Wild West enjoyed among Americans – a lawless terrain where the normal rules of civilization did not apply. The conflict that resulted in Churchill's participation in the Malakand campaign of 1897 certainly had its origins in the disaffection among the frontier Pashtun tribes that had been provoked by the establishment of the Durand Line. One of the most serious tribal revolts concerned the small British garrison at Chitral, the northernmost town of any size on the British frontier at its closest point to the Indian Empire's border with Russia. Close to the snow-covered wastes of the Hindu

Kush, the most inaccessible point of the entire frontier formed the backdrop for Rudyard Kipling's Great Game novel *Kim*. It had proved physically impossible for the British to find any means of establishing their new border north of the Khyber Pass in a three-cornered region abutting Russia and Afghanistan. Instead they garrisoned an isolated force at Chitral to keep a watchful eye on Russian activities on the other side of the border.

The British presence at Chitral dated back to 1870, when the Indian government intervened after George Hayward, a former army officer and explorer who had been commissioned by the Royal Geographical Society to investigate the frontier tribes, was murdered after falling out with one of the local maliks, or chieftains. A recipient of one of the Society's gold medals for his exploits, Hayward was one of the less well-known members of the golden age of Victorian exploration that included more familiar names such as Livingstone and Stanley. In the autumn of 1869 Hayward had set off on an expedition to locate the sources of the Oxus, a subject of keen interest to British policy-makers. But in the course of his explorations he fell foul of the local malik, and paid with his life. Today his body rests in an overgrown British cemetery in Gilgit, together with the remains of numerous British soldiers, officials and adventurers who perished in the surrounding mountains. The headstone on his grave pays tribute to 'a gallant officer and accomplished traveller' who was 'cruelly murdered'.

The British avenged Hayward's death by sending a punitive expedition to expel the offending malik, who was then replaced by a pro-British tribesman, Aman-ul-Malk. The new malik signed an agreement with the Indian government in 1877 whereby, in return for pledging his loyalty to the British, he was guaranteed protection from hostile Afghan tribes and granted an annual allowance of 6,000 rupees. Durand was appointed the British Agent for the area, basing himself at Gilgit, a border town around 140 miles to the east of Chitral. Durand increased the malik's allowance to 12,000 rupees a year, 'contingent on good behaviour' and on condition the malik and his sons 'accepted the advice of the British Agent on all matters'.[31] The arrangement was similar to the bribes the Americans and their allies would later pay to various Afghan leaders to buy their loyalty in the aftermath of the September 11 attacks.

This cosy agreement came to an abrupt end in 1892 when Aman-ul-Malk died, sparking a spate of fratricide as rival members of his family fought over the succession. It eventually passed to Nizam-ul-Mulk, one of the dead malik's many sons, but only after he had overcome the challenge of his younger brother Sher Afzal, who had murdered fifteen of his younger brothers in his quest for the title. Afzal fled to Kabul, where he was placed under 'surveillance' by Abdur Rahman, who no doubt thought his new guest might be a useful ally in stirring up trouble against the British. Nizam, meanwhile, cemented his relationship with Durand by promising to help the British build a telegraph line to Chitral, a vital link to the outside world for the isolated garrison. But Nizam's alliance with the British, together with their increasing interference in local tribal affairs, was deeply resented by many of the neighbouring tribal leaders, particularly Umra Khan, another powerful malik who controlled most of the Swat Valley and the district of Bajaur. In *The Story of the Malakand Field Force* Churchill describes Umra Khan as 'the most important man between Chitral and Peshawar'.[32] Matters finally came to a head on 1 January 1895 when Nizam was murdered while out hawking – probably on the orders of Umra Khan, who himself was in league with Abdur Rahman, for the amir never ceased in his anti-British scheming from the safety of his palace in Kabul. Within weeks Umra Khan had moved a force of between 3,000 and 4,000 tribesmen to confront the small British contingent at Chitral, with Abdur Rahman running guns freely to the rebels across Britain's newly created frontier. In addition, the British received reports that the Afghan amir was actively encouraging the maliks of all the frontier tribes to attack the British, in return for which they would receive ammunition and compensation for any losses suffered.

By 3 March the beleaguered British garrison at Chitral found themselves facing a Rorke's Drift-style battle for survival, surrounded by an enraged mob of hostile tribesmen hell-bent on their destruction. At first the local Chitralis, who had benefited from the generous British allowances, opposed Umra Khan. But, in characteristic tribal fashion, they soon changed sides, prompting British suspicions that the Chitralis had invited Umra Khan to make the attack on their base in the first place, but had tried to conceal their treachery lest they were subjected to reprisals by the British.[33] After the initial British pre-emptive attack that resulted in the defenders suffering twenty-five killed and thirty wounded, they were forced to regroup and wait out the siege in the hope that a relief force could be sent from India to save them. Ammunition was so low that the soldiers, who were drawn primarily from the Indian regiments of the 14th Sikhs and 4th Kashmiri Rifles, were limited to 300 rounds each for the duration of the siege. After two weeks food rations had diminished to the point where they had no alternative but to kill their ponies and live off horseflesh. The defenders made frantic efforts to reinforce the fort's defences, such as strengthening the two parapets, improving the head cover to afford better protection against enemy snipers and increasing the protection for the water-gate that led to the Chitral river, the fort's main water supply. Meanwhile Sher Afzal, one of the prime instigators of the revolt, returned from Kabul and offered to make peace on condition the British evacuated the fort and returned to India. But fearing they would be double-crossed and massacred once they left the fort, the surviving officers opted to stay and await the arrival of the relief force. 'To rescue them was imperative,' Churchill states in the introduction to his account of his own adventures on the North-West Frontier.[34]

'The besiegers . . . were thoroughly versed in every trick and artifice of besieging forts similar to that in Chitral,' noted

Captain W. R. Robertson of the 3rd Dragoon Guards, whose official account of the siege was published in 1898.[35] Frustrated by the refusal of the British to surrender, the tribesmen responded by making intermittent attacks, on one occasion trying to burn the fort down by placing red-hot embers and a bundle of faggots close to the gun tower. 'The enemy showed great courage and enterprise in firing our tower, and our sentries showed great slackness and want of vigilance,' one of the officers later recalled.[36] When, in mid-April, the tribesmen learned that the British relief force was on its way to save the garrison, the attackers intensified their efforts to break down the defences. 'They now commenced an almost incessant beating of *tom-toms* and playing of pipes' to drown out the noise of gangs of workmen working furiously to dig a mine under the fort's defences. The British responded by sending out a raiding party which, despite being under a constant barrage of fire, succeeded in blowing up the mine with 110lb of explosive, for the loss of twenty-one British killed and wounded out of a hundred men.

Two days later, on 18 April, realizing that the British were in no mood to surrender, and that a much larger relief force would soon arrive, the tribesmen quietly withdrew and abandoned the siege, which had lasted for forty-six days. The British had lost a total of 104 killed or wounded out of a garrison – including all the camp followers – that originally numbered more than 500. In addition another 85 were incapacitated by disease. The siege was lifted after a small British force under Colonel Kelly made an epic march across the snow-covered passes from Gilgit, a manoeuvre of extraordinary bravura, which entailed pushing mules laden with guns up mountains and fording rivers while all the time fighting off raiding parties of Pashtun fighters. Captain Robertson wrote in his official account of the siege that, when the relief force arrived, 'All seemed to think, from Kelly downwards, that their march was a mere trifle, their hardships undeserving of reference.' After the siege was lifted Lord Elgin, who had taken up the position of Indian

Viceroy, wrote to the *Gazette of India* stating that 'the steady front shown to the enemy, the military skill displayed in the conduct of the defence, the cheerful endurance of all the hardships of the siege, the gallant demeanour of the troops, the conspicuous examples of heroism and intrepidity recounted, would ever be remembered as forming a glorious episode in the history of the Indian Empire and its army'.[37] Several of the young officers who participated in the campaign received the Victoria Cross, the highest military award for valour 'in the face of the enemy', while many received other awards or were mentioned in dispatches.

Churchill came in search of similar honours when he volunteered to fight on the wild frontier two years later.

CHAPTER THREE

A SUBALTERN AND A GENTLEMAN

'It seemed to my youthful mind that it must be a
thrilling and immense experience to hear the whistle
of bullets all around.'
Winston S. Churchill, *My Early Life*

Before Churchill could even think about going to fight in Afghanistan, his first priority on leaving Sandhurst was to get himself commissioned into a cavalry regiment. His father would not have approved, having tried his hardest to secure his son a commission in the 60th Rifles, which he regarded as 'one of the finest regiments in the army'. Indeed, so determined was Lord Randolph that Winston should join the infantry that, during a race meeting at Newmarket, he extracted a promise from the Duke of Cambridge, the army's commander-in-chief, to get his son into the 60th when he left Sandhurst. And this was how matters stood at the time of Lord Randolph's death.

Winston, however, had never shared his father's enthusiasm for what he called 'those old Rifles'. The young cadet's head had been turned by the glamour and dash of the cavalry, and now that his father was no longer able to impede his ambition, he threw all his energy into securing a cavalry commission. At Sandhurst, Winston had advanced a number of arguments for the cavalry over the infantry, the most forceful being that the cavalry was better suited to his temperament and physique. Churchill was well aware how his deficiencies could hinder his prospects in the infantry, 'in which physical weaknesses will render me nearly useless on service and the only thing I am showing an aptitude for athletically – riding – will be no good for me'.[1] There were other reasons why an ambitious young cadet might prefer to join the cavalry: promotions were quicker than in the infantry (the 60th Rifles having the slowest promotion rate in the entire army), commissions were obtained faster and the 4th Hussars, his preferred regiment, was due shortly to deploy to India, where lay the promise of medals and glory.

Winston's enthusiasm for the cavalry, and the 4th Hussars in particular, was partly due to his admiration for the charismatic Colonel John Brabazon, who had recently taken command of the regiment at their Aldershot depot. Brabazon was an impoverished Irish landlord who had nevertheless enjoyed a distinguished military career and had befriended Winston's parents when they lived in Ireland. Churchill, who increasingly displayed an independent frame of mind, enlisted Brabazon's support to make sure that, on leaving Sandhurst, he joined the Hussars, rather than the dreaded 60th Rifles. As an expert horseman in his own right, Brabazon often officiated at military riding examinations, which enabled him to keep a watchful eye on his protégé. When Winston wrote to Brabazon as a cadet – taking care not to let his father know what he was up to – he set out persuasive arguments for joining the cavalry. Brabazon responded by inviting him to spend a weekend with the Hussars and dine with him in the regimental mess.

The dinner can be seen as a seminal moment in young Winston's life, one he long remembered and cherished into adulthood. As Churchill recalls in *My Early Life*,

> In those days the Mess of a cavalry regiment presented an impressive spectacle to a youthful eye. Twenty or thirty officers, all magnificently attired in blue and gold, assembled round a table upon which shone the plate and trophies gathered by the regiment in two hundred years of sport

and campaigning. It was like a State banquet. In an all-pervading air of glitter, affluence, ceremony and veiled discipline, an excellent and lengthy dinner was served to the strains of the regimental string band. I received the gayest of welcomes, and having it would seem conducted myself with discretion and modesty, I was invited again on several occasions.[2]

Also present at this dinner was Captain Julian Byng, the future hero of Vimy Ridge who, as Viscount Byng of Vimy, became Governor General of Canada. The young scion of the Marlborough dynasty evidently felt very much at home among the glamour and tradition of a British cavalry regiment.

Brabazon's background may also have had a bearing on Churchill's desire to prove himself in combat on the North-West Frontier. Brabazon, who had won the War Medal fighting in Africa, saw active service in Afghanistan with another cavalry regiment, the 10th Hussars. He had participated in the Second Afghan War, helping Roberts to retake Kabul in 1879, and was Cavalry Brigade Major at the Battle of Kandahar the following year, winning a clutch of medals in the process. Brabazon was in every sense the archetypal hero for an impressionable young army cadet. Churchill thought him 'one of the brightest military stars in London society. He was exactly the right height for a man to be. He was not actually six feet, but he looked it. Now, in his prime, his appearance was magnificent. His clean-cut symmetrical features, his bright grey eyes and his strong jaw, were shown to the best advantage by a moustache which the Kaiser might well have taken as his unattainable ideal.'[3] A lifelong friend of the Prince of Wales, he was known as 'Brab' to his friends, though the troopers of the 4th Hussars referred to him behind his back as 'Bwab' because of his inability to pronounce the letter 'r'.

By choosing the 4th Hussars, Churchill had joined one of England's elite cavalry regiments, one that enjoyed an impeccable fighting pedigree. The 4th (Queen's Own) Hussars, to give the regiment its full title, was regarded as a 'smart' cavalry regiment, a reputation that benefited from Brabazon's own social connections, and had been in existence for more than two centuries. Formed on 17 July 1685 during the reign of King James II, it was originally named Berkeley's Dragoons after its first colonel, the Honourable John Berkeley. The regiment went through various manifestations until it emerged as a distinctive unit during the Napoleonic Wars, where it earned its first battle honours under the Duke of Wellington in the Peninsular War. The 4th Hussars fought in the First Afghan War of 1839–42, taking part in the storming of the fortress at Ghazni, where the British had their first experience of the Afghan suicidal religious fanatics. But its most renowned exploit took place during the Crimean War of 1854–6, when the 4th Hussars were one of the cavalry regiments that took part in the infamous Charge of the Light Brigade, leading a suicidal charge against well-defended Russian artillery positions. A French officer who witnessed the carnage commented, 'The Charge of the Light Brigade may have been folly, but it was certainly magnificent.'[4] During the engagement the 4th succeeded in silencing the Russian guns at the end of the valley, but at a terrible cost. Of the 600 cavalrymen who took part in the charge, half were killed, wounded or taken prisoner. Among those captured was Private Samuel Parkes, who was awarded the Victoria Cross after his repatriation to Britain, the only member of the regiment to be so honoured in its entire history.

Churchill's intrigues to get himself commissioned into the 4th Hussars did not meet with universal favour. Prince Arthur, Duke of Connaught, who was Queen Victoria's seventh child and a distinguished soldier in his own right, was displeased to learn that young Winston was not keen to join the 60th, especially as, like his elder brother the Duke of Cambridge, he had made a personal recommendation on the cadet's behalf. Lord Randolph, despite his declining health, had also been unhappy with Brabazon's intervention, particularly as he had already obtained a personal promise from the Duke of Cambridge. 'Brabazon, who I know is one of the finest officers in the Army, had no business to go and turn that boy's head about going into the 4th Hussars,' Lord Randolph remonstrated.[5] But Lord Randolph's death meant that the strong-willed Winston 'was in the main the master of my fortunes', and he would not be dissuaded from pursuing his ambition. He even believed that Lord Randolph, in the final days of his life, had reconciled himself to his son's chosen course. 'One of the last remarks he made to me was, "Have you got your horses?"' Churchill recalled.[6]

It was left to Winston's mother, the recently widowed Jennie, to undertake the delicate mission of persuading the Duke of Cambridge, in his capacity as head of the army, to allow Churchill to make the transfer from the infantry to the cavalry. Having secured Brabazon's assurance that there was an opening for Winston, Jennie wrote to the Duke, who was holidaying on the Riviera, seeking the necessary consent. In the event the Duke, who deeply mourned the loss of 'poor Randolph', was more than happy to oblige. 'The 4th Hussars is a very good Cavalry Regiment, and Colonel Brabazon an excellent Commanding Officer so I think your selection is in that respect a very good one,' the Duke wrote to Jennie in February 1895. 'I am delighted to hear that your son has passed so well out of Sandhurst, a proof that he has made good use of his stay at the College.'[7] Not many young officers of Churchill's generation can have received their commission with such a ringing endorsement from their commander-in-chief, but then Churchill, as he sought to demonstrate from the outset of his military career, was no ordinary recruit.

*

Churchill's commission into the 4th Hussars – motto *Mente et Manu*, Might and Main – was published in the *London Gazette* of

19 February 1895, with an effective date of 20 February, and was signed by Queen Victoria and H. Campbell Bannerman, the Secretary of State for War. The assistance Jennie provided in helping her son to join his regiment of choice highlighted the deepening relationship between Winston and his mother. Winston, who from a young age had been in awe of his mother's beauty and charm, still remained in her thrall. 'How I wish I could secrete myself in the corner of the envelope and embrace you as soon as you tear it open,' he wrote in one particularly Oedipal outburst.[8] Now they became close allies, not least because of the precarious financial position in which the family had been left by Lord Randolph. After his father's substantial debts had been paid off to the Rothschild Bank, there was little left to maintain Jennie and her two boys in their customary style. This was a particular problem for Winston, who had been relying on financial support from his parents to supplement his meagre army salary of £120 per annum – less than £10,000 at today's values.

Lord Randolph had warned Winston repeatedly about the added expense of joining a cavalry regiment, and by joining the 4th Hussars he had chosen one of the smartest the army had to offer. The uniform was blue with gold trim and a brown fur hat called a busby, similar to the 'bearskin' worn by guardsmen, with a dashing red plume. The cavalry might be more glamorous and offer faster promotion, but it was also a great deal more expensive. Colonel Brabazon, who was on first-name terms with the royal family, set the regiment's high social tone, and Winston had difficulty meeting the costs of his uniform, horses, mess subscriptions and other social obligations. Winston calculated the total cost of his uniforms, equipment and mess bills at just over £653. Most of Churchill's contemporaries – many of whom came from wealthy families – could expect to draw on annual allowances of £500 or more. But Jennie could offer no more than £400, and often struggled to find this amount, leaving Winston to fret over paying his mess bill.

Duchess Lily, Winston's favourite aunt, herself the daughter of a US navy commodore, helped him out with £200 to buy a horse. Formerly Mrs Lillian Hammersley, she was the widow of the 8th Duke of Marlborough, who had died suddenly in 1892. In the summer of 1895 the widowed Duchess married Lord William Beresford, another war veteran who had won the Victoria Cross fighting the Zulus and had also served with distinction in India, thereby helping to consolidate Churchill's connections to the senior echelons of the British military. The help of their well-connected relatives notwithstanding, the Churchills were condemned to a hand-to-mouth existence for the foreseeable future, with Jennie frittering away what remained of the family inheritance on expensive gowns and parties, and responsibility for balancing the books falling on the shoulders of her eldest son. The Churchills' financial predicament did not cause a family rift: rather it brought mother and son closer together. 'My mother was always at hand to help and advise,' Churchill recalled. 'She never sought to exercise parental control. Indeed she soon became an ardent ally, furthering my plans and guarding my interests with all her influence and boundless energy. She was still at forty young, beautiful and fascinating. We worked together on even terms, more like brother and sister than mother and son.'[9]

And when it came to money, Jennie and Winston were as bad as each other. When Jennie took herself off to Paris to recuperate from the trauma of nursing Lord Randolph, she travelled with her maid and butler. Then she bought a new house at 35A Great Cumberland Place, just north of Hyde Park, which she insisted was redecorated from top to bottom at great expense, and had all the latest modern luxuries fitted, such as electric light and hot water. While the house was being made ready, the Churchills were reduced almost to the status of refugees, staying at the country houses of their friends, or else putting up in smart hotels. Winston, meanwhile, spent money as though he had a sizeable private income to supplement his modest army pay, which meant that he was forever writing pleading letters to his mother asking for more funds, money which she simply did not have. The family's parlous finances meant that, from a young age, Churchill understood the imperative of earning a healthy income.

The death of Mrs Everest, Winston's long-serving nanny, in the summer of 1895 came as another bitter blow. The kindly Mrs Everest had effectively brought up Winston and his younger brother due to their parents' constant absenteeism and neglect. Winston had protested bitterly when, for financial reasons, Lord and Lady Randolph terminated Mrs Everest's employment in 1893. Winston had kept in touch with her after her retirement, sending her a cheque for more than £2 – which he could ill-afford – when he learned that she had suffered a fall and broken her arm. And when, in the summer of 1895, Mrs Everest died, he paid for a headstone to be erected on her grave at the City of London Cemetery in Manor Park bearing the simple inscription: ERECTED IN MEMORY OF ELIZABETH ANNE EVEREST WHO DIED 3RD JULY 1895 AGED 62 BY WINSTON SPENCER CHURCHILL AND JACK SPENCER CHURCHILL. The death of his beloved nurse, coming so soon after that of his father, left Winston feeling very much alone in the world, and drew him even closer to his mother. 'I shall never know such a friend again,'[10] he wrote of Mrs Everest, and for many years afterwards he paid an annual sum to the local florist for the upkeep of the grave.

*

Churchill applied himself with rigour to the demands of life with the 4th Hussars. Although he had proved himself an accomplished horseman at Sandhurst, he found the training at his new regimental headquarters very demanding. As a young officer Winston was expected to undergo the same training as non-commissioned recruits. Some of the more challenging exercises included mounting and dismounting from a bare-backed horse at the trot or canter, and making the horse jump over a high bar without any stirrups or saddle, often with the rider's hands tied behind his back. Just like the other recruits, Winston suffered his fair share of falls, the indignity of being dumped on the riding-school floor made all the greater by the furtive grins of the recruits surrounding him as he attempted to refasten his little gold-braided pork-pie cap, which was tied to the chin by a bootlace strap. Winston's exertions were made more difficult by a bad injury he had sustained to his thigh muscle, which meant that he suffered 'tortures' while undergoing the training. But for all the discomfort, he took it in his stride, remarking many years later that 'I am all for youth being made willingly to endure austerities'.[11] In the 4th Hussars' official regimental history, S. Hallaway, who was a lance corporal at the time, remembers Churchill's first appearance at the regimental stables. 'Mr Churchill walked over the squadron parade ground towards my stable. I thought how odd he looked. His hair and his gold lace forage cap the same colour . . . I had to tell him all I knew about my troops, men and horses and stable management. He kept me very busy asking questions.' According to Hallaway, Aldershot, where Churchill did his training, was a most agreeable posting in 1895. 'There is no other station like it for a cavalry man; lovely country, grand rides, very good food and lots of fun.'[12]

Another contemporary description of Churchill at Aldershot by the journalist Richard Harding Davis records:

He was just of age, but seemed much younger. He was below medium height, a slight delicate looking boy; although as a matter of fact extremely strong, with blue eyes, many freckles and hair which threatened to be a decided red . . . His manner of speaking was nervous, eager, explosive. He had then and still has (in 1906) a most embarrassing habit of asking many questions, embarrassing,

sometimes, because the questions are so frank, and sometimes because they lay bare the wide expanse of one's own
ignorance.[13]

Churchill's letters home to his family show he clearly enjoyed
the military life, which began with breakfast in bed at 7.45
before undertaking various riding and military drills. Although
he was pushed to the limits of his endurance by the regimental
riding master, Winston quickly proved himself to be a better
horseman than many other young officers of his rank. Before
long he had taken up steeplechasing, a dangerous sport that
resulted in him being laid up in bed for three days following a
bad fall he sustained when his horse refused a jump. He also
became a fan of the more aristocratic, and more expensive,
pursuit of polo. 'It is the finest game in the world,' he wrote to
his mother from Aldershot, 'and I should almost be content
to give up any ambition [in order] to play it well and often.'[14]
Because of the family's financial position, Winston struggled to
meet the costs of maintaining the ponies he needed for the sport.
    Winston's love of equestrian pursuits, though, was perfect
training for Afghanistan, where expert horsemanship could make
all the difference between life and death. The Hussars were a
light cavalry regiment, used mainly for reconnaissance missions.
The cavalry of the British army was divided into three classes
based on the weight and size of the rider and horse. Heavy
cavalry with men five feet eight inches and above were sought
by regiments such as the 1st and 2nd Life Guards and the Royal
Horse Guards. Medium cavalrymen of around five feet seven
inches in height joined the Dragoon regiments, which were
trained to fight on foot, or Lancers, who were distinguished by
the use of the lance as their primary weapon. Light cavalry, such
as the 4th Hussars, comprised the smallest cavalrymen of around
five feet six inches – about Winston's height. The light cavalry
was made up of thirteen regiments of hussars, which specialized
in actions such as reconnaissance where speed was of the essence.

Churchill, who maintained his links with the regiment until long after the end of the Second World War, is today remembered as 'the Greatest Hussar of them all', and his youthful portrait features prominently on the regimental website. The regiment survived as a traditional cavalry unit through the First World War, where it won twenty-one battle honours and nearly a hundred awards for gallantry. It eventually mechanized in 1936, becoming part of the Royal Armoured Corps, and saw extensive action during the Second World War in Greece, North Africa and Italy. After he became prime minister Churchill was the regiment's colonel-in-chief from 1941 until it was amalgamated into the Queen's Royal Irish Hussars in 1958. Known more simply as The Queen's Royal Hussars, it was designated as the British army's senior light cavalry regiment and saw service in Bosnia, Kosovo and Iraq. In early 2012 it was deployed to southern Afghanistan as part of NATO's mission to defeat the Taliban, the descendants of the tribesmen Churchill fought in 1897. On several occasions in the current conflict the Hussars took part in joint combat operations with the Afghan army against the Taliban.

As a young Hussar at Aldershot, not all Churchill's time was spent wisely. One escapade led to his name being linked to an unsavoury sporting scandal in which it was claimed that a team of riders from the 4th Hussars – including Winston – had 'fixed' the result of a horse race in order to pocket the proceeds of a bet on the winner. Winston had taken part in the race, borrowing the horse of a fellow subaltern for his first competitive ride in the 4th Hussars Subalterns' Challenge Cup. He came third, and wrote to his younger brother Jack of his exhilaration at jumping the high fences. But the experience was tarnished by accusations that the winner, a 6–1 outsider, was in fact a horse that had been substituted at the last minute to beat the 5–4 favourite, which came second. The officers of the 4th Hussars who took part in the race were accused of fixing the result, and all the participating horses banned from future National Hunt events.

A potentially more damaging slur on Churchill's name arose over allegations that Winston and some other officers had attempted to bully a young man called Alan Bruce into resigning his commission from the 4th Hussars because they had formed an unfavourable opinion of him. Having invited Bruce to dinner, they proceeded to inform him that his annual allowance of £500 was not sufficient to maintain the style of a cavalry officer, which was a bit rich coming from Winston – the group's main spokesman – whose own allowance fell well short of that sum. Such odious conduct was not uncommon in elite British army regiments. The previous year another young officer had been roughly handled and dumped in a horse trough by colleagues who objected to his presence in the regiment. On that occasion the victim had resigned his commission. Bruce, on the other hand, enlisted the help of his father, who proceeded to turn the incident into a national issue. The 4th Hussars' conduct was the subject of a parliamentary debate, and publicly condemned in the press. Churchill, perhaps because of his name and his father's own notoriety, was singled out for his role in demanding Bruce's resignation, and matters took an ugly turn when Bruce's father went so far as to allege that his son knew Winston had participated at Sandhurst in 'acts of gross immorality of the Oscar Wilde type'. In May 1895 Wilde had been jailed for two years for committing acts of 'gross indecency', and the suggestion that Churchill had indulged in similar activities had potentially disastrous implications for his prospects. Lord Randolph's louche lifestyle had often fuelled gossip that he enjoyed homosexual liaisons. There was, for example, the occasion when he attended an all-male soirée at the Berkeley Square home of Lord Rosebery, the homosexual Liberal prime minister, at which the elder brother of Lord Alfred Douglas, Wilde's lover, had been present.[15] Fortunately for Winston, Bruce had overstepped the mark, and when, four days after the accusation was made public, Winston sued for libel, he received a complete withdrawal and apology, as well as £500 in damages.

Like any spirited young man, Winston was going to find himself involved in the occasional scrape. Before Sandhurst he had experienced two potentially life-threatening escapades, the first when he almost drowned while swimming in a lake near Lausanne. On another occasion he had nearly killed himself after falling almost thirty feet during a spirited game of hide-and-seek at Bournemouth. But as a Churchill, it was also important that he maintain his good reputation. Even at this early stage in his career he took a keen interest in politics. In 1893, while studying for the Sandhurst entrance examination, Winston had squeezed into the Distinguished Strangers' Gallery at Westminster to hear Prime Minister William Gladstone wind up the debate on the Home Rule Bill. Afterwards the precocious eighteen-year-old had been invited to dine with the Unionist politician Edward Carson. Following his commission into the 4th Hussars he received an invitation to address the electors of Barnesbury constituency just two weeks after he arrived at Aldershot. Churchill was clear in his own mind that his military career was very much a means to an end. Although he enjoyed soldiering and the camaraderie of his regiment, 'I feel convinced that it is not my metier,' he wrote to his mother. Politics was what really inspired him, and he saw the military as a constructive way of occupying his time until an opportunity to pursue a political career presented itself. 'It is a fine game to play – the game of politics, and it is well worth waiting for a good hand – before really plunging.' As for the military, 'Four years of healthy and pleasant existence, combined with both responsibility and discipline, can do me no harm – but rather good.' To make sure that his mind did not stagnate, 'I try to raise myself by reading and re-reading Papa's speeches – many of which I know almost by heart.'[16]

Winston was well aware that, because of his indifferent

performance at school, he had much ground to make up on his Oxbridge-educated contemporaries if he was to be successful in politics. To this end he explored the possibility, in addition to his military training, of taking a tutor for one or two hours a week to study Economics or History. Churchill was determined that his Hussar career would be short. Not for him the slow progress from subaltern to captain, from captain to major, eventually reaching the pinnacle of regimental command. Even as a newly commissioned subaltern Churchill sought a wider stage, a national name and political stature. One indication of where Winston's true ambitions lay became evident in his first venture in the world of journalism, an article he wrote for *Pall Mall Magazine* on life at Sandhurst. He signed the article with the pseudonym, 'A Cornet of Horse', a title that had previously been attributed to William Pitt, Earl of Chatham, another great wartime British prime minister.[17]

Churchill drew encouragement from the knowledge that he could make use of the extensive network of social and political contacts he had inherited from his father – about the only useful legacy he received from Lord Randolph. While on leave from Aldershot he attended Duchess Lily's wedding to Lord Beresford, who had introduced Winston to General Sir Bindon Blood, the commander-in-chief of the British military expedition at the time of the relief of the garrison at Chitral. He attended the races at Newmarket, where he met the Prince of Wales, an old family friend. 'The whole world' had been in the stand, Winston excitedly reported to his mother, 'all most civil and agreeable too'.[18] He joined the Bachelors' Club in London and had so many invitations he boasted that he could go to a ball every night if he wished to. He dined with the Duke and Duchess of York, later King George V and Queen Mary, when they attended the Field Day at Aldershot, at which he also had a long talk about politics with the Duke of Connaught. It was through this impressive list of social contacts that he had his first, fleeting encounter with the land where he was soon to make his name. In June Churchill was afforded the honour of joining the escort of the Duke of Cambridge to welcome Nasrullah Khan, the son of Abdur Rahman, the amir of Afghanistan, who had arrived in England on an official visit. 'I was seven hours on horseback without dismounting or taking off my busby,' Churchill later complained to his mother, 'and two more hours after lunch – but it was a great honour to have been selected'. It was worthwhile, for at the official lunch Churchill 'generally made myself sociable to the foreigners on the staff'.[19] He also saw the Prince of Wales and had a long talk with Lord Roberts, the hero of Kandahar, who had just been made a field marshal. The next time Winston came across some Afghan tribesmen, the circumstances would not be quite so cordial.

*

As a Tory, Churchill was thrilled with the result of the general election in July 1895, in which Lord Rosebery and the Liberals were defeated, and the Tories under Lord Salisbury formed the new government. On a personal level, however, he must have had some mixed feelings about the result. Rosebery, despite his radical political leanings, had remained a true friend to Lord Randolph until the end of his life, whereas Salisbury had effectively ended Lord Randolph's political career by accepting his intemperate resignation, and making sure he spent the remainder of his days languishing in a political wilderness. Certainly the ignominious end to his father's career acted as a constant reminder to Winston of the vicissitudes of political life. The close interest he took in political affairs meant he had a precocious talent for spotting potential flashpoints. Even though Salisbury's government had won a commanding Commons majority of 150 seats, Winston warned, 'They are just the sort of Government to split on the question of Protection.'[20] This is precisely what happened a few years later over the Tory demand for a tariff system to protect imperial trade against foreign competition. Churchill, by then a newly elected Conservative

MP, achieved political prominence as a leading opponent of the tariffs.

So far as the 4th Hussars were concerned 'we were all delighted' by the change of government, Churchill later recalled, as 'the Liberals were very unpopular at this time in Aldershot' because they had been kept in office by the Irish Nationalists, 'who everyone knew would never be satisfied till they had broken up the British Empire'.[21] With his impressive social contacts, Winston was invited to a party held at Devonshire House to meet the new ministers, who all turned up 'looking very smart in their blue and gold uniforms', then the traditional dress of government ministers. He had a long conversation with George Curzon, the future Viceroy of India and a long-standing friend of his parents, who had been made a junior minister at the Foreign Office. Curzon had just returned from a memorable tour of the North-West Frontier and Afghanistan at the same time that the British were establishing the Durand Line. Entirely through his own endeavours, he had secured an audience with the Afghan amir, making him the first Englishman to visit Abdur Rahman as a private individual. Curzon travelled very much in the manner of Elphinstone and Burnes, the British adventurers who earlier in the century had endeavoured to establish cordial relations between Britain and the Afghans. But unlike his predecessors, whose advice was often ignored by officialdom, Curzon told Winston that he hoped to have a share in making foreign policy instead of only defending and explaining it.[22] A lifelong imperialist – Curzon once described the British Empire as 'the greatest instrument for good the world has seen' – the Eton- and Oxford-educated Curzon truly believed it was his destiny one day to be prime minister. Curzon became Britain's Foreign Secretary following the First World War, but he never achieved his ambition of becoming leader – unlike the ambitious young subaltern from the 4th Hussars.

Curzon's personal investment in gaining first-hand knowledge of the complex issues concerning the North-West Frontier proved very useful in helping the new British government to formulate its policy towards Afghanistan and its troublesome border. Curzon called his trip to Central Asia a 'last wild cry of freedom', as he had sensed that when he got back to England the Liberal government would collapse and he would be back in office. Having already published books on Persia and the Far East, Curzon was a respected explorer in his own right, subsequently receiving the Royal Geographical Society's gold medal for his research on the origins of the River Oxus during his trip to the North-West Frontier.

On arrival in India Curzon immediately set off for the isolated British garrison at Chitral, which he described as 'this small chink in the mountain palisade'. He travelled with Francis Younghusband, Britain's political agent at Chitral, and the pair reached their destination in the autumn of 1894 having crossed the fast-flowing Oxus by means of hazardous rope bridges, made of birch or willow twigs twisted together into a cable which, as Curzon complained, had 'a detestable habit of swinging'. Pompous and self-regarding, Curzon's attitude grated on the young soldiers living solitary lives in this most inhospitable corner of the world. But annoying as he could be, Curzon was nevertheless a great defender of Britain's imperial interests, and he shared the troops' fears that the Russians were preparing to create trouble along the frontier. He was insistent that Chitral must not be occupied by the tsarist army, a view that no doubt influenced the new Conservative government's approach. At Chitral Curzon met one of the half-brothers of the pro-British tribal chief, Nizam-ul-Mulk, whom he described as 'a sullen and repulsive figure, with long black locks and a look of gloom'.[23] A few weeks later this same half-brother murdered Nizam-ul-Mulk while he was out hawking, provoking the outbreak of border hostilities that would ultimately bring Churchill to the North-West Frontier.

Curzon's resourcefulness enabled him to secure a personal audience with Abdur Rahman, whose often indifferent allegiance to Britain had a direct bearing on the fortunes of the

young British soldiers camped on the Afghan border. To ensure
he made a good impression on the amir, Curzon had taken the
precaution of visiting a theatrical costumier in London and
hired an enormous pair of gold epaulettes, together with several
glittering foreign decorations. He bought a pair of patent leather
boots in India, and borrowed a gigantic curved sword from the
commander-in-chief of the Indian army. Thus attired, he presented himself to the amir, who was suitably impressed, and
asked inquisitively about the sparkling array of medals without
for a moment doubting their authenticity. Curzon later
described Abdur Rahman as 'a sort of Afghan Henry VIII', and
saw him as a tyrant and a man of blood. Yet he appreciated the
amir's 'shrewd but untutored intellect' and applauded his skill
in welding the Afghan tribes into a unity which they had never
previously enjoyed. 'At once a patriot and a monster, a great
man and almost a fiend,' Curzon concluded that, had the amir
lived in an earlier age, he 'might have founded an Empire, and
swept in a tornado of blood over Asia and even beyond it'.[24]

Curzon remained as Abdur Rahman's guest for a fortnight,
and was summoned for daily audiences that lasted for several
hours. Speaking in Persian through an interpreter, the amir
discoursed on such disparate subjects as the lost tribes of Israel
and the efficacy of cruelty as a punishment. He discussed the
Russian threat to their borders, and asked pointedly why he did
not receive more weapons from the British to defend his people
against a common enemy. Curzon was too diplomatic to give
the obvious answer, that any British weapons sent to Kabul
would inevitably end up in the hands of tribesmen on the
Afghan frontier, and be used against British soldiers. The visit
ended with Curzon inviting the amir to visit London, an
invitation he never took up for fear that his absence from Kabul
might cause a palace coup. But he sent his son instead, which
was how Churchill came to be invited to participate in the
welcoming parade. Curzon's visit proved to be invaluable preparation for his new post, in which one of his tasks was to

maintain Abdur Rahman's allegiance, even when there was clear evidence that the amir was actively plotting against British interests in India. In his official dealings with the amir, Curzon formed the view that the best way to deal with the recalcitrant monarch was through a mixture of pressure and blandishment, a policy that modern-day rulers of Afghanistan would no doubt recognize. But he also acknowledged the futility of trying to keep the amir in check, admitting that his correspondence with his 'old friend' was 'about as fruitless an occupation as throwing pebbles in the ocean'.[25]

The election of a Tory government in London certainly had a direct and immediate bearing on British policy towards the North-West Frontier. Following the relief of the siege at Chitral in April 1895, the Liberal government under Lord Rosebery had been keen to remove the British force as soon as possible, in keeping with its policy of maintaining a healthy distance from the quarrelsome Afghans. But just as the relief force was about to pack up and return to India, the new government ordered it to stay put while it undertook a thorough policy review. The Tories, no doubt encouraged by Curzon's reports of his recent travels, supported the Forward Policy argument that, without adequate protection, Chitral could easily fall into Russian hands, leaving India at Moscow's mercy. An urgent intelligence assessment was commissioned, which showed that the Russian front line was just fifty miles from Chitral in a direct line, and a hundred miles by road. With a force of 2,500 men it would be possible for the Russians to stir up the frontier tribes against the British if Chitral were not properly defended. For that reason it was necessary to maintain a force at Chitral of sufficient size 'to delay a Russian advance' through the mountain passes until reinforcements could be brought up from India.[26] As is so often the case in Afghanistan, though, the result was a fudge, with London ordering the troops to stay put until a firm decision could be reached. This meant that the troops sent to relieve Chitral were to remain deployed along the main relief road, with a detachment stationed on the Malakand Pass, so that reinforcements could quickly be sent to Chitral if trouble flared again. The order sent to British commanders in August 1895 stipulated that they should 'make no permanent arrangement for cantonment on Malakand and neighbourhood until further details, both of cost and numbers, can be sent home'.[27] For the next two years the troops had no idea whether they were going or staying, and this was the situation when Churchill arrived in Malakand to take part in a fresh round of fighting against the frontier tribes.

Churchill's regiment had received its orders in August 1895 to deploy to India the following year to join the British garrison permanently stationed there. The 4th Hussars would be gone for nine years, which was the average length of time British soldiers and officials were expected to serve overseas in the nineteenth century. During preparations for departure, officers were free to take the five-month allocation of annual leave they were due. Cavalry subalterns were encouraged to spend the winter fox-hunting and in other social pursuits. But Winston had neither the money nor the inclination to kick his heels until the time came for his regiment to embark for India. While he enjoyed army life, Winston fretted that it might lead to a state of mental stagnation 'quite in accordance' with the spirit of the army. He was more interested in making up for the education he had missed by not attending university, and began reading serious works on political economy which would, at the very least, give him a grasp of the 'first principles'. But at a time when the world was generally at peace, Winston yearned to be in the thick of the action. 'From very early youth I had brooded about soldiers and war, and often I had imagined in dreams and day-dreams the sensations attendant upon being for the first time under fire,' Churchill recalled in *My Early Life*. 'It seemed to my youthful mind that it must be a thrilling and immense experience to hear the whistle of bullets all around and to play at hazard from moment to moment with death and wounds.'

1. A *Vanity Fair* sketch of the 7th Duke of Marlborough, Winston Churchill's grandfather.

2. Winston's father, Lord Randolph Churchill, who was once tipped as a future prime minister, but whose political career ended in spectacular fashion.

3. Jennie Churchill, a notable society beauty who included some of young Winston's direct contemporaries among her coterie of lovers.

4. Jennie with her two sons, Winston and Jack. Her neglect of her children was considered awful even by the standards of her generation.

5. But Winston was devoted to his mother, describing her as 'a fairy princess: a radiant being possessed of limitless power and riches.'

6. Churchill (left) as a cadet at the Royal Military Academy at Sandhurst, where he excelled and made many life-long friends.

7. Churchill's regiment, The 4th (Queen's Own) Hussars, was regarded as one of the British Army's 'smart' cavalry regiments.

8. General Sir Bindon Blood, Churchill's commanding officer during the Malakand campaign, was a distinguished veteran of frontier warfare.

9. Churchill's desire to acquire the best polo ponies caused him frequent financial problems.

10. The headstone on the grave of George Hayward at Gilgit. Hayward's murder by tribesmen on the North-West Frontier in 1870 prompted the British to occupy the area.

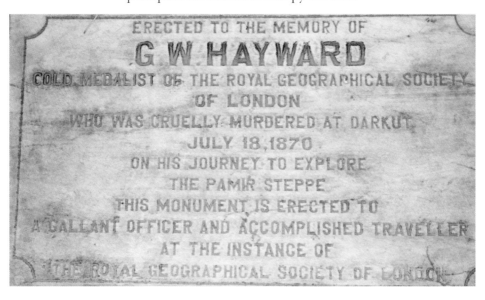

ERECTED TO THE MEMORY OF
G. W. HAYWARD
GOLD MEDALIST OF THE ROYAL GEOGRAPHICAL SOCIETY
OF LONDON
WHO WAS CRUELLY MURDERED AT DARKUT
JULY 18, 1870
ON HIS JOURNEY TO EXPLORE
THE PAMIR STEPPE
THIS MONUMENT IS ERECTED TO
A GALLANT OFFICER AND ACCOMPLISHED TRAVELLER
AT THE INSTANCE OF
THE ROYAL GEOGRAPHICAL SOCIETY OF LONDON

11. Soldiers from the 1st Battalion East Kent Regiment (the Buffs), who rescued Winston's unit from being overrun during fierce fighting on the frontier.

12. Locally-raised native regiments such as the 15th Sikhs formed the backbone of the Indian Army.

13. The arrival of the Sikh cavalry at Chitral in 1895 saved the beleaguered British garrison from wholesale slaughter.

14. A British mountain battery in action at Chitral.

15. British and native officers at the Malakand Pass.

16. A British cavalry detachment making its way through a narrow defile where the tribesmen often tried to mount surprise attacks.

There was also the small matter of the high esteem that distinguished military service attracts. 'It was the swift road to promotion and advancement in every arm,' Churchill wrote. 'It was the glittering gateway to distinction. It cast glamour upon the fortunate possessor alike in the eyes of elderly gentlemen and young ladies.' Rather than waiting for a conflict that required his professional participation, Churchill resolved to find one that he could observe at close quarters, 'a private rehearsal, a secluded trial trip, in order to make sure that the ordeal was not unsuited to my temperament'.[28]

*

That autumn the Spanish colony of Cuba was in the midst of a bloody war of independence, and Churchill decided he would be far better employed that winter dodging bullets in the Caribbean than chasing hapless foxes around the muddy English countryside. For this escapade he enlisted the support of a fellow subaltern, Reggie Barnes, who, as General Sir Reginald Barnes, later commanded several British army divisions in France during the First World War. Barnes, like Churchill, was a young lieutenant in the 4th Hussars who had been commissioned two years previously and became one of Churchill's dearest friends and closest confidants during his military career. (He was appointed the regiment's honorary colonel in 1918, and was succeeded in that position by Churchill in 1941.) Churchill described Barnes as 'a good friend of mine . . . who is one of the senior subalterns and acting adjutant and very steady'.[29] The two young officers discussed their scheme in the mess and received the support of their fellow officers, including Colonel Brabazon. Jennie Churchill was less than impressed at the idea, especially as her son presented his plan to her as a fait accompli. 'Considering that I provide the funds,' she remonstrated, 'I think that instead of saying "I *have* decided to go" it may have been nicer and perhaps wiser to have begun by consulting me.'[30] But the twenty-year-old Winston was too headstrong to be dissuaded by his mother, who accepted that it would be a good, if expensive, experience for her son, and even offered to pay for his ticket as a birthday present. As Churchill himself later wrote, 'Twenty to twenty-five! These are the years! Don't be content with things as they are. "The earth is yours and the fullness thereof." '[31]

Churchill was not averse to pulling strings to ensure the trip was a success, a trait that would become more pronounced as he strove to make his name. Shamelessly drawing on his mother's acquaintances, he contacted everyone, from the head of the army to the British ambassador to Madrid, to enlist their help. Field Marshal Lord Wolseley, the army's new commander-in-chief, put him in touch with the Director of Military Intelligence, who helpfully showed the two young men maps detailing the military campaign in Cuba and asked that, in return, they collect information on the conduct of the war, in particular 'the effect of the new bullet – its penetration and striking power'.[32] Sir Henry Drummond Wolff, the British ambassador to Spain and another long-standing family friend, lobbied for the two subalterns to be allowed access to Marshal Martínez Campos, the Spanish forces' commander. Meanwhile Churchill secured a letter of introduction to Mr Akers, *The Times* special correspondent in Cuba, from Sir Donald Mackenzie Wallace, the Director of the Foreign Department of *The Times*, who had previously served as a private secretary to the Viceroys of India. Wallace asked Akers if he could help the two young travellers by 'placing the stores of your local knowledge at their disposal', although in the event Akers was away on another assignment in Venezuela when Churchill and Barnes arrived in Havana. Churchill was aware of the influence the press brought to bear in international affairs, in terms of both reporting events and informing public opinion. He was eager to do both and, mindful that any extra funds would be extremely useful for financing the trip, he persuaded the populist *Daily Graphic*, for which his father had previously written during a visit to South Africa, to let him send regular dispatches from the 'seat of war' in Cuba for the princely sum of five guineas per article.

Churchill's first port of call on his way to Cuba was New York, where Jennie's family connections proved immensely useful in providing him with an introduction to American high society. He sailed to New York on the steamship *Etruria*, one of the fastest and most luxurious vessels on the transatlantic route at the time, and his main recollection of the voyage was that he and Barnes were never seasick and never missed a meal, despite having a rough crossing. Winston was met at the dockside in New York by Bourke Cockran, an Irish-American Democratic congressman who had befriended Jennie in Paris earlier that year. Born in County Sligo, Cockran was a man of eloquence and charm who alternated between running his New York legal practice and representing his city for a number of unconnected terms. With his grey hair, deep-set blue eyes and big powerful nose, he was not a man who was easily ignored. He was an outstanding orator, one contemporary observing that 'listening to him . . . was like being transported to the Roman Senate in its best days'.[33] Jennie's friends believed she had formed a romantic attachment with Cockran in Paris earlier that summer. Whether true or not, Cockran certainly made a deep impression on Churchill, who developed a lifelong attachment to a man he regarded as an inspiration, mentor and father figure.

Cockran hosted Churchill at his 763 Fifth Avenue apartment while he explored the city and its surroundings with his American cousins. Churchill's cousin 'Sunny', who three years earlier had succeeded his father to become 9th Duke of Marlborough, had just married the American heiress Consuelo Vanderbilt. The wedding took place in New York on 6 November 1895, while Churchill and Barnes were sailing across the Atlantic, and they arrived three days after the nuptials. Churchill's social connections meant that the young officers received the best possible introduction to *fin-de-siècle* New York society. On their first night in the city they had dinner with a group of lawyers,

were then taken to a nightclub and finished off with supper at
the Waldorf. Everyone was 'very civil', Winston reported back
to his mother, and he and Barnes had 'engagements for every
meal for the next few days about three deep'.[34] The next day
they spent the afternoon with Consuelo Vanderbilt's uncle, the
celebrated businessman Cornelius Vanderbilt II.

For the duration of his stay in New York Winston busied
himself with a variety of activities. Cockran, aware of Winston's interest in military matters, arranged for him to visit an
American warship, the cruiser *New York*, the American army
headquarters of the Atlantic Military District and the West
Point Military Academy – the Sandhurst of the United States.
The Sandhurst graduate was horrified by the discipline at West
Point. 'They are not allowed to smoke or have any money in
their possession,' he told his brother, 'nor are they given any
leave except two months after the first two years.' Churchill was
outraged by this 'positively disgraceful' state of affairs, and
fulminated that 'young men of 24 or 25 who would resign their
personal liberty to such an extent can never make good citizens
or fine soldiers. A child who rebels against that sort of control
should be whipped – so should a man who does not rebel.'[35] He
was more impressed with the American sailors he met – 'while
any nation can build a battleship, it is the monopoly of the
Anglo-Saxon race to breed good seamen'. Thanks to Cockran's
influence in the city, New York's Fire Commissioner was prevailed upon to give the young men a tour of four or five fire
stations, which impressed Winston greatly. 'On the alarm bell
sounding the horses at once rushed into the shafts – the harness
fell on to them – the men slid half dressed down a pole from
their sleeping room and in five and a half seconds the engine
was galloping down the street to the scene of the fire.' The
following day he was invited by a judge he had met at dinner
on his first night at Cockran's apartment to sit on the bench at
his side while he presided over the trial of a defendant accused
of shooting a man who had seduced his sister. Winston's

whirlwind tour of New York, and the robust discussions he had each night over dinner with Cockran, gave him a lasting affection for a country that would occupy a seminal position in his political outlook. 'This is a very great country my dear Jack,' he wrote to his younger brother. 'Not pretty or romantic but great and utilitarian. There seems to be no such thing as reverence or tradition. Everything is eminently practical and things are judged from a matter of fact standpoint.'[36]

Not everything was to young Winston's taste, however. He took a violent dislike to the American currency, claiming the paper dollars he used in everyday transactions were possibly 'the most disreputable "coin" the world has ever seen', while he took a similarly dim view of American journalism, which he dismissed as 'vulgarity divested of truth'. He did not wish to appear over-censorious, though, and conceded 'that vulgarity is a sign of strength. A great, crude, strong, young people are the Americans – like a boisterous healthy boy among enervated but well bred ladies and gentlemen.' Churchill's views on America, while diverting, should not be taken too seriously, but rather seen in the context of an impressionable, intelligent and exuberant young man desperate to make his mark on the world.

The most lasting legacy of Churchill's initial introduction to the United States was his friendship with Cockran, who, he told his mother, was one of the most charming hosts and one of the most interesting men he had ever met. During his week-long stay in New York they had deep and wide-ranging discussions together on every conceivable subject from economics to yacht racing. Winston was particularly interested in Cockran's oratorical skills, and listened to Cockran in his library while he read his favourite speeches aloud. Cockran taught his young protégé the importance of timing and drama and sincerity when making speeches, and ensuring the argument was presented with clarity and grandeur, and instilled in Churchill the need to defend individual liberty. During the breaks in their intense discussions they ate oysters and hominy together, and Cockran later told

Jennie that he was 'profoundly impressed' with Winston's responses to his speeches.[37] Without a son himself, Cockran was more than happy to take the young man under his wing and nurture his potential.

Many years later Churchill told Adlai Stevenson, the Democratic contender for the US presidency, that Cockran 'inspired me when I was 19 and taught me how to use every note of the human voice like an organ. He was my role model. I learned from him how to hold thousands in thrall.' Stevenson was surprised by this revelation, because, as a boy, he had known Cockran. 'He wasn't a great statesman, just an Irish politician with the gift of the gab, but Winston called him a statesman.'[38]

From New York, Churchill and Barnes travelled by train to Key West in Florida, and then caught a steamer to Havana, checking in to the Gran Hotel Inglaterra on 20 November. Winston took a characteristically dramatic view of his arrival.

'When first in the dim light of early morning I saw the shores of Cuba rise and define themselves from dark-blue horizons, I felt as if I sailed with Long John Silver and first gazed on Treasure Island. Here was a place where real things were going on. Here was a scene of vital action. Here was a place where anything might happen. Here was a place where something would certainly happen. Here I might leave my bones.'[39]

When Churchill and Barnes arrived in Cuba Spain had deployed 250,000 men to suppress a revolt against Spanish rule that had flared intermittently since 1868. Marshal Martínez Campos's expeditionary force had attempted to suppress the revolt by occupying the main towns, but this proved ineffective as the rebels controlled the countryside, which meant they could disrupt Spanish supply lines and communications at will. Spain's military intervention in Cuba was deeply unpopular in the US, where uncorroborated stories – the first examples of 'yellow journalism' – frequently appeared in newspapers owned by the press barons William Randolph Hearst and Joseph Pulitzer alleging

that the Spanish committed what would now be designated as
war crimes – torture, rape and mass pillaging by the Spanish
forces, with heaps of dead men, women and children regularly
left on the side of the road. The pattern of the conflict in Cuba
was not dissimilar to what the British were experiencing in faraway Afghanistan. Just like the Afghan tribesmen, the Cuban
rebels were poorly armed and trained, but had the enormous
advantage of knowing the terrain. Staging ambushes and conducting hit-and-run raids were their forte, but if they felt an
engagement was going against them they had no shame about
running away. They used the mountains and forests as refuges
into which they simply disappeared when confronted or cor-
nered. These guerrilla-style tactics proved highly effective against
more conventional, slow-moving armies, and so the Spanish
experienced very similar problems fighting the Cuban rebels as
the British did against the Afghans on the North-West Frontier.

Because of the political sensitivities surrounding the conflict,
Churchill and Barnes were designated 'guests' of the Spanish
army, which meant they could use weapons only to defend
themselves. The young officers were keen to get to the thick of
the action, and immediately went to see the British consul
general who introduced them to the Spanish military governor,
who in turn telegraphed to the commander-in-chief that they
had arrived. The following day Churchill and Barnes set off by
train to join the Spanish forces, a journey that was not without
incident. The rebels regularly attacked the trains and wrecked
the line to impede the movement of the Spanish troops, and it
took two days for the British travellers to meet up with Marshal
Martínez Campos's forces. Winston's account of his Cuban
adventures later appeared in the form of five dispatches to the
Daily Graphic under the heading 'Letters from the Front', which
were signed 'WSC'. In the first dispatch, written while he was
still travelling to the front, Churchill concluded that the Cuban
rebels 'possess the sympathy of the entire population, and hence
have constant and accurate intelligence. On the other hand

Spain is equally determined to crush them, and is even now pouring in fresh troops by the thousands. How it will end is impossible to say, but whoever wins, and whatever may be the results, the suffering and misery of the entire community are certain.'[40] Martínez Campos received the two subalterns at his temporary headquarters in Santa Clara, about one hundred miles east of Havana, and seconded them to his Chief of Staff, General Suárez Valdés, at Sancti Spiritus, forty miles further on. The route was under constant attack from the rebels, and it took Churchill and Barnes another three days to get there. Eventually they caught up with Suárez Valdés, a 'General of Division', who was about to lead a considerable force – four battalions comprising about 3,000 infantry, two squadrons of cavalry and a mule battery – through the mountains to the various Spanish garrisons. When Churchill met up with the mobile column, as the Spanish called it, he found 'the troops looked fit and sturdy and none the worse for their marches. They were dressed in cotton uniforms which may originally have been white, but now with dirt and dust had toned down to something very like khaki. They carried heavy packs and double bandoliers, and wore large straw Panama hats.'[41]

Churchill and Barnes received a warm welcome from General Suárez Valdés, who, speaking through an interpreter, said what an honour it was for him to have two distinguished representatives of a great and friendly power attached to his column, and how highly he valued the moral support which this gesture of Great Britain implied. As Britain had remained steadfastly neutral in the conflict, and British public opinion was generally more sympathetic to the rebel cause than the Spanish, Churchill needed to be diplomatic in his response. 'We said, back through an interpreter, that it was awfully kind of him, and that we were sure it would be awfully jolly.'[42] The next morning, 26 November, the two British soldiers set off with Suárez Valdés's column to the north-east and into the heart of rebel territory. For the next four days the column moved forward without incident, and though Churchill was keen not to cause offence to his hosts, he was starting to feel increasingly ambivalent about his position as a war correspondent. 'The more I see of Cuba,' he wrote in his second dispatch for the *Daily Graphic*, 'the more I feel sure that the demand for independence is national and unanimous. The insurgent forces contain the best blood in the island, and can by no perversion of the truth be classed as banditti. In fact, it is a war, not a rebellion.'[43]

Then, on 30 November, Winston's twenty-first birthday, his circumstances changed dramatically when, for the first time in his life, he came under hostile fire. Churchill later wrote: 'The 30th November was my 21st birthday and on that day for the first time I heard shots fired in anger and heard bullets strike flesh or whistle through the air.'

The column had just stopped for breakfast in a small clearing, and as Winston stood gnawing on the remains of 'a skinny chicken' a group of rebels opened fire from behind the surrounding trees. They were quickly driven off, but not before one of their bullets had passed close enough to Churchill's head to generate a healthy breeze. 'I began to take a more thoughtful view of our enterprise than I had hitherto done,' wrote the special correspondent of the *Daily Graphic*.[44] During the course of the next week Winston came under fire on several more occasions. The rebels shot at him while he was bathing in a river with two Spanish officers, and when they returned to their headquarters half a mile away they found another skirmish was taking place, which was also repulsed. Then, later that day, the rebels attacked again while the troops were asleep. 'One bullet came through the thatch of the hut in which we were sleeping and another wounded an orderly outside,' he recorded with obvious satisfaction in another of his dispatches.[45] The following morning, on 2 December, General Suárez Valdés, finding the rebels occupying an entrenched position on a ridge in open country, decided to launch a conventional assault, a skirmish that later became known as the Battle of La Reforma. The troops started off at first light, and the rising mist, Churchill wrote in his subsequent account of the battle, 'gave cover to the rebel marksmen, who saluted us as soon as we got across the river with a well-directed fire'. The general, 'a very brave man in a white and gold uniform on a grey horse – drew a great deal of fire'.[46] Churchill and Barnes stayed close to Valdés throughout the action, which meant, as Winston later explained with some relish to his mother, that they were 'in the most dangerous place in the field'. The fighting was so intense that Churchill believed the Spanish were lucky not to lose more soldiers, but this was because 'as a rule the rebels shot very high'. After ten minutes of heavy firing, the rebels, realizing they were heavily outnumbered, abandoned their positions and withdrew into 'impenetrable woods'. No pursuit by the Spanish was attempted, and the column withdrew to its original fortified starting point. Churchill's first experience of the battlefield was at an end.

As Churchill was to discover, the challenge of waging conventional warfare against lightly armed Cuban rebels was similar to the British experience of fighting the Afghans on the North-West Frontier. And although Winston won his first medal fighting with the Spanish – he and Barnes were awarded the Red Cross by Martínez Campos for their gallantry at La Reforma – he entertained few doubts as to the futility of the exercise in which they had participated. 'Here you have a General of Division,' he wrote in his final dispatch for the *Daily Graphic*, 'and two thousand of the best troops in the island, out for over ten days in search of the enemy, overcoming all sorts of difficulties, undergoing all sorts of hardships, and then being quite contented with taking thirty or forty rebels and taking a long grass hill which was destitute of the slightest of importance.' He now had first-hand experience of the limitations of fighting what today might be called a counter-insurgency campaign. And while Churchill was clearly indebted to his Spanish hosts for allowing him to be blooded in a war zone, he left no one in any doubt as to where his true sympathies lay. Cuba, he wrote, had been 'overtaxed in a monstrous manner for a considerable period'. The Spanish had taken so much money from the country that its 'industries are paralysed and development is impossible'. Bribery and corruption pervaded the administration 'on a scale almost Chinese'. Consequently, 'a national and justifiable revolt is the only possible result of such a system'.[47] A year later Churchill wrote to his mother saying he reproached himself for being so supportive of the Cuban rebels, at the expense of his Spanish hosts.

After Churchill had arrived safely in New York for the return voyage to London, he found himself the centre of much press attention. Before setting off for Cuba he received his first mention in the *New York Times*, the newspaper in which his American grandfather had owned a considerable stake several decades earlier, under the heading, 'Randolph Churchill's son in Cuba'.[48] Lord and Lady Churchill had always been the focus of much interest in the American press, and the American-born Jennie had even been the subject of a full-length feature article in *Vanity Fair* when she participated in an election campaign in support of Lord Randolph.[49] Following his Cuban adventure, the American press started to take an interest in Winston in his own right. On 6 December the *New York Times* reported that 'especial mention' had been made in the battle reports of the 'valorous conduct' of Churchill and Barnes in Cuba. But some of the more critical papers in New York spread rumours that, by going to Cuba, Churchill and Barnes had been acting as secret emissaries of the British government, an observation which, in view of their brief to collect information on behalf of the Director of Military Intelligence, was not that wide of the mark. This was a sensitive subject for the Americans, for it suggested that Britain was breaking the rules of the Monroe Doctrine, which gave the United States exclusive responsibility for handling disputes in Latin America.

The suggestion that Churchill was meddling in American affairs made for some feisty exchanges when he was mobbed by reporters on the Cunard pier in New York on 14 December as he prepared to board the *Etruria* for the homeward voyage. The *New York World* reported that he exclaimed 'Rot!' when asked about the political significance of his visit to Cuba. This may explain the generally pro-rebel tenor of his comments on the conflict, for the *New York World* recorded that Churchill had returned from the Cuban war 'without a wound and with a conviction that there are few occupations more salubrious than that of a Cuban insurgent'.[50] Another publication, the *New York Herald*, described Churchill as 'a pleasant faced young officer' who answered the reporters' questions 'in straightforward fashion, with his beardless, boyish face flushed with eagerness'.[51] Before boarding the ship, he concluded the dockside interview by predicting that the Spanish would fail to inflict a comprehensive defeat on the rebels, and that the United States would eventually be forced to intervene. In normal wars, Winston remarked, it took an average of 200 bullets to kill a soldier, whereas in Cuba 200,000 rounds was closer to the mark. The secret of the rebels' strength was their 'ability to harass the enemy and carry on guerrilla warfare'. As for the Spanish, 'I make no reflections on their courage, but they are well versed in the art of retreat.' He believed 'the upshot of it will be that the United States will intervene as peacemaker'.[52] In the event, the US went to war with Spain, defeating the Spaniards and creating an independent Cuba in 1901. As a reward for their help defeating the Spanish, the Americans were granted a perpetual lease of Guantanamo Bay.

Churchill returned to England in December 1895 with a souvenir bullet in his pocket that had killed a Spanish soldier standing next to him at La Reforma. He also came home with his reputation greatly enhanced. He had left his boyhood behind him, for the young officer who arrived back in London had been under fire and lived to tell the tale. Churchill had achieved several important personal ambitions with his Cuban adventure. He had gained recognition on the world stage, he had won his first medal and he had covered his costs by earning twenty-five guineas, the total sum he was paid for his dispatches for the *Daily Graphic*, as well as the occasional sketches he had provided of the conflict. He later had another article published in the *Saturday Review*, which Joseph Chamberlain, the Colonial Secretary, praised as 'the best short account I have seen of the problems [with] which the Spaniards have to deal, and agrees with my own conclusions. It is evident that Mr Winston kept his eyes open.'[53] Winston made sure he sent a copy of the article to Bourke Cockran. In Cuba Winston had taken a significant step towards his goal of achieving fame and fortune, one that he would seek to replicate in Afghanistan.

CHAPTER FOUR

PASSAGE TO INDIA

'My life here would be intolerable were it not for the
consolations of literature.'

Winston S. Churchill, 17 April 1897

After all the excitement of New York and Cuba, Churchill
found it difficult to summon much enthusiasm for his regiment's
posting to India. When he first had the idea of joining the
Hussars, one of the main attractions had been that they were
about to deploy overseas, where the prospect of fresh adventures beckoned. But his interest waned when he learned the
Hussars were being sent to the sleepy garrison town of Bangalore in southern India, some 2,000 miles from the North-West
Frontier and about as far as it was possible to get from the
main area of conflict on the Indian subcontinent. As soon
as Winston realized he was to be abandoned to this remote
imperial backwater he embarked on a frantic effort to be posted
somewhere else. As he complained to his mother, he wanted
'to sail in a few days to scenes of adventure and excitement – to
places where I could gain experience and derive advantage –
rather than to the tedious land of India'. He found the prospect
of spending the foreseeable future at a nondescript military
outpost 'utterly unattractive'. Being posted to India with his
'unfortunate regiment' was a 'useless and unprofitable exile'.[1]

According to Randolph Churchill, Winston's eldest son and
official biographer, the reason his father was so reluctant to
accompany his regiment to Bangalore was because, following
his return from Cuba, he had already made up his mind to

pursue a career in politics. Winston's visit to America had been a great success. He had seen his first newspaper articles published, and he was keen to develop his journalistic profile further, not least because he needed the money. Churchill's ambition was encouraged by the realization that, unlike many of his contemporaries, he had inherited no estate when he came of age on his twenty-first birthday and, as the son of the younger son of the Marlborough dynasty, had little prospect of so doing. His mother, meanwhile, continued to fritter away the little that remained of the family's wealth. As Winston confided to Jennie, he feared being left behind by his contemporaries, because 'others as young are making the running now and what chance have I of ever catching up'.[2] By setting sail for India, Churchill was undertaking a journey roughly equal in distance to the transatlantic crossing between Britain and America. But there the similarities ended, for Winston was firmly of the opinion that, by being consigned to the monotony of garrison life in southern India, his career prospects were heading in the wrong direction.

Churchill's predicament was further complicated by the fact that, as a young gentleman from a good family, his options for earning a decent living were limited. In late-nineteenth-century English high society, occupations such as trade, commerce and the Stock Exchange were still frowned upon. For those, like Winston, who did not have the academic qualifications to go to the Bar, or did not have the contacts to be hired by a firm of merchant bankers, there were few alternatives. He could choose the Church, the army or the navy, none of which was financially rewarding. After the success of his Cuba trip, though, Churchill was convinced he had found a way to avoid the conventional military career path by pursuing his interest in journalism and politics. His first foray into the highly competitive world of British journalism had been a marked success. His articles for the populist *Daily Graphic*, together with some sketches he had drawn of the Spanish campaign, were well received by editors and readers alike. On his return to London he received a warm letter of thanks from William Thomas, the paper's managing editor. 'Allow me to congratulate you on the result (as I imagine of your first experiences) as a Special Correspondent and artist combined. Your letters were very interesting and to the point and the sketches useful . . . I am sorry that your time was so limited and so preventing your sending more.'[3] Churchill's dispatches from Cuba proved to himself that he could write, and whetted his appetite for new opportunities that would both build his reputation and generate much-needed income. But he was hardly likely to achieve these goals if he ended up in some distant corner of empire where the greatest hazard he faced was a heavy fall from his polo pony.

After Cuba Churchill wanted to find new conflicts where he could satisfy his thirst for adventure and self-promotion. Prior to embarking for India all the officers were given generous allowances of free time to sort out their personal affairs in preparation for a long overseas posting. As Churchill had no desire to absent himself from British public life for long, he devoted all his free time to exploring any opportunity that might spare him exile to southern India. Living with his mother, who had moved into the new family home at 35A Great Cumberland Place, near Marble Arch, Winston was required to visit the regimental base at Hounslow Barracks only two or three times a week, which he did by travelling on the recently opened tube line to Hounslow Barracks station.[4] In Churchill's day the barracks were occupied by regiments preparing to deploy to India. More than a hundred years later they were used by British troops returning from combat operations in Afghanistan. Unfortunately for the modern soldiers, the barracks' living quarters had seen little improvement since the 1890s, prompting a number of MPs to complain that the conditions were so bad that troops housed in tents in Afghanistan enjoyed better living conditions. One tabloid newspaper reported the scandal in graphic detail: 'Squaddies Living in Squalor: Conditions in barracks "worse than Afghanistan"; Rat-infested and Mouldy: No Hot Water in Slum'.[5]

While seeking new opportunities for his soldiering career, Churchill made the most of London high society. During the day he spent much of his spare time playing polo at Hurlingham and Ranelagh. He had acquired five 'quite good ponies', and showed considerable promise as a player. He played with gusto, and enjoyed the sport so much that he continued playing until the age of fifty-two. He was keen to buy a pony – 'a really first class animal' – that would enable him to win a place in the regimental polo team. The only snag was that he could not afford the £200 it would cost, and he pleaded with his mother to loan him the money. At night, meanwhile, he made the most of the amusements of the London Season, attending glittering parties and balls which 'comprised all the elements which made a gay and splendid social circle in close relation to the business of Parliament, the hierarchies of the army and navy, and the policy of the State'.[6] He rubbed shoulders with prominent statesmen of the day, such as Lord Salisbury, the Conservative prime minister, and famous sportsmen. The turf was an all-consuming passion for the English aristocracy, and Churchill was impressed to learn that Salisbury scrupulously avoided calling a Cabinet meeting when there was a race meeting at Newmarket. Moving in such elevated circles, it was little wonder that he felt so wretched about his impending banishment to a dreary garrison town in southern India.

What set Churchill apart from so many of his contemporaries at this time was his all-consuming passion to make his name. While most young men of twenty-one with few commitments might have looked with enthusiasm on a posting to India, this was not sufficient for Winston's restless nature. He wanted to be at the centre of events, and he exploited his family connections to get his way. After Cuba his father's friends and political associates took more interest in him. The banker Natty

Rothschild, one of Lord Randolph's closest friends, asked him often to visit Tring. On other occasions he dined with some of London's leading socialites. At dinner given by Mrs Adair, a leading American hostess, he met Joseph Chamberlain, the Colonial Secretary, with whom he had a long conversation about events in South Africa. He also conversed with Field Marshal Lord Wolseley, commander-in-chief of the British army and a veteran of the Indian Mutiny in 1857. At other events he met two future prime ministers – Asquith and Balfour – as well as many of the other leading politicians of the day.

While it was useful to make these contacts, it did not help Churchill's immediate predicament, which was to find an alternative posting to Bangalore. On this score he turned to his mother and his aunt, Duchess Lily, whose new husband, Lord William Beresford, did his best to help. Bill Beresford, as Churchill called him, had recently returned to England after sixteen years working as an aide-de-camp and military secretary to four successive Viceroys of India. Churchill was fond of Beresford, who had 'every quality which could fascinate a cavalry subaltern'. Apart from his distinguished service in India, Beresford shared Winston's love of equestrian pursuits. 'He was a grand sportsman who had lived his whole life in companionship with horses,' Churchill recalled. 'Polo, pig-sticking, pony-racing, horse-racing, together with shooting big game of every kind, had played a constant part in his affairs.'[7] Winston was a frequent visitor to the couple's new home, 'the beautiful Deepdene' near Dorking in Surrey, and it was during one of these visits that he had first met General Sir Bindon Blood, who was visiting England following his participation in the campaign to relieve the siege at Chitral.

Born in Scotland in 1842 to a military dynasty, Sir Bindon was the descendant of the infamous Colonel Thomas Blood, who had organized the daring attempt to steal the Crown Jewels from the Tower of London in 1671. Sir Bindon, who was one of Beresford's closest friends from their time together in India, had enjoyed a varied career soldiering upon the outposts of the British Empire, serving in Egypt, India, Afghanistan and South Africa. He had seen action at the Battle of Tel el-Kebir in Egypt and the Anglo-Zulu war in Africa as well as various engagements against the Afghans on the North-West Frontier. Winston regarded him as 'one of the most trusted and experienced commanders on the Indian frontier. He had come home fresh from his successful storming of the Malakand Pass in the autumn of 1895. If future trouble broke out on the Indian frontier, he was sure to have a high command. He thus held the key to future delights.' Winston made a point of befriending Blood and, one Sunday morning on the sunny lawns of Deepdene, extracted a promise from the general that if he ever commanded another expedition on the Indian frontier, 'he would let me come with him'.[8] It would not be long before Winston held Blood to his promise.

For the moment, though, all was quiet on the Indian frontier, so that it held no great attraction for Churchill. Rather his attention was focused on other potential sources of adventure. When the Greek population of Crete resumed their campaign for independence from Turkish rule, Churchill wrote to the *Daily Chronicle* asking to be sent as a special correspondent to cover the conflict. The *Daily Chronicle* was a Liberal-supporting newspaper which included Sir Arthur Conan Doyle among its reporting staff. The newspaper declined to take up his offer, although it did suggest that if Winston decided to go under his own steam, it might be prepared to publish his reports 'at the rate of ten guineas a letter', which was twice the fee he had received for his Cuban dispatches.

Next Churchill turned his attention to Egypt, where General Sir Horatio Herbert Kitchener was preparing a punitive expedition along the Nile against the Mahdi. The fanatical Sudanese leader had massacred the British garrison in Khartoum ten years previously, placing the decapitated head of General Gordon in the branches of a tree so that the natives

could look upon it with disdain. Churchill was desperate to be
sent to the Sudan as a 'galloper' to Kitchener. When his efforts
failed he then persuaded his mother to write to Lord Lansdowne, the Secretary of State for War, asking permission for
her son to be allowed to travel to South Africa, where a British
force was attempting to suppress the native uprising in Matabeleland. Jennie even wrote to Field Marshal Lord Wolseley
making the same request, but to no avail. In July Lord Lansdowne wrote to Jennie saying the War Office was not involved
in the management of the operations in South Africa, which
meant 'we can do nothing to find employment for Winston'.[9]

Churchill made one last bid to get himself seconded to active
service in South Africa. He wrote to the colonel of the 9th
Lancers asking to be one of the two or three extra subaltern
officers who would be attached from other cavalry regiments if
they were sent to fight in Matabeleland. He even persuaded
Lord Beresford to wire the regiment's colonel on his behalf. As
he told his mother, the South African campaign was an opportunity to lay the foundations for a career in politics. He reasoned
that, rather than being stuck in India where he would have
neither 'the pleasures of peace [nor] the chances of war', he
could spend a few months in South Africa where he was
guaranteed to win at least two medals, the South Africa Medal
and the British South Africa Company's Star. Once the campaign had finished he could then move on to Egypt where, with
a bit of luck, he might return with two more decorations,
enabling him to 'beat my sword into an iron dispatch box' and
launch his career in politics.

But it was not to be. For all Churchill's fervent entreaties
and resourceful lobbying, no place could be found for the restless
young cavalryman, and by the end of August it was clear that
he must reconcile himself to his fate and join his comrades in
the 4th Hussars for the long journey to India. Winston blamed
his mother for this woeful state of affairs. 'I cannot believe with
all the influential friends you possess and all those who would

do something for me for my father's sake that I could not be allowed to go,' he remonstrated. 'You really ought to leave no stone unturned to help me at such a period. Years may pass before such chances occur again.'[10] His doleful mood is evident in the last letter he wrote before sailing for Bombay. 'I fear I shall not be back in England for at least three years as it is very hard to get leave,' he told his grandmother, the Dowager Duchess of Marlborough.[11]

*

When Churchill sailed for India with the 4th Hussars on 11 September 1896, Britain enjoyed complete military and political domination of the subcontinent. In the hundred and fifty or so years since Clive of India had established Britain as the paramount imperial power, the British had steadily consolidated their grip through force of arms. The Indian Mutiny of 1857 had come as an enormous shock to the British, who had wrongly assumed the Indians enjoyed being subjected to imperial rule. After the Mutiny had been put down, a new set of constitutional arrangements was devised in which the British Crown assumed direct responsibility for the administration of its Indian possessions, an arrangement that was formally sealed in 1877 when a vast gathering of Indian notables was convened at Delhi Ridge to solemnize Queen Victoria's assumption of the title Empress of India. In her crown was set the world's largest diamond, the Koh-i-noor, for centuries the jealously guarded jewel of Afghan kings that had recently come into the British Crown's possession. The Koh-i-noor (which means 'Mountain of Light' in Persian) is believed to have originated in India but, having been captured by the rulers of Persia and Afghanistan, it eventually came into the possession of the Sikh ruler of the Punjab, and was handed to the British when they annexed the province in 1849. Lord Lytton, the Viceroy, noted the presence of 'sixty-three ruling princes' and 'three hundred titular chiefs and native gentlemen', maharajas, rajas, raos, nawabs, sheikhs, dewans, rawals, tharkurs

and deais from Cape Comorin to the Hindu Kush and from the
deserts of Sind to the hills of Assam. The Viceroy received three
salutes of thirty-one guns apiece with a *feu de joie*, in which
formations of troops fire their guns in rapid succession between
the salutes. General Frederick Roberts, who was soon to depart
for the North-West Frontier to fight in the Second Afghan War,
recalled that the noise of the shooting was too much for the
elephants. 'As the *feu de joie* approached nearer and nearer to
them they became more and more alarmed, and at last scam-
pered off, dispersing the crowd in every direction.' When order
was eventually restored, and the elephants brought back, the
princes took it in turn to pledge their allegiance to the Crown.
The first to speak was His Highness the Maharaja of Sind
Province: 'Shah in Shah Padishah. May God Bless You. The
Princes of India bless you, and pray that your sovereignty and
power may remain steadfast forever.'[12]

For all the Indians' protestations of loyalty, the legacy of the
Indian Mutiny, when Indian sepoys butchered their British
comrades-in-arms, made the British a lot more cautious in their
dealings with their Indian subjects, particularly where the military was concerned. The majority of the soldiers serving in the
Indian army were of native descent, but London now insisted
that a significant proportion of the fighting force was drawn
from British regiments, such as Winston's 4th Hussars. The
British worked on a formula by which one-third of the army
was British, and the other two-thirds Indian. This meant that
out of a total strength of around 190,000, about 60,000 were
British. In post-Mutiny India, British units were stitched into
Indian brigades to ensure their 'reliability', a procedure that
continued through both the First and Second World Wars.

Bangalore, where Churchill was to be stationed, had, in
common with the rest of southern India, been largely unaffected
by the trauma of the Mutiny. The city was located in the heart
of the princely state of Mysore, which had retained a degree of
autonomy after its conquest by the British at the end of the

eighteenth century. The only controversy of any note to have affected Bangalore in the decades prior to Churchill's arrival was the so-called 'Bangalore conspiracy' during the winter of 1831–2. The unrest was caused by disaffected followers of the Raja of Mysore, when an 'unaccountable excitement pervaded the minds of the lower classes of Muslims that their religion was in some danger' and that the British intended to convert them to Christianity. The plotters wanted to trigger a widespread anti-British uprising by contriving an outrage in which a mosque was defiled by having a pig's head and a cross placed in front of it. The plot misfired, thanks to the help of informers, and the British resolved to make an example of the ringleaders in order to discourage the 'ignorant, bigoted and disaffected'. In the presence of huge crowds and a large contingent of troops, and against the sounds of the Dead March from Handel's *Saul*, the condemned men were led to an open space where some were shot, some hanged and some blown from cannon.[13]

Sixty years on, however, Indian opposition to the British Raj was more sophisticated, a consequence of the traditions of liberalism, free speech and the rule of law that they had acquired from their British overlords. British officials contended that there was no such thing as public opinion in India, as only an estimated 4–5 million of the country's 300 million citizens were literate. For this reason they opposed the notion that the Indians might one day be allowed to govern themselves, an attitude Churchill himself maintained right up to Indian independence in 1947. The attitude of the British Raj was summed up by Lord Salisbury, who remarked, 'The principle of election or government by representation is not an eastern idea, it does not fit eastern tradition or eastern minds.'[14] But the rapid spread of the telegraph, railways and the postal system, as well as an explosion in the number and circulation of newspapers, had a profound impact on the development of India's fledgling middle classes, who increasingly demanded representation. This resulted, in 1885, in the formation of the Indian

National Congress, which would eventually lead the country to independence.

The rapid development of Indian political discourse was reflected in the vibrancy of the Indian press, to which Churchill contributed during his spell on the North-West Frontier. The expansion was helped by the relaxation of restrictions on political comment in native-language newspapers in 1880. By 1885 there were thirty-nine vernacular titles with a total circulation of 150,000, and they pulled no punches when it came to criticizing and abusing British officialdom. In 1889, for example, the Punjabi newspaper *Halisahar Patrika* published an unflattering profile of Sir George Campbell, the province's Lieutenant Governor. The British official was described as, 'The baboon Campbell with a hairy body . . . His eyes flash forth in anger and his tail is all in flames.'[15] The English language press, which was mainly read by representatives of the Raj, responded in kind. Rudyard Kipling's newspapers, the *Allahabad Pioneer*, to which Churchill contributed articles, and the *Civil and Military Gazette*, never missed the chance to criticize the leaders of the Indian National Congress in similar vein.

The vibrancy of the political debate between educated Indians and their stiff-necked British masters made little impression on sleepy Bangalore, more than 1,000 miles away from the heart of the imperial government in Calcutta. Today Bengaluru, as it is now known, is India's third largest city and is known as the Silicon Valley of India because of its dominance of the IT market there. But in the late nineteenth century it was very much the backwater that Churchill had feared. Bengaluru, which literally means 'town of boiled beans', takes its name from the legend of an old woman who once served cooked pulses to a lost and hungry king, who named the place accordingly as a token of his thanks. Prior to the arrival of the British, Bangalore had been the stronghold of several Hindu dynasties, including the Gangas, Cholas, Hoysalas and the Vijayanagara Empire. Following the conquest of the kingdom of Mysore in 1831, the

British decided to move their regional administrative base to Bengaluru, renaming the city Bangalore in the process. Situated at more than 3,000 feet above sea level with a tropical savannah climate, the city quickly became a popular destination for the subcontinent's burgeoning European population, as well as tens of thousands of Indians who flocked to the city in search of work. Under British rule it acquired the first manifestations of a modern city, linked to the rest of the country by the arrival of the railway and telegraph. Nominal control of Mysore was handed back to the Wadiyar dynasty in 1881, who took up residence in the newly constructed Bangalore Palace in 1887. But the British maintained a large military presence at their specially built cantonment until Indian independence.

The cantonment itself covered an area of some thirteen square miles. It was, in effect, a self-contained city-state built on the edge of the old town, complete with all its own amenities including hospitals and shops, bars and restaurants as well as a cathedral, St Mark's, which has been described by one Indian ecclesiastical historian as 'the ugliest church building ever constructed'. The massive parade ground formed the heart of the base, and in Churchill's time the Bangalore garrison was the largest British military cantonment in southern India, with a permanent garrison that included three artillery batteries and regiments of cavalry, infantry, sappers, miners, mounted infantry, supply and transport corps, as well as the Bangalore Rifle Volunteers, a locally raised regiment. The street names, many of which survive, reflected the occupation of their residents: Artillery Road, Brigade Road, Infantry Road and Cavalry Road, where Churchill's own regiment was based. The area south of the parade ground was one of wide shaded streets lined with fine residences, gardens and parks which gave Bangalore its lasting image as a garden city. The cantonment also boasted great open spaces, including five polo grounds and a steeplechase course.

'The appearance of the cantonment from the rising ground

outside is certainly very pretty,' wrote Captain Albert Hervey of the 41st Madras Native Infantry. 'The substantial buildings, the neatly trimmed hedges, the well made roads, and the church peeping out from among the trees, the soldiers' quarters and other barracks, and public stores, all form a striking picture to the eye of the stranger. There is a large force maintained here . . . to hold the Mysoreans in check.'[16] This quintessentially English suburban scene was maintained until the start of the First World War, even though there was very little in the way of real soldiering to keep the cantonment's inhabitants occupied. Having escaped the convulsions of the Indian Mutiny, southern India was too remote and underdeveloped to make any mean- ingful contribution to India's new generation of political leaders in northern cities such as Bombay, Delhi and Calcutta. More- over, so far as the military garrison in Bangalore was concerned, all the action was taking place some 2,000 miles away on the North-West Frontier, far removed from the cosy routine of everyday life in this remote outpost of empire. In his valedictory letter to his grandmother Churchill seemed to understand per- fectly well the unchallenging nature of the posting that awaited him: 'We are going to Bangalore – a station in the Madras Presidency – and one which is usually considered an agreeable place to soldier in,' he wrote, making little attempt to hide his lack of enthusiasm.[17]

For the majority of British officers and men dispatched to serve in one of India's many military cantonments the principal challenge was to find 'entertainments' with which to occupy their spare time. This was particularly the case for young, single officers like Churchill, for whom the regimental mess and the sports field provided the principal outlets for their leisure activi- ties. At one level the mess, with its strict dress code and abundance of native domestic servants in club livery, sought to maintain the standards and etiquette observed in the best London clubs. But it could also be a place where exuberant young men, far removed from their families and friends, let off steam. High jinks in the officers' mess were often so raucous that university-educated civil servants were advised to wear their second-best suit of dinner clothes, as their best set might be ruined by flying plates of food. One young officer recalled how, one night after dinner, well-trained servants 'appeared by magic to remove all the breakable furniture . . . replacing it with a special set of chairs and tables made to smash. Senior officers bolted away to play bridge: the rest of us, who were young in years or heart, began to enjoy ourselves according to the ancient custom.' On one occasion a young officer with a Punjabi regiment 'brought in a little bazaar pony and made it jump sofas'.[18] Rudyard Kipling, who anticipated Churchill's arrival in India by a decade, frequently visited the mess of British regiments stationed at the equally massive Mian Mir cantonment on the outskirts of Lahore, which provided him with the inspiration for many of the characters in his stories about life on the North-West Frontier.

Hunting was another favoured pastime for these under-employed young men marooned far away in a foreign land. When the British first arrived in India great expanses of the country were almost unpopulated and teemed with game. Shooting expeditions, or *shikar*, were extremely popular with officers of all ages, who hunted a wide variety of animals including tiger, cheetah and, in the foothills of the Himalayas, deer. For those who could afford it, shooting tiger from a howdah on an elephant's back, which became the classic sport of viceregal India, was particularly fashionable, and groups of officers would often disappear for a month at a time to bag their prey. In the absence of the traditional English country pursuit of fox-hunting, pig-sticking, where a mounted man armed with a steel-tipped bamboo spear went in pursuit of a wild boar, was regarded as an acceptable alternative. But, as with fox-hunting, these pursuits were not without their human casualties. In one year one English regiment lost three of its officers to sporting accidents – a tenth of its officer strength.[19]

This, then, was the world that awaited young Winston when, with heavy heart, he set sail for India with his regiment. Churchill's passage to India was undertaken on the coal-fired steamship *Britannia*, which was owned and operated by the Peninsular and Oriental Steamship Navigation Company, the oldest British line east of Suez. P&O, as it was and is still more familiarly known, ran regular routes from Brindisi on the heel of Italy to Port Said in Egypt, a route often referred to as the Imperial Highway. The ships were also used at troop transporters, a far more appealing alternative to the more utilitarian 'trooper' vessels – specially designed military ships that had come into service in the 1870s to facilitate the passage of large numbers of British soldiers to and from India. Prior to the commissioning of the troopships, sailing to India could be both a lengthy and hazardous enterprise. In the late eighteenth century it had taken the young Arthur Wellesley eight months to reach Calcutta from England, and while the introduction of modern iron-built steamers improved the journey time, it was still by no means safe. When the troopship *Birkenhead* foundered off the coast of South Africa in 1852, 454 of the 693 passengers aboard were lost. The opening of the Suez Canal in 1869, which meant ships no longer had to make the lengthy and hazardous voyage around the Cape of Good Hope, dramatically improved journey times, and meant that large numbers of men could be shipped quickly and safely between Britain and her most important colony.

Winston seems to have enjoyed the voyage. His mentor, Colonel Brabazon, did not sail with the regiment, having relinquished his command. He was replaced by Colonel William Alexander Ramsay, who, in contrast to his predecessor, was a quiet and unspectacular officer who suffered the misfortune of never having seen action in nearly thirty years of military service. Churchill sailed with Reggie Barnes, his travelling companion to Cuba and America, who had been confirmed as adjutant the previous May, and Hugo Baring, the son of Lord Revelstoke, a member of the famous Baring banking dynasty and the great-great-grandfather of Diana, Princess of Wales. Another of Churchill's companions on the voyage was Captain Ronald Kincaid-Smith, who was rumoured to have been romantically attached to Winston's mother.[20] There were nearly a hundred other officers on board, so there was no shortage of company. For much of the passage Churchill played cards and chess, and spent a lot of the time peering through his telescope, 'a very powerful glass' that was 'in great demand and constant use'. He wistfully told his mother, 'This voyage is a very different experience to crossing the Atlantic in a Cunarder last winter,' but was consoled by the fact that he and his fellow officers 'make a very cheery party ourselves'.[21]

When the ship docked at Bombay harbour Churchill and the other soldiers were grateful to be free of their nautical confinement. 'It may be imagined how our whole shipful of officers and men were delighted after being cooped up for nearly a month to see the palms and palaces of Bombay lying about us in a wide crescent,' he recorded.[22] Indeed, such was Churchill's enthusiasm to escape the ship's claustrophobic surroundings that he managed to dislocate his shoulder while trying to go ashore, when his landing craft suddenly swung away from the dockside just as he was grabbing hold of the iron steps. 'I scrambled up alright, made a few remarks of a general character, mostly beginning with the earlier letters of the alphabet, hugged my shoulder and soon thought no more about it.' In fact the accident-prone Winston had suffered yet another of his youthful misadventures, only this time the injury would plague him for the rest of his life. It meant that he had to play polo with the upper part of his arm strapped against his shoulder, and once he nearly suffered a repeat dislocation when he gave too expansive a gesture in the House of Commons while making a speech. It also meant he had to strap his arm to his side when riding into battle, a handicap that made his feats of daring on various battlefields all the more courageous. It was, as he wrote in *My Early Life*, an injury 'which was to cripple me at polo, to prevent me from ever playing tennis, and to be a grave embarrassment in moments of peril'.[23]

After a few days' rest at Poona, Churchill and his regiment travelled by train to Bangalore, where even impecunious young subalterns like himself were able to live in considerable comfort and style. He shared a bungalow with Barnes and Baring, 'a magnificent pink and white stucco palace in the middle of a large and beautiful garden', as he described it to his mother. Winston had three large rooms to himself, including a writing table covered with photographs and memories of family. Yet again Churchill, who as a boy had been abandoned by his parents at various institutions, found himself stationed thousands of miles away from home and hearth and his homesickness was self-evident. 'The house is full of you – in every conceivable costume and style,' he wrote to Jennie. But he warned her against making a visit herself because of the recent outbreak of bubonic plague in Bombay. And he tried to put a brave face on his new habitat, declaring, 'I think I shall like this place and enjoy the time I spend here.'[24]

The new arrivals certainly lacked for nothing in terms of their personal comfort. Each officer had his own butler, whose duties were to wait at table, manage the household and supervise the stables. They had their own 'dressing boy', as well as sharing the services of two gardeners, three water carriers, four washermen – or dhobis – and a watchman. Winston soon settled into the undemanding routine of garrison life. He rose for early breakfast at five, followed by parade at six. Second breakfast, bath and 'such papers as there are' followed at eight before proceeding for an hour of stables. After that the officers were left to their own devices until polo at 4.15, which Winston played with great passion until the shadows began to lengthen over the polo ground, and 'we ambled back perspiring and exhausted to hot baths, rest, and at 8.30 dinner, to the strains of the regimental band and the clinking of ice in well-filled glasses.'[25]

Winston found India 'in every respect the exact contrast of America', he wrote in his first letter home to his younger brother, Jack. 'The obsequious native servants replace the uncivil "freeborn citizens". Labour here is cheap and plentiful. Existence costs but little and luxury can be easily obtained.' He asked his mother to send him a card table and equipment for collecting butterflies, a childhood hobby he wanted to revive. The bungalow's garden was filled with a wide variety of the creatures – 'Purple Emperors, White Admirals & Swallowtails and many other rare and beautiful insects,' he told Jack.[26] An entirely new interest was provided by gardening, particularly the growing of roses. The bungalow's previous occupants had left a magnificent collection of standard roses in the garden, including 'La France', 'Gloire de Dijon' and 'Maréchal Niel'. India inspired Churchill's lifelong passion for gardening, leading him to construct his own rose garden at Chartwell House, the Churchill family home at Westerham, Kent. Churchill later wrote that, in India, the clement weather conditions produced perfect specimens. 'The roses of Europe in innumerable large pots attain the highest perfection of fragrance and colour. Flowers, flowering shrubs and creepers blossom in glorious profusion. Snipe (and snakes) abound in the marshes; brilliant butterflies dance in the sunshine, and nautch-girls by the light of the moon.'[27]

Polo, or 'the emperor of games' as Churchill called it, was Winston's main sporting pursuit in India. He was by now a prominent member of the regimental polo club, which decided to buy the entire stud of twenty-five ponies from the Poona Light Horse to help their bid to win the Inter-Regimental Tournament, the most prestigious polo event in India. Never in the history of the tournament had the cup been won by a cavalry regiment from southern India, and Churchill and his comrades resolved to rectify this omission. They trained every day for hours at a time, with Churchill playing in every chukka he could get into, and they announced their arrival as serious contenders for honours by winning a tournament at Secundera-bad within a month of their arrival from England, a feat never before achieved by a newly arrived regiment. The victory attracted much attention in the Indian press, and Winston told his mother, 'The entire population turns out to watch and betting not infrequently runs into thousands of rupees. Our final match against the Native contingent was witnessed by eight or nine thousand natives who wildly cheered every goal or stroke made by their country men – and were terribly disappointed by the issue.'[28]

It was through polo that Winston met Pamela Plowden, the first great love of his life, who was the daughter of the British Resident at Hyderabad, 700 miles and a twenty-four-hour train ride from Bangalore. Pamela, a great society beauty, was intro-duced to Winston when he was playing at Secunderabad, ten miles from her father's headquarters, and Winston was love-struck. Before meeting Pamela, Churchill had an intense dislike of Anglo-Indian society, referring to it as a 'godless land of snobs and bores'. He was particularly dismissive of the womenfolk he met at a point-to-point meeting. 'I saw a lot of horrid Anglo Indian women at these races,' he told his mother. 'Nasty – vulgar creatures all looking as if they thought themselves great beauties. I fear me they are a sorry lot.'[29] For Winston, the Anglo-Indian ladies would never surpass Jennie's looks. After meeting Pamela, though, he appears to have revised his opinion. 'I must say she is the most beautiful girl I have ever seen – "Bar none", as the Duchess Lily says . . . We are going to try to do the City of Hyderabad together – on an elephant. You dare not walk or the natives spit at Europeans – which provokes retalia-tion leading to riots.'[30]

The ride through the city of Hyderabad on an elephant with

Miss Plowden was duly accomplished, the beginning of a deep mutual affection that lasted the rest of their lives. Winston was invited to dine with the Plowdens at Hyderabad and enjoyed himself immensely. 'A civilised dinner with ladies present is delightful in this country after nearly three months of messes and barbarism.'[31] He was clearly smitten by Pamela Plowden, and henceforth she was constantly in his thoughts. When, in 1899, Churchill made his dramatic escape from captivity having been taken prisoner during the Boer War, Pamela was one of the first people to cable his mother offering her congratulations. When he finally got back to London he noted, 'Politics, Pamela, finances and books all need my attention.'[32] That Winston should list his priorities thus was not lost on Miss Plowden, who eventually ended the courtship in 1902 when she married Victor, 2nd Earl of Lytton. She feared she would always play second fiddle to Winston's love of politics – a not unreasonable conclusion – and she doubted his boasts that he would one day make his fortune.

Winston was heartbroken by her decision, having proposed marriage to her previously, even though he was well aware that his lack of money posed a significant barrier to their union. Recently released correspondence from Pamela's descendants shows that, when Winston wrote to her from Calcutta in 1899, he began 'My dear Miss Pamela' and told her: 'I have lived all my life seeing the most beautiful women London produces . . . Never have I seen one for whom I would forego the business of life. Then I met you . . . Were I a dreamer of dreams, I would say . . . "Marry me – and I will conquer the world and lay it at your feet." For marriage two conditions are necessary – money and the consent of both parties. One certainly, both probably are absent. And this is all such an old story . . .'[33] Despite rejecting him in marriage, Pamela remained devoted to Winston for the rest of his life. When Churchill was appointed to his first ministerial post in 1906, Lady Lytton, as she had become, told

Churchill's private secretary, 'The first time you meet Winston you see all his faults, and the rest of your life you spend in discovering his virtues.'[34]

However hard Winston tried to embrace his new life in India, he found it difficult to leave behind the interests that had excited him in London. In many respects India should have been the perfect posting for Churchill. His father had served as Secretary of State for India, and the new government of Lord Salisbury was determined to reassert its authority over its restless colony. Lord Curzon, a long-standing friend of the Churchill family, was shortly to be made Viceroy, with responsibility for administering the entire subcontinent. Many other family acquaintances, such as Bill Beresford and John Brabazon, had served with distinction in India, making a name for themselves in the process. If ever an ambitious young subaltern was well suited to serving the Queen-Empress in her favourite colonial possession, it was Winston Churchill.

But Winston simply could not shake off the feeling that he had been consigned to some godforsaken colonial backwater and that his prospects of personal and political advancement were fast diminishing. In the same letter in which he told his mother about meeting Pamela Plowden, he expressed his unhappiness that he was not in London to put his name forward to contest a forthcoming by-election in the north of England. 'I see there is a vacancy in East Bradford,' he remarked when he had been in India little more than a month. 'Had I been in England – I might have contested it and should have won – almost to a certainty. Rather than being an insignificant subaltern I should have had opportunities of learning those things which will be of value to me in the future.' He no longer made any pretence of liking his posting. 'I will not disguise from you that life out here – is stupid dull and uninteresting.' Unlike Cuba, where he had milked his contacts to gain access and acquire knowledge, no one was going to take him seriously without good letters of introduction. If he had come out as an elected member of parliament, 'I should know more than as a soldier in five years.' His lowly status meant he was denied access to the great and the good: 'It is a poor life to lead and even its best pleasures are far below those obtainable in England. I meet none but soldiers and other people equally ignorant of the country and hear nothing talked but "shop" and racing.'[35]

In *My Early Life*, written more than thirty years later, Churchill gives a rather rose-tinted view of his Indian sojourn, writing warmly of the joys of polo and the friendly camaraderie of the mess, with its formal dinners and social chit-chat. But this fondness is not reflected in his letters home of that period, which show he had developed a deep dislike for his surroundings, missed his family and yearned for news and social gossip. By Christmas 1896 his homesickness is apparent when he refers to 'the Blenheim festivities' in the press, where the Prince of Wales had distinguished himself in a family shooting competition.[36] He complains that, apart from his mother and brother, 'no one else has sent me a line', and begs his mother to send him details of her social activities in England. As for India, he grows more critical by the day. When he travels to Calcutta at Christmas to take part in a polo tournament, he writes that, whenever he meets British expatriates in India, 'I immediately desire to flee the country. It is only in my comfortable bungalow, among my roses, polo ponies and butterflies, that I feel that philosophical composure which alone can make residence in India endurable.' He was glad to have seen the city 'for the same reason Papa gave for being glad to have seen Lisbon, namely "that it will be unnecessary ever to see it again"'.[37]

*

Churchill was determined to escape his Indian predicament. Before travelling to Calcutta he wrote to Sir Evelyn Wood, the Adjutant General, making yet another request to join Kitchener's force in Egypt before it began its expedition up the Nile. 'I revolve Egypt continuously in my mind,' he wrote to Jennie, who promised to try to use her own influence on Winston's behalf. Jennie, still short of funds, hoped that through constant promotion of Winston's cause the family's fortunes would be revived. She advised Winston to write to the War Office directly, and even though she expected his application to be ignored, it would give her the excuse to approach Kitchener. 'I am looking forward to the time when we shall live together again and all my political ambitions shall be centred in you,' she wrote to her son on Christmas Eve.[38] But Jennie was concerned that her son's restless nature could be his downfall. She insisted that, if she did manage to secure his re-posting to Egypt, he must give a firm commitment to stay with the Egyptian army for at least two years 'and there will be no getting out of it if you don't like it . . . Life is not always what one wants it to be but to make the best of it as it is the only way of being happy.' Kitchener, who became Secretary of State for War at the outbreak of the First World War, had a reputation for being a meticulous military planner, and was not the kind of commander to offer a placement purely on the recommendation of a pushy mother. For his part Winston continued to regard his time in India as 'utterly barren . . . Poked away in a garrison town which resembles a 3rd rate watering place, out of season and without sea, with lots of routine work and a hot and trying sun – without society or good sport – half my friends on leave and the other half ill – my life here would be intolerable were it not for the consolations of literature.'[39] The first stirrings of the 'black dog' moods that would affect him in later life, when he suffered bouts of depression, were evident during his stay in southern India.

The discovery of literature was an important consolation for Churchill at this time. An indifferent student at school, he knew that the gaps in his knowledge put him at a disadvantage with his contemporaries. From Bangalore he wrote to Jack, who was still at Harrow, urging him to 'try and get hold of a certain amount of knowledge. I only wish I had worked more.'[40] In

Bangalore, with so much spare time on his hands, 'The desire for learning came upon me,' as he later recalled.[41] Rather than wasting his time idling like his fellow officers, Winston became an autodidact, embarking on a radical course of self-improvement, avidly devouring the heavy political, historical and philosophical tomes that were more familiar to Oxbridge undergraduates. He had begun his self-education programme at Aldershot, starting with Henry Fawcett's *Manual of Political Economy* before ploughing through Gibbon's *Decline and Fall of the Roman Empire*. Once settled in India he immersed himself in other classics, including twelve volumes of Macaulay – eight of history and four of essays – as well as Plato's *Republic*, Aristotle's *Politics*, Darwin's *On the Origin of Species*, and two volumes of Adam Smith's *Wealth of Nations*. Schopenhauer, Malthus, Pascal and Saint-Simon soon followed.

Jennie supported her son's literary interests, regularly sending books to Bangalore, together with back copies of the *Annual Register of World Events*, a yearly analysis of global current affairs. In addition Winston made time to read and reread his father's speeches, learning many of them by heart, as well as the letters and speeches of his American mentor, Bourke Cockran. He corresponded with both Cockran and his former headmaster at Harrow, the Reverend J. E. C. Welldon, who was pleased to hear of Churchill's interest in self-education. 'I would not forgo your India experience for the world,' Welldon wrote to Churchill, adding, 'Gibbon is the greatest of Historians, read him all through.'[42] In his letters to Cockran and his mother, the first intimations of Churchill's political outlook are evident. He is an enthusiastic proponent of 'Tory Democracy', the cause advocated by his late father. When Lord Rosebery resigned the leadership of the Liberals in late 1896, Winston tells his mother that Rosebery would be a worthy leader of a revived 'Tory Democracy' movement. He is critical of the decision by Lord Lansdowne, the Secretary of State for War, to increase the size of the army, arguing that the money would be better spent on developing 'an unequalled navy', a cause he would pursue with vigour in his later political career as First Lord of the Admiralty.

Churchill provided his mother with a running commentary on the authors he was reading and the progress he was making. 'I have been reading a great deal lately. Fifty pages of Macaulay and twenty-five of Gibbon every day. There are only a hundred of the latter's 4,000 odd left now.'[43] Churchill developed a particular liking for Gibbon, whom 'through the glistening hours of the Indian day, from . . . stables till the evening shadows proclaimed the hour of Polo, I devoured'.[44] Churchill's constant need for intellectual stimulus was noted by his fellow soldiers. Sergeant Hallaway, Churchill's troop sergeant in the 4th Hussars, recalled, 'The great thing about him was the way he worked. He was busier than half the others put together. I never saw him without pencils sticking out all over him. And once when I went up to his bungalow, I could scarcely get in what with books and papers foolscap all over the place.'[45] Winston understood the need to maintain his demanding reading schedule. He needed to build up 'a scaffolding of logical and consistent views which will perhaps tend to the creation of a logical and consistent mind'. As the British military historian Sir John Keegan has written, 'The young Churchill, in his leap to self-education, must have been the most unusual cavalry subaltern in any European army.'[46]

For all his enthusiasm for self-improvement, Winston, unlike his famous contemporary Rudyard Kipling, showed little interest in learning about Indian history or culture, nor could he be bothered to learn the native languages. 'I shall not learn Hindustani,' he informed his mother. 'It is quite unnecessary. All natives here speak English perfectly and I cannot see any good wasting my time acquiring a dialect I will never use.'[47] Indeed, he showed little interest in the people of India, and the only Indians he got to know were those serving in the military. Perhaps, had he taken the time to learn more about the Indian people, Churchill might have been more sympathetic to their campaign for independence in the twentieth century, instead of becoming one of its most implacable opponents.

Churchill's anti-social habit of locking himself away with his books did not always endear him to his fellow officers, many of whom found his behaviour decidedly odd. One evening, during some horseplay in the mess, they showed their resentment by trying to squash Winston under a large sofa. He wriggled free, telling them they would never be able to keep him down.[48] On other occasions, though, he was more gregarious. The official history of the 4th Hussars recalls how he organized a concert party to raise money for the regimental fund. Sergeant Hallaway deemed it 'the best show in India, which put all the travelling shows in the shade'.[49] Churchill opened the concert himself with the song 'Oh, listen to the band', wearing morning dress with a carnation in the buttonhole. The chorus was dressed as guardsmen in scarlet, with 'pill-box' hats. The cast included a strongman, a card-sharper and a conjuror, and the repertoire included folk songs and Negro spirituals. The concert party performed all over the district and raised a substantial amount for the regiment. An entry in the Regimental Betting Book shows Winston was not completely detached from mess life. 'Lt. Winston S. Churchill bets Captain F. Lee Rupees 100 that Moreton Frewen is in possession of a head (stag) which was within the last three years exhibited at White's Club for a period of some months: and that the head had fifty-two (52) distinct points. The bet to be decided by Lt-Col. F. De Moleyns or, in default, by the Secretary of White's Club.' The book does not record whether Churchill won his bet.[50] The 4th Hussars' complaint book is filled with remarks by Churchill and his friend Reggie Barnes on various issues, such as recommending that the mess should buy some new carpets, since the 'present state of discomfort is intolerable'. Churchill takes issue with the 'dirty, filthy, beastly tank water', unclean tablecloths and inferior cigarettes. There is even a recommendation on how the kitchen should serve his eggs on toast at breakfast in a way that prevents 'the toast getting all sodden'.

Churchill tried to make the most of his 'unprofitable exile', but his burning ambition remained to see action and make his name. His hopes of escaping the tedium of Bangalore were thwarted in December when Kitchener made a lukewarm response to Jennie's request for Winston to join the British force in Egypt. 'I will note your son's name for special service . . . I have however no vacancies in the cavalry but I will have his name put down on the list.'[51] For the time being Winston had to reconcile himself to the tedium of regimental life. But he was clear in his own mind that if a new opportunity arose for him to experience military combat, he would grab it with both hands.

CHAPTER FIVE

THE SEAT OF WAR

'You should always kill an Englishman. First comes one as
a hunter, then two to make a map, and then an army
to take the country, so better to kill the first one.'

Pashtun proverb

'I was on the lawns of Goodwood in lovely weather and winning
my money, when the revolt of the Pashtun tribesmen on the
Indian frontier began.'[1] So Churchill wrote of the event that
would transform his life, providing him with the opportunity he
so desperately sought to escape his dreary confinement in
Bangalore and give him his first taste of front-line combat.
Despite his earlier misgivings that he might not be able to return
to England for up to two years, he nevertheless managed to
secure three months' leave in the summer of 1897, ostensibly to
enjoy 'the gaieties of the London season'. And Winston was
doing precisely that, attending glittering balls in London and
spending enjoyable days at race meetings, when news arrived in
early August that the tribesmen of the North-West Frontier had
launched a new rebellion against the British. This time their
target was the newly established fort at Malakand, which was
under construction to protect the all-important road to Chitral
following the tribes' rebellion two years earlier. The moment he
heard about the uprising Churchill realized this was an opportunity he dare not miss. Scores of young British officers had
made their names fighting against the fierce tribesmen of the
Afghan frontier and winning medals, and Winston was determined that his should now be added to their ranks.

Until the outbreak of the revolt Winston had spent the year growing increasingly impatient for adventure. From early January he agitated to return to England for the summer. 'I long for excitement of some sort,' he had written plaintively to his mother in March.[2] This was despite his superiors' interest in the promise he was displaying as an officer. He was awarded temporary promotion to adjutant, and then brigade-major, where he had responsibility for managing the regiment's everyday affairs. Winston boasted that his superiors regarded him as 'one of the two most efficient officers of my rank', but not even these achievements diminished his desire to leave Bangalore at the earliest opportunity. Nor was his mood improved when his commanding officer refused to allow the 4th Hussars' polo team to travel to Meerut for the Inter-Regimental Tournament for which they had trained so hard. There had also been a worrying moment when he came close to suffering serious injury while supervising shooting practice with his troopers. In a freak accident he was hit by flying slivers of metal after one of the bullets hit the iron edge of the target. The shrapnel was eventually extracted after 'an abominable twenty minutes', and Winston suffered considerable discomfort until the wounds healed. When, in April, his leave was finally approved, Winston could hardly contain his excitement about 'seeing civilisation again after the barbarous squalor of this country'.[3]

Then, as he prepared to return to England, the possibility arose that he might travel as a war correspondent to cover the crisis between Greece and Turkey over the question of Crete. Always on the lookout for an opportunity to repeat the success of his Cuban adventure, Churchill was excited at the prospect of renewed fighting between the island's Greek and Turkish communities. The crisis had all the potential to ignite a major war between the main European powers, particularly after Britain and its European allies imposed a naval blockade of the island to prevent the shipment of arms that might have inflamed tensions further. Churchill wanted to cover the conflict as a 'special correspondent', and asked his mother to use her social contacts to get him a commission to write for one of the leading newspapers. Ever conscious of the need to make money, Winston thought he should be paid between £10 and £15 per article – twice the amount he had received from the *Daily Graphic* for his Cuban dispatches – and stated that his preference was to write for either *The Times*, the Establishment newspaper, or the *Morning Post*, a Conservative-supporting title to which Rudyard Kipling contributed occasional verse. Failing everything else, Winston said he would once again write for the populist *Daily Graphic*. He set sail from Bombay on 8 May with the intention of going to cover the war in Crete, but his hopes of new adventure ended in frustration. Within three days of setting off for Brindisi, from where he planned to secure a passage to Crete, the Greeks and Turks agreed a ceasefire, so that by the time he reached Italy the threat of war had receded. Disappointed, he amused himself by doing a mini version of the Grand Tour, visiting Naples, Pompeii and Rome before returning home.

Summer 1897 brought Queen Victoria's Diamond Jubilee, and all the leading aristocratic families competed to stage extravagant parties in her honour. Winston attended many of these affairs, including the Duchess of Devonshire's famous fancy dress ball at Devonshire House in Piccadilly, which was seen as the highlight of the celebrations. 'Of all the private entertainments for which the Jubilee has provided the occasion none is comparable with the magnificent fancy dress ball given last night at Devonshire House by the Duke and Duchess of Devonshire,' reported *The Times*.[4] Jennie, who had begun an affair with a young Grenadier Guards officer only five years older than Winston, went as the Empress Theodora, the former courtesan who became the wife of the Emperor Justinian I. It is not recorded how Winston was attired, except for the fact that he was wearing a sword, which was no doubt useful when he was asked to act as a 'second' to his brother Jack, who was challenged to a duel in the course of the night's festivities.[5]

Churchill also went to a number of high-society race meetings, such as the Derby at Epsom and Royal Ascot. In his youth Churchill often attended such events, mainly because he saw them as wonderful networking opportunities, where he could mingle with the great and the good in the royal enclosure.

With time on his hands, Winston decided the summer of 1897 might be an opportune moment to make his first public speech. He had already contacted a family acquaintance working at Conservative Central Office, declaring his interest in becoming a candidate. The upshot was that Winston received an invitation to address a rally of the Primrose League, a grass-roots organization dedicated to spreading Conservative principles throughout Britain. The meeting was held near Bath, and on 26 July Churchill made his maiden political speech in support of providing working men with compensation if they suffered injury or sickness, a cause very much in keeping with his late father's Tory Democracy beliefs. The speech was generally well received, and *The Lady* reported that 'an auspicious debut on the platform was made the other day by Mr Winston Churchill, elder son of the late Lord Randolph Churchill ... [who] is strikingly like his late father in features and colouring'.[6] Not all the press coverage was positive, though. One local newspaper reported that, while Churchill was 'anxious to take a part in public affairs', he was 'in danger of being spoilt by flattery and public notice'.[7]

Fresh from his Bath triumph Winston went to stay with Duchess Lily and Bill Beresford at Deepdene for the Goodwood races, another highlight of the racing season. And it was at Goodwood that he read in the newspapers about the tribal unrest that had erupted on the North-West Frontier. It was just the opportunity Winston had been seeking, and he was even more encouraged to discover that the British force sent to confront the rebels was commanded by General Sir Bindon Blood. From Deepdene Winston telegraphed Blood immediately, reminding the general of his promise to find him a position on his staff if trouble flared again. But such was his desperation to get to the front that, rather than waiting to find out if Blood could honour his commitment, he set off at once on the long return journey to India.

*

As he made his way to Victoria station to catch the boat train to Brindisi, Winston no doubt had in mind the recent exploits of one of his direct contemporaries, Viscount Fincastle. Winston had met Fincastle, like himself a young cavalry officer, during his visit to Calcutta the previous Christmas. Born Alexander Murray, the eldest son of the Earl of Dunmore, Viscount Fincastle was three years older than Winston, and had enjoyed the kind of military career that the younger cavalryman desperately sought for himself. Not only had Fincastle's family connections secured his appointment as aide-de-camp to Lord Elgin, India's Governor General, but Fincastle had also managed to get himself seconded to Kitchener's campaign to the Sudan, where he had seen action in the war against the Mahdi. Barely able to conceal his envy, Winston had told his mother that Fincastle 'has got 3 medals out of Egypt, and hardly saw any fighting'.[8] Now it was to be Winston's turn for medals and glory.

Before leaving for India, Winston had once more sought the help of Lord Beresford, in his capacity as a close acquaintance of Blood, to reinforce his appeals to the general to be allowed to join his campaign. 'These Beresfords had a great air,' recalled Churchill. 'They made one feel that the world and everyone in it were of fine consequence. I remember the manner in which he announced my purpose to a circle of club friends many years my seniors. "He goes to the East tonight – to the seat of war." '[9] His mother, meanwhile, was encouraged to use her own contacts to make sure Blood accommodated her son. Churchill left in such a hurry that he did not even have time to see his younger brother Jack, who was spending the summer in Paris with Jennie's relatives. Jack was due to return to London in late August, but Winston could not wait, and wrote Jack a deeply apologetic letter, suggesting that his brother join him in India later in the year. Winston was very close to Jack, and wrote to him often, but in his last, hurriedly written letter before leaving London there was no hint of the potential dangers he faced if he succeeded in joining Blood's force. His only concern was that Jack continued to write to him. Short of money himself, Winston nevertheless enclosed a cheque 'for a fiver which I hope will be welcome'.[10] The suddenness of his departure meant he left a typical Winston-like mess behind him. Only when he was aboard the steamship heading for Bombay did he remember that he had left his polo sticks behind, forgotten to return the badges loaned to him by the Primrose League for his speech and failed to pick up the books he had ordered containing the speeches of Disraeli and Gladstone, as well as leaving one or two bills unpaid. But perhaps his biggest oversight was to leave Peas, his little dog, which he had intended to take with him to Bangalore to keep him company.

As Churchill rushed back to India, he still had an anxious wait to see whether Blood would honour his promise. Winston travelled to India at the hottest time of the year, and the hand-pulled *punkahs*, a length of cloth hanging from the ceiling that acted as a fan, did little to relieve the discomfort. He complained that the ship provided neither tolerable food nor adequate ventilation. Sailing through the Red Sea, Winston signed one letter home, 'your liquefied, evaporating, but devoted son'.[11] By sailing for India without a firm commitment from Blood, Winston risked wasting three weeks of his valuable leave, as well as incurring significant expenditure that he could ill afford. At each port of call he eagerly sought news from Blood, but none was forthcoming. By the time he returned to his regiment at Bangalore he was getting desperate. 'I have heard nothing more from

Sir Bindon Blood,' he wrote to his mother. 'I cannot think he would willingly disappoint me and can only conclude that someone at Headquarters has put a spoke in my wheel.'[12] A week later he was even more despondent. 'I am still disgusted at my not being taken. Sir Bindon Blood has never replied to any of my wires.'[13]

It was not until the end of August that Winston finally received the news he had been hoping for. 'My Dear Churchill', Blood wrote from his military camp in the Upper Swat Valley. 'I should advise your coming as a press correspondent, and when you are here I shall put you on the strength on the 1st opportunity.'[14] Much to Winston's irritation Blood had already found a position for Viscount Fincastle, his great rival for fame and glory on the battlefield. Blood had appointed Fincastle to replace an officer who had been killed in action with the Corps of Guides, the specially created British regiment raised in Peshawar in 1846 to police the North-West Frontier. If nothing else, Winston could replicate the success he had enjoyed in Cuba by writing newspaper articles about the campaign. And if he was lucky, he might even get himself to one of the fighting regiments and experience his first real taste of combat.

Churchill had already taken the precaution of sounding out the leading national newspapers about the possibility of covering the campaign as a war correspondent, instructing Jennie to approach the editors on his behalf. George Buckle, the editor at *The Times*, was a family acquaintance. Under Buckle's editorship the 'Thunderer' had become increasingly conservative and pro-empire, a policy that suited Winston's own outlook. Buckle had at one time been one of Lord Randolph's allies, although he had never forgotten his difficult encounter with Winston's father over the episode of his resignation letter. To his irritation, Winston discovered that Buckle had already hired Viscount Fincastle to be his special correspondent for the military campaign. Fincastle seemed to steal a march on Churchill at every turn. Buckle wrote apologetically to Jennie, saying that 'our appointed correspondent must have preference'. But by way of encouragement he said of Winston that 'it would be very strange if he did not inherit ability, resource, and the power of expression'.[15]

Jennie did succeed in persuading Edward Lawson, the editor of the *Daily Telegraph*, to take a number of her son's dispatches. By comparison with *The Times*, which had been founded on 1 January 1785, the *Daily Telegraph* was a relative newcomer to the Fleet Street scene. Founded in 1855, its first proprietor, Colonel Arthur Sleigh, had set up the *Daily Telegraph and Courier* to pursue a grudge against Prince George, who was commanding British Forces during the Crimean War. But by September Sleigh had been obliged to hand over control of the title to his printer, Joseph Moses Levy, after his competitors cut their cover price to put him out of business. Levy appointed his son, Edward Levy Lawson, as the new editor, and Lawson took responsibility for managing the title as well. The new owners cut the cover price by half to 1d, dramatically undercutting its main rivals. From its inception the paper was directed at Britain's educated and wealthy middle classes, and under Lawson's leadership became one of the most successful of the Victorian era, combining populist appeal with a strong imperial outlook. But the newspaper's racy coverage of events, such as the dispatches of George Augustus Sala, one of the newspaper's most distinguished journalists and a protégé of Charles Dickens, on foreign conflicts such as the American Civil War, prompted the respected Victorian cultural critic Matthew Arnold to denounce what he called 'Telegraphese', which he saw as being representative of the philistinism of the middle classes. Winston moved in the same social circles as Lawson's son, Harry, who would later take control of the paper when his father was made a life peer by Arthur Balfour, the Conservative prime minister. Winston had met Harry Lawson in Calcutta the previous Christmas, when Harry and his wife were touring India 'endeavouring to collect material to pass as an authority on India', as Churchill sarcastically remarked. Winston took Mrs Harry Lawson to a dinner in Calcutta while her husband was otherwise occupied, and found her 'a nice woman'. But he was less complimentary about Harry, remarking, 'He is a fool, but harmless, and amiable.'[16]

Whatever his personal views concerning the owners of the *Daily Telegraph*, they did not prevent Winston from accepting a commission to be the paper's war correspondent on the North-West Frontier, even if it meant doing so for far less money than he had expected. The *Daily Telegraph* prospered during the late Victorian era because the Lawson family, keen to avoid a repetition of the financial disaster that had nearly killed the paper at its inception, kept a very tight grip on its finances. Lawson agreed to pay Winston £5 (about £300 today) an article – the same amount that he had received for his Cuban dispatches – even though he had expected to receive at least twice as much. Only a few months previously the *Daily Chronicle* had offered him ten guineas an article to cover the war in Crete, and Winston complained that the *Telegraph* offer was not enough, especially as he had to pay all his own travelling expenses, which were considerable, as he was travelling to the front as a private citizen, and not as a serving officer. Jennie promised to take the matter up with Lawson personally, to 'try and shame the old devil to pay you properly'.[17] She did not succeed, but Churchill's war dispatches were the beginning of a lifelong association with various owners of the *Daily Telegraph*. At the end of the Second World War, when Churchill realized he did not have enough money to run Chartwell, the family home in Kent, Lord Camrose, who had bought the paper from the Lawson family in 1927, organized a group of wealthy well-wishers to donate £5,000 each to allow the Churchills to keep their home on condition it was left to the nation on Winston's death, an undertaking Clementine Churchill fulfilled after her husband's death in 1965.

From India Winston also made his own arrangements to

write for the *Allahabad Pioneer*, Kipling's old newspaper. Thus armed with his telegram from Blood and his commissions to write for the *Daily Telegraph* and the *Pioneer*, all that remained was for him to seek permission from his commanding officer, Colonel Ramsay, to travel to the Afghan border to join Blood's campaign. 'I presented in much anxiety Sir Bindon Blood's telegram to my commanding officer,' Churchill recalled. 'But the Colonel was indulgent, and the fates were kind. Although the telegram was quite informal and unofficial, I was told I could go and try my luck.'[18] Presumably Colonel Ramsay encouraged the desire to acquire martial experience among his junior officers. Winston owed an enormous debt of gratitude to Reggie Barnes, his Cuban travelling companion, whom he regarded as 'one of the best friends I shall ever have – perhaps *the* best'.[19] As the more experienced officer, Barnes had an equally legitimate claim to be allowed to join the campaign. 'Barnes behaved splendidly about my leave,' Winston told his mother, 'as he would have loved to go himself and it was due to his efforts as adjutant that I got it'.[20]

Winston now had to travel virtually the entire length of the Indian subcontinent to reach Blood's force. Accompanied by 'my dressing boy and campaigning kit', he arrived at Bangalore railway station and inquired about a ticket to Nowshera, the main military railhead for the Malakand expedition, which sounded like a more than passable imitation of 'nowhere'. 'I had the curiosity to ask how far it was,' Churchill wrote. 'The polite Indian consulted a railway time table and impassively answered, 2,028 miles' – similar to the distance that separates the east and west coasts of the United States. This meant a five-day train journey in the worst of the summer heat, although Winston did manage to travel first class in 'large leather-lined Indian railway carriages, deeply shuttered and blinded from the blistering sun and kept fairly cool by a circular wheel of wet straw which one turned from time to time . . . I spent five days in a dark padded moving cell, reading mostly by lamplight or by some jealously admitted ray of glare.'[21] Captain Kincaid-Smith, Winston's senior officer in the Hussars and a close friend of Jennie, wrote to reassure her that Winston would not be exposed to too much danger. 'Your son started last night for the frontier and I am delighted he will have a chance and I don't think there will be very much risk.'[22]

*

While Churchill took the slow train journey to the front, Blood's force was already engaged in a brutal conflict with the Pashtun tribesmen who controlled the forbidding mountain terrain of the Afghan border. Trouble had been brewing since the inconclusive end to the Chitral campaign in 1895. Having defeated the tribes, the British could not decide whether to maintain a permanent military presence at key strategic points, such as the makeshift fort at Malakand, to protect the main supply road to Chitral. But after Lord Salisbury's Tory government took office in the summer, advocates of the Forward Policy were again in the ascendant, and opted to make the encampment at Malakand a permanent fixture to safeguard the all-important Malakand Pass, thereby guaranteeing protection of the Chitral road. Work began on construction of the fort, but the decision to make the British presence at Malakand permanent served only to stoke fears among the local tribes that the British, as their mullahs were constantly telling them, were preparing to annex their territory and place it under the control of the Indian government, thereby depriving them of their freedoms and ancient customs. As the solid stone walls of the fort that would enable the British to dominate the surrounding valleys began to take shape, the mullahs had no difficulty in persuading the local tribes to stage yet another rebellion.

The unrest centred principally on the Pashtuns, the distinctive ethnic group that since the first century BC has inhabited the vast mountain ranges that straddle the border between Afghanistan and Pakistan. Today there are around 50 million

Pashtuns, about a third of whom live in Afghanistan and the remainder in Pakistan. Their number and distinctive culture have led many prominent Pashtuns to campaign for the creation of an independent Pashtunistan state on the Afghan-Pakistan border. Experienced in the art of leadership, Pashtuns have dominated Afghan politics since the middle of the eighteenth century, and nearly every Afghan leader has come from one of the main Pashtun tribes. Abdur Rahman, the amir who ruled Afghanistan when Churchill was fighting on the North-West Frontier, came from a prominent Pashtun tribe, and Pashtuns have also held senior positions in the Pakistani government since independence in 1947, including three presidents, as well as distinguishing themselves in the arts and sport, such as cricket. Imran Khan, the former Pakistan cricket captain and leader of the country's Movement for Justice political party, is one of the country's most celebrated Pashtuns.

Churchill's memorable remark that, on the North-West Frontier, 'tribe wars with tribe . . . Every tribesman has a blood feud against his neighbour' was particularly true of the Pashtuns. During Dost Mohammed's reign in the earlier part of the nineteenth century British officials were inclined to favour the Pashtun tribes, whom they believed were more trustworthy than the violent Afghans. The British thought they detected traits in the character of the Pashtuns that set them apart from the treacherous Afghans, even though most Afghans in fact came from Pashtun families. The arduous life they lived amid the mountains gave them an air of hardy independence, and when the British looked a Pashtun in the eye they believed that they saw a man, not a scoundrel. But the British soon learned that the Pashtun strict honour code, or Pashtunwali, created problems of its own. Pashtunwali is an ancient self-governing tribal system that regulates nearly all aspects of Pashtun life ranging from community to personal conduct. One of the code's better known tenets is *melmastia*, which obliges Pashtuns to provide hospitality and asylum to all guests seeking help. Another of the code's key principles is *badal,* which means that any perceived injustice merits swift revenge, which makes it all the more confusing that 'Revenge is a dish best served cold' is a popular Pashtun saying. All Pashtun males are charged with protecting *zan, zar* and *zameen* (women, gold and land). The only concession the code makes to promoting peaceful coexistence is *nanawati,* the humble admission of guilt for a wrong committed, which should result in automatic forgiveness from the wronged party.

The Pashtuns invariably used violence to resolve their differences, which led to feuds between families lasting for generations. The Pashtun language even contains a specific word to define revenge between cousins. In many respects these frontiersmen were warriors in the Homeric sense, enjoying fighting for its own sake, often internecine, for the blood feud was central to their way of life. They took offence easily, were jealous of their personal honour and savagely cruel to any opponent no longer able to defend himself. They tortured, mutilated and killed without compunction. The British both admired and feared them, and enlisted them in the Indian army well aware that, when the mood took them, they could turn on their allies with a terrible fury, shooting, knifing or even castrating British soldiers as if they were their lifelong enemies. When Pashtuns joined the army their officers were told not to send them on leave at the same time, since they tended to pursue their ancient blood feuds, which often resulted in them losing their lives.

Nor were the British under any illusions that the Pashtuns might change allegiance at any moment. The Pashtuns had provided crucial support to the British when they were nearly overwhelmed during the Indian Mutiny of 1857. But in their dealings with some of the main Pashtun tribes controlling the principal mountain passes to India, the British had a more chequered experience. In the late 1870s, for example, when they had agreed to pay the Afridi tribe tens of thousands of rupees to allow them safe passage through the Khyber Pass, the British still found themselves having to fight their way to safety after the tribesmen reneged on the deal. More than a hundred years later, American and British soldiers were to suffer similar experiences when Pashtun recruits to the Afghan army and police force turned their guns on the foreign soldiers who were trying to help them.

Indeed, it is worth reflecting on how the Pashtun honour code has had an important influence on the present-day conflict with the Taliban. The American-led intervention in Afghanistan in 2001 was undertaken after Mullah Omar, the Pashtun leader of the Taliban movement, offered *melmastia*, or refuge, to Osama bin Laden and his al-Qaeda supporters when they were expelled from Sudan in 1996. Having committed himself to protect the mastermind of the September 11 attacks, Mullah Omar was honour bound to do so, and therefore would not comply with Washington's demand to hand over those responsible for carrying out the attacks. When coalition forces defeated the Taliban and drove Mullah Omar and bin Laden's followers across the border into Pakistan, the Pashtun code of *badal* was applied, and very soon thousands of young Pashtuns on both sides of the border volunteered to fight for the Taliban, which remains predominantly a Pashtun movement. Thus a conflict that began as one between the West and an extremist group of Taliban ideologues soon escalated into a full-scale revolt of the Pashtuns against the foreign invaders. As the British found during their two disastrous military interventions in Afghanistan in the nineteenth century, the Pashtuns do not take kindly to foreign armies trampling through their territory.

The modern conflict has certainly been made a great deal more complex by the influence brought to bear by Pashtun tribesmen on both sides of the Afghan–Pakistan border. Mullah Omar's obligation to protect bin Laden's al-Qaeda fighters resulted in them seeking shelter in north Waziristan, a remote mountain region in the heart of the Pashtun tribal belt over which neither the Afghan nor Pakistani government exercises effective control. The Taliban movement also received invaluable support from Pakistan's Inter-Services Intelligence agency, which has many Pashtun officers serving in its senior ranks, and who regard the Taliban as a vital ally in protecting Pakistan's interests. The prospects of negotiating a settlement to the conflict were undermined by the refusal of Pashtuns from the more influential tribes to accept Washington's appointment of Hamid Karzai as the country's president in 2002. Karzai's family come from the Popalzai tribe in Kandahar, which is not regarded as one of the Pashtuns' 'royal' tribes (all previous leaders had been drawn from one of the major Durrani tribes). Just as, in the nineteenth century, most conflicts in Afghanistan were fought over which Pashtun tribe governed the country, a significant factor in the modern Afghan conflict was the power struggle between the country's Pashtun president and rebel Pashtun tribesmen, led by Mullah Omar, who questioned his legitimacy.

*

The uprising of 1897 mainly involved the Afridi and Orakzai frontier tribes, and the issue that caused most concern to the great-great-grandfathers of the modern Taliban was the arbitrary division of their ancestral tribal lands by the establishment of the Durand Line, which was agreed between the British government and the Afghan amir in November 1893. Even though Abdur Rahman had put his name to the agreement that sought to mark the 1,640-mile border between Afghanistan and the Indian subcontinent, he continued to express his deep unhappiness about the terms of the settlement, and never ceased in his attempts to have them reversed. In his view, large swathes of Afghan territory had been surrendered to British control. In many places the nature of the mountainous terrain meant that it was physically impossible to mark the border. But in the inhabited areas, its arbitrary division of the Pashtuns' tribal lands was to cause resentment and conflict for many decades. It

is said that there has now been more conflict over the Durand
Line than any other border in the world. And when modern
politicians tried to distinguish between the Taliban in Afghanistan and the Pakistani movement of the same name, they soon
realized that they were dealing with people who come from the
same families and the same tribes, the only difference being that
they have been separated by an antiquated, and arbitrarily
imposed, colonial boundary.

The attack on the Chitral garrison of early 1895 was caused
as much by Pashtun resentment over the Durand Line as the
desire to prevent the British from extending their influence over
the tribes any further. The end of the siege had resulted in the
capture of Sher Afzal, the tribal chief who had murdered fifteen
of his own brothers in his bid to rule Chitral. He was seized by
the pro-British Khan of Dir, who handed him over, and Sher
Afzal and his followers were then taken by the British to India
as prisoners of war while the issues raised by the Chitral uprising were considered. The Khan of Dir received a payment of
25,000 rupees from the Indian government for his trouble. But
as Captain Robertson, who wrote the official account of the
expedition, noted, the arrangement 'was not altogether satisfactory: the population was almost entirely in sympathy with Sher
Afzal, and manifested an extreme dislike of the British'.[23] Meanwhile Umra Khan, another powerful tribal chief – described by
Churchill as 'the most important man between Chitral and
Peshawar' – who had supported Sher Afzal's bid to seize Chitral,
fled to Kabul seeking the amir's protection there. The British
soldiers who had fought to save the Chitral garrison expressed
their frustration that Umra Khan did not stand and fight, opting
instead to slip across the newly established Afghan border. 'Our
enemies do not usually act as we desire,' one British officer
ruefully noted.[24] Britain installed a fourteen-year-old prince,
Shaja al-Mulk, as Chitral's new leader, an appointment that
suggested the British had no intention of relinquishing control
of their frontier town.

Having retained control of Chitral, the British agonized over whether they should build a new road to the isolated border town to enable the swift movement of military reinforcements should trouble flare again. From a purely military perspective, a road was essential for the British to dispatch reinforcements, either from Rawalpindi, the main British military supply base for northern India, or Abbottabad, the other significant supply depot in the area located some 500 miles from Chitral. Abbottabad had been established in 1853 and named after General James Abbott, a British army officer who spent the majority of his career in India as a soldier and colonial administrator. Abbott chose the site for his new military cantonment because of its strategic location and pleasant climate. Used today as a major training academy for the Pakistani military, Abbottabad came to international prominence in 2011 when it was found to be the hiding place of Osama bin Laden, who was killed instantly when a team of US Navy Seals stormed his compound.

Opponents of the road scheme argued that it would cause unnecessary distress to the local tribes, and further inflame anti-British feelings on the frontier. But their objections were overruled when Lord Salisbury's government agreed to strengthen Britain's hold on the area. Teams of British engineers began work on building the new road to Chitral at the same time as construction started on the new fort at Malakand. George Curzon was one of the government's most vocal supporters for building the road. After completing his personal fact-finding mission to the North-West Frontier, the new Under-Secretary of State for Foreign Affairs argued that if the British did not maintain their hold on Chitral, it would be seized by the Russians, with all the implications that would have for the security of the Indian Empire. Acting on Curzon's advice, the British strengthened the garrison at Chitral, while two battalions of reinforcements were stationed at Malakand to guard the passes and ensure that the road was kept open. Churchill himself was a proponent of the Chitral road, which he thought represented the best hope for spreading the values of the empire. 'As the sun of civilisation rose above the hills,' he wrote, 'the fair flowers of commerce unfolded, and the streams of supply and demand, hitherto congealed by the frost of barbarism, were thawed'.[25] Not everyone, though, regarded construction of the road as a necessity. Sir Lepel Griffin, a veteran of the Indian Civil Service and a firm opponent of the Tories' Forward Policy, wrote to *The Times* denouncing the folly of the scheme. 'This policy consists in spending a quarter of a million annually on a post of defence and observation which defends and observes nothing, and on the maintenance of a road which leads nowhere.'[26] In the event Curzon's cautious approach appears to have been justified. In the spring of 1898 a British officer on a shooting expedition in the Hindu Kush by chance met a Russian frontier official, who informed him that the Russians had 'very complete' plans for the immediate possession of Chitral if the British ever decided to vacate it.[27] Today the Chitral road, which cuts through the breathtaking scenery of the Hindu Kush, is marketed by Pakistan as a major tourist attraction for cyclists and hikers.

The construction of the Chitral road, together with the strengthening of Britain's military presence at places like Malakand, were important factors in provoking the rebellion of 1897 that brought Churchill to the North-West Frontier. Although the British offered to pay compensation to the local tribes, who could no longer raise tolls, and paid them handsomely for supplies of grain and fodder, they failed to reassure the tribal leaders that they had no desire to annex their land to India. Consequently they were unable to contend with the violent, anti-British rhetoric of the mullahs. After the controversy of the Durand Line, the mullahs had no trouble in persuading the tribes that they were about to suffer a further erosion of their independence and culture. The Pashtuns are Sunni Muslims, and generally adhere to Sharia law, the codified system of Islamic justice, so long as it does not conflict with the tenets of Pashtunwali. This meant that for centuries tribesmen living in remote, inhospitable mountain regions were susceptible to the preaching of the wandering Islamic scholars, the Talib-ul-ilms, the forerunners of the modern Taliban, who moved from village to village giving their own interpretation of events taking place in the faraway world. In the Swat Valley the influence of Mullah Sadullah – who was known as the 'Mad Mullah' or 'Mad Fakir' by British soldiers – was particularly effective, especially his call for a widespread jihad against the British to prevent the conquest of their lands and the conversion of their people to Christianity.

In his own account of the origins of the conflict in *The Story of the Malakand Field Force*, Churchill was particularly critical of the mullahs' role in inciting the local tribes to rise against the British. 'The priesthood of the Afghan border instantly recognised the full meaning of the Chitral road,' he wrote. 'The cause of their antagonism is not hard to discern. Contact with civilisation assails the ignorance, and credulity, on which the wealth and influence of the Mullah depend. Here Mahommedanism was threatened and resisted.'[28] In Churchill's view, the threat posed by Western civilization aroused a bloodthirsty impulse in the followers of Islam.

> The Mahommedan religion increases, instead of lessening, the fury of intolerance. It was originally propagated by the sword, and ever since, its votaries have been subject, above the people of all other creeds, to this form of madness . . . the more emotional Pashtuns are powerless to resist. All rational considerations are forgotten. Seizing their weapons they become *Ghazis* – as dangerous and as sensible as mad dogs: fit to be treated as such . . . The forces of progress clash with those of reaction. The religion of blood and war is face to face with that of peace. Luckily the religion of peace is usually the better armed.[29]

Churchill's real bêtes noires, though, were the Talibs, the religious students, who were greatly influenced by the Ottoman

Empire, the pre-eminent Islamic power at the time. He denounced the Talibs as 'a host of wandering Talib-ul-ilms, who correspond with the theological students in Turkey, and live free at the expense of the people'. When they stayed in remote mountain villages they took advantage of their position to demand droit de seigneur over the womenfolk, so that no man's wife or daughter was safe.[30]

Viscount Fincastle, Churchill's great rival on the North-West Frontier, who wrote his own account of the campaign, took a more measured view of the causes of the uprising. While he acknowledged the role the 'Mad Fakir' had played in rousing the Pashtuns to revolt against the British, he stressed the devious role played by the Afghan amir, Abdur Rahman, in stirring up trouble. Britain's handling of the Durand Line negotiations still rankled with Abdur Rahman, who complained that 'in your cutting away from me these frontier tribes, who are people of my nationality and my religion, you are injuring my prestige in the eyes of my subjects, and will make me weak, and my weakness will be injurious to your government'.[31] In public, though, Abdur Rahman continued to profess his loyalty to the British Crown, while in private lending his support to any tribal leader who was prepared to raise his banner against the British. So strong was Abdur Rahman's supposed allegiance to the British that Queen Victoria awarded him two of the country's highest decorations, the Star of India (1885) and the Order of the Bath (1893), a rare royal honour which he received in acknowledgement for his contribution to the Durand Line Agreement. But as Fincastle noted, 'Another belief that the tribesmen were firmly embued with, was that the amir would support them, and there were many factors that lent colour to this supposition in the eyes of the people, among them being the titles which Abdur Rahman, in endeavouring to pose as the head of the Mohammedans of the East, has lately assumed.'[32]

The belief among the frontier tribesmen that Abdur Rahman was planning to lead a rebellion against the British gained in strength when he convened a pan-Islamic festival in Kabul in the spring of 1897, to which all the acknowledged religious leaders of the region were invited. After claiming the Afghan throne in 1880, Abdur Rahman exploited his subjects' Islamic faith to his advantage. He declared himself to be an imam, as well as being an amir, thereby conveniently uniting the powers of spiritual and temporal leadership in his own person. In addition Abdur Rahman declared himself Zia-ul-Millat-Wa-ud-Deen (Light of Union and Faith), as well as a Caliph of Islam, a gesture designed to consolidate his claim to be the undisputed leader of Muslims in the East. The only reason he did not break completely with the British was that, without their protection, he would be at the mercy of the Russians. So rather than criticize the British in public, the amir's agents left letters in mosques claiming the amir would 'liberate Afghanistan for Islam from the English', and extolling the virtues of jihad. Every mullah on the frontier received copies of the amir's letters, which then passed from hand to hand throughout the border region. In calling for a holy war against the British, Abdur Rahman used the same arguments and quotations from the Koran that, many years later, Osama bin Laden would employ to urge Muslims to wage war against the West. Abdur Rahman urged his Muslim subjects to place the demands of jihad over their family, tribe and property, an argument that resonated with the Pashtun tribesmen. Similar arguments were later used by Mullah Omar and his supporters at madrasas in Pakistan to brainwash young Pashtuns to join the Taliban.

The new rebellion against the British which erupted in the summer of 1897 began in the Swat Valley, one of the northernmost points of the Indian Empire which today forms part of Pakistan and is located close to the Afghan frontier. The revolt was led by the 'Mad Mullah' Sadullah, who rallied the local tribes to launch an attack against the infidel British and drive them from the sacred land of the Prophet. Sadullah, who was also known as the Mastun Mullah (Ecstasy Mullah) or the

Sartor Fakir (Bare-headed Saint), came from a long line of self-proclaimed Islamic prophets who enjoyed close links with the extremist Wahhabi sect of the Arabian peninsula. Osama bin Laden was a Wahhabi, as were many of his followers, and in the nineteenth century the sect had acquired a large following among India's Muslim population, particularly in the Hindustan region of northern India. Known by the British as the Hindustani fanatics, they played a prominent role in the Indian Mutiny of 1857, and the British singled them out for their role in murdering 'our poor women and children'. Thousands of Hindustani fanatics were subjected to summary execution in Delhi after the revolt was suppressed.

The British then fought another battle against Wahhabi-inspired fanatics during the Ambeyla campaign of 1863, when a British force ventured into the Swat Valley to confront large numbers who had been attacking the settled areas of British-controlled northern India. General Josiah Harlan, the first American adventurer to enter Afghanistan and the inspiration for Kipling's classic story 'The Man Who Would Be King', encountered these fanatics while fighting with the Sikh army. 'Savages from the remotest recesses of the mountain districts . . . who were dignified with the profession of the Mahomedan faith, many of them giants in form and strength . . . concentrated themselves around the standard of religion, and were prepared to slay, plunder, and destroy, for the sake of God and the Prophet, the unenlightened infidels.'[33] The British had little experience of fighting in the Swat Valley, mainly because the Akhund of Swat, a revered figure who exercised both political and religious control, persuaded the local Pashtun tribes to avoid provoking the British. The Akhund disliked the Wahhabi fanatics, but he was equally unhappy when the British moved into the area of the Swat Valley controlled by the Buner tribes, or the Bunerwals, in pursuit of the Islamic extremists. The Akhund responded by mobilizing the Pashtuns, with the result that the Ambeyla campaign was won by the British only with some difficulty, although it did achieve its aim of destroying the base used by the Hindustani fanatics, many of whom were killed. Just like the suicidal Ghazi fighters the British encountered during their two Afghan campaigns, the Hindustanis showed no fear on the battlefield, and often dressed in their best white robes and velvet jackets in readiness for martyrdom. Before leaving Bunerwal territory the British found that the Islamists' hideout was far larger than had been expected, and contained a barracks for the soldiers, stabling and a gunpowder factory. The complex was not dissimilar to the training camps al-Qaeda fighters established in the same border territory more than a century later.

Whether Mullah Sadullah had links to these Hindustani fanatics is unclear, although his views did reflect their uncompromising Wahhabi agenda. Prior to leading the anti-British revolt in the summer of 1897, he claimed he had been visited by a number of saints, and had been ordered by them to turn the British out of the Swat Valley and neighbouring areas, including Chitral and Malakand. Those who joined the jihad, he proclaimed, need have no fear, for the saints had informed him that the bullets of the British would turn to water and the barrels of their guns would melt. Furthermore, he was reinforced by a heavenly host, massed but hidden from human sight on a 9,000-foot high peak overlooking the Swat Valley. As for supplies, the single pot of rice he had with him was sufficient to feed a multitude. In fact the bowl-of-rice pledge turned out to be nothing more than an elaborate con trick, as Fincastle discovered. 'Every man of his following brought him daily a handful of rice, as is the custom when visiting a holy man. Of this, the Mullah, with considerable acumen, took advantage, stating that he would feed his followers, who numbered several thousands, out of the contents of a small jar which he kept outside his abode, and it apparently never occurred to the people that they were but receiving back their own offerings.'[34]

The legend of the Mad Mullah caught Churchill's imagination.

For him, the mullah's message spread like a bush-fire through the mountain ranges. 'The mountains became as full of explosives as a magazine. Yet the spark was lacking,' he wrote. 'The mine was fired. The flame ran along the ground. The explosions burst forth in all directions . . . As July advanced the bazaar at Malakand became full of tales of the Mad Fakir. A great day for Islam was at hand. A mighty man had arisen to lead them. The English would be swept away.'[35]

The British officers at Malakand and the nearby garrison at Chakdara, which guarded the crossing-point of the Swat river, had forewarning that the local tribes were growing restless. The previous month resentment over the Durand Line in nearby Waziristan had resulted in a 300-strong British force being attacked without warning during talks with tribal leaders. The mood before the attack, in which four British officers died, had been so convivial that a Scottish piper had been playing during a break in the talks at the request of the tribal elders. All along the border tribes were stirring. In the Swat Valley the British garrisons made the necessary preparations for an attack, but otherwise continued with their normal routine. On the day Mullah Sadullah issued his rallying cry, British officers from the Malakand garrison were playing an important polo match at the nearby town of Khar. Sadullah had prophesied that by the rising of the new moon in ten days' time the British would be driven from Malakand. Unperturbed by these dire threats, the British decided to proceed with the fixture. 'The game was a good one, and the tribesmen of the neighbouring village watched it as usual in little groups, with a keen interest,' Churchill recalled in his account of the battle, which was drawn from interviews he later conducted with the participants. 'Nothing in their demeanour betrayed their thoughts or intentions. The young soldiers saw nothing, knew nothing, and had they known would have cared less.' It was not until the last chukka that a 'strange incident occurred, an incident eminently characteristic of the frontier tribes', wrote Churchill. 'The Pash-

tun grooms attending the officers' ponies were warned by their
fellow tribesmen to go home as there was going to be a fight.
They knew, these Pashtuns, what was coming. The wave of
fanaticism was sweeping down the valley. It would carry them
away. They were powerless to resist. Like one who feels a fit
coming on, they waited. Nor did they care very much. When
the Mad Fakir arrived, they would fight and kill the infidels. In
the meantime there was no necessity to deprive them of their
ponies.'36 As a young polo-playing subaltern, Churchill knew
where his priorities lay.

When Mullah Sadullah raised his banner in the Swat Valley
and summoned the surrounding tribes to arms, the British were
just finishing their polo match. Lieutenant Haldane (Harry)
Rattray, a young cavalry subaltern five years older than
Churchill who commanded the nearby Chakdara fort, was
leaving the polo ground to return to his post when he met two
cavalry troopers galloping in the opposite direction. They
informed him that a tribal army was advancing on Malakand
down the left bank of the Swat river with banners flying and
drums beating. Rattray, whose father had raised the regiment
known as Rattray's Sikhs (today a battalion in the modern
Indian army), put spurs to his horse and rode right through the
tribesmen to reach his post at Chakdara, where he managed to
send a telegram to Major Harold Deane, the political officer at
Malakand, warning him of the impending danger. Rattray's
action probably saved the Malakand and Chakdara garrisons
from annihilation, as his prompt action enabled Deane to send
a message to the Corps of Guides, the main relief force at
Mardan thirty-two miles away, calling for immediate reinforcements. No sooner had the message been sent than the line was
cut and every telegraph pole along the new British road burnt
to the ground.

The officers of the Guides were sitting at dinner on the night
of 26 July when the commanding officer, Colonel Adams,
received a telegram informing him that Malakand was under

attack by overwhelming numbers of tribesmen. Formed in the 1840s, the Guides, which combined infantry and cavalry units in a single regiment, was designed specifically for frontier warfare, and prided itself on its ability to respond quickly to any emergency. Within three hours of receiving the telegram the officers had abandoned their dinner and set off for Malakand. They completed the gruelling, thirty-five-mile march from Mardan to Malakand in just sixteen hours in the fierce Indian heat, and their prompt arrival most likely saved the British garrison from being overrun.

At the neighbouring fort of Chakdara, meanwhile, a force of only 200 men – mainly British officers with Indian sepoys – were engaged in a desperate fight for survival against overwhelming numbers of hostile Pashtuns. The fort, which is today known at 'Churchill's Picquet', was built on a rocky, steep-sided hillock. It was difficult to assault, but was overlooked all around by hills, most of them within rifle range, enabling the enemy to fire into the compound day and night. The attack began at about 10 p.m. on 26 July and continued almost uninterrupted until 2 August. A small relief cavalry unit arrived the day after the siege began, having undertaken a desperate ride from Malakand, fording a river and crossing paddy fields, where the horses sank deep in the mud while 'the bullets of the enemy made watery flashes on all sides', Churchill recorded.[37] For the next six days the enemy, which at times numbered between 12,000 and 14,000 men, made repeated attempts to storm the fort, while their marksmen, well concealed in the surrounding hills, maintained a constant volley of fire at the fort's inhabitants. During the day massed ranks of Pashtuns would appear, carrying ladders to scale the walls and bundles of grass to throw on the barbed wire. At night the tribesmen advanced with shouts, yells and the beating of drums. At the height of the fighting the attackers carried '200 standards whose gay colours were representative of every tribe on the border'. But despite the ferocity of these assaults the beleaguered garrison managed to beat them off, even though, as Churchill recounted, 'Many Ghazis, mad with fanaticism, pressed on carrying standards, heedless of the fire, until they fell riddled with bullets under the very walls.'[38]

While there were many individual acts of bravery among the British contingent, their survival prospects were greatly enhanced by their possession of two Maxim guns, arguably the first weapons of mass destruction to be deployed on a modern battlefield. Developed in the 1880s, the Maxim gun, with its automatic recoil mechanism which enabled a spent cartridge to be replaced immediately with a live one, meant that the defenders were able to handle the enemy's overwhelming numbers. After each attack the bodies of up to seventy tribesmen were piled against the walls of the fort. But despite their heavy losses, still the enemy pressed their attack. At one point in the battle they succeeded in capturing the hospital close to the fort's defences and, encouraged by this success, thousands more Pashtun volunteers joined the fight. During breaks in the fighting brave groups of Indian sepoys climbed to the top of the signal tower to send messages by heliograph, a small solar panel that signals by using flashes of sunlight reflected by a mirror. Despite being under constant fire from the surrounding hills they still managed to send messages asking for reinforcements to be sent. After nearly a week of incessant fighting, and with water supplies running low, the signallers sent one final, despairing message in Morse code which simply read: 'Help us'.

On the last day of the siege a tremendous force of Pashtuns assembled for one final attempt to storm the fort and put the inhabitants to the sword, thereby inflicting a humiliating defeat on the British Empire equal to the massacre of General Gordon and his men in Khartoum the previous decade. Several men inside the fort were killed by the hail of bullets that were directed against it and then, just as the fighting approached crisis point, the cavalry of the relieving British column appeared on a nearby ridge, and the enemy began to turn and run. With relief at hand, Rattray and his men flung open the gate of the fort and charged the hospital that had earlier been captured by the Pashtuns. 'The hospital was recaptured,' recalled Churchill. 'The enemy occupying it, some thirty in number, were bayoneted. It was a finish in style.'[39] The cavalry made one last charge against the enemy, killing many and driving the rest 'in rout and ruin'. In his account, Viscount Fincastle writes that the cavalry 'dashed in among the panic-stricken tribesmen, pursuing them without a check for over three miles, and the numerous bodies which strewed the route bore witness to the splendid execution done by lance and sword'.[40] In the last moments of the battle, recorded Churchill, 'a retreating Pashtun shot Lieutenant Rattray in the neck, but that officer, as distinguished for physical prowess as military conduct, cut him down. This ended the fighting. It is not possible to think of a more fitting conclusion.'[41]

The British lost a total of 20 men, compared with Pashtun losses in excess of 2,000, a testament to the lethal destructiveness of the British army's new weapon. As the Victorian poet Hilaire Belloc remarked on the overwhelming superiority of British firepower:

> Whatever happens, we have got
> The Maxim gun, and they have not.[42]

Rattray, who in a distinguished army career rose to become the regiment's lieutenant colonel, was awarded the VSO for his bravery, one short of the much-coveted Victoria Cross, which was just the kind of award young Churchill hankered after. A fearless soldier all his life, Rattray was killed in 1917 trying to storm a heavily defended Turkish position in Mesopotamia – modern Iraq – during the First World War.

The garrison at Malakand experienced a similarly fierce battle. Here the Mad Mullah personally led the advance to storm the British garrison, with crowds of unarmed teenage boys pushed ahead of him. Among them was one aged thirteen or fourteen whose head was bound with a turban. Sadullah claimed the boy was Shah Sikander (Alexander), the last of the Mughal dynasty and the rightful heir to the throne in Delhi who would again rule over India once the British had been defeated. The boy was killed instantly as he and the other unarmed teenagers were encouraged to attack the British positions. Today his body is said to rest in a well-preserved tomb that can be seen beside the Malakand road. According to Fincastle, during the assault on Malakand, 'Bands of Ghazis, worked up by their religious enthusiasm into a frenzy of fanatical excitement, would charge our breastworks again and again, leaving their dead in scores after each repulse, while those of their comrades who were unarmed would encourage their efforts by shouting with much beating of tom-toms and other musical instruments.'[43] The attack subsided after Sadullah himself was wounded – the rumour among the tribesmen was that he had been killed – and another mullah slain, together with several hundred tribesmen. The arrival of a relief force comprising Guides infantry and Sikhs raised the spirits of the beleaguered garrison, even though, having made a punishing march right through the heat of the day, the relief force suffered twenty-one deaths from sunstroke and apoplexy. During the week-long siege the Malakand garrison suffered 28 dead and more than 150 wounded, while the Pashtuns' losses were in their hundreds, if not their thousands.

As the beleaguered garrisons at Chakdara and Malakand fought for their lives, the government in India responded by calling for the establishment of a military force to undertake punitive raids against all the tribes that had supported the anti-British revolt. On 30 July, four days after the uprising had begun, the government announced: 'The Governor General in Council sanctions the dispatch of a force, to be styled the Malakand Field Force, for the purpose of holding the Malakand and the adjacent posts, and operating against the neighbouring tribes as may be required.'[44] The force would be commanded by Brigadier General Sir Bindon Blood, who knew the region well having served as Chief of the Staff during the relief of Chitral in 1895. Promoted to the temporary rank of major general, Blood set off immediately, and on the 31st took command at Nowshera – the final destination of Winston's epic train ride – before setting off for the fort at Malakand, where he arrived on 1 August.

The fighting was over, and the two garrisons had been saved. Blood now turned his attention to arranging punitive expeditions against those tribes that had supported the revolt. Churchill summed up the position thus: 'A surprise, followed by a sustained attack, has been resisted. The enemy, repulsed at every point, have abandoned the attempt, but surrounded and closely watch the defences. The troops will now assume the offensive, and the hour of reprisals will commence.'[43] If he could get to the front in time, it was possible that Winston himself might take part in the 'reprisals'. Kincaid-Smith's reassuring note to Jennie Churchill that there would be 'not much risk' to her son if he went to fight on the North-West Frontier seemed wide of the mark. During the fierce battles at Malakand and Chakdara many young subalterns of Churchill's age had been fighting for their lives in the worst outbreak of anti-British violence on the North-West Frontier for many decades. Some of them had perished, while others had distinguished themselves and would win medals. Their ranks would shortly be bolstered by the arrival of Lieutenant Winston Churchill of the 4th (Queen's Own) Hussars.

CHAPTER SIX

KNIGHT OF PEN
AND SWORD

'We march tomorrow, and before a week is out there
will be a battle.'

Winston S. Churchill, 5 September 1897

Sitting in his dark, padded cell of a railway carriage, Churchill
fretted about whether he would make it to the front in time to
join the action. After the disappointments of not getting to Egypt
and missing the war in Crete, he feared that he was destined
never to see active service, and that any injuries he received
were more likely to be the result of his own foolhardiness than
enemy combat. His badly dislocated shoulder, the cuts and
bruises he sustained from falls from his polo ponies; all had been
the result of his recklessness, while thousands of miles away
on the North-West Frontier his contemporaries were engaged in
truly heroic exploits, where they frequently risked their lives
and, if they survived, were rewarded with honours and medals.
By the time Winston set off for the North-West Frontier in late
August, nearly a month had passed since the heroic defence
of the Malakand and Chakdara garrisons, and there was no
guarantee he would be involved in any fighting when he
eventually got there. As the train neared its destination,
Churchill wrote to Jack that he had 'perhaps a good chance of
seeing active service and securing a medal. But the future is
vague and somewhat uncertain.'[1]

Churchill often gave the impression that he was bored with

army life, and would give it up at the first opportunity. And yet his military career in the 4th Hussars was deemed to be a success. In uniform Winston was a conscientious officer who had taken to heart his late father's admonishment that, 'The army is the finest profession in the world if you work at it and the worst if you loaf at it.'[2] In India Winston did 'work at it', and gave his full attention to his military duties, which he did not find too taxing, and which his abundant energy and natural intelligence enabled him to master easily. Sergeant Hallaway, Churchill's troop-sergeant in the 4th Hussars, recalled the young subaltern was popular with his troopers. Whether supervising his men's training courses, inspecting them at stables or commanding them in drill and on exercises, he went about his duties in a cheery and positive manner. 'Mr Churchill was a real live one,' Hallaway recalled. 'Not stuffy like some of the other officers, if you know what I mean. Easy going, and always ready for a joke. He hated to see chaps punished. The officers used to inspect the stables every day but we never knew when they were coming. But Churchill would whisper to me, "Eleven-thirty, sergeant-major." '[3]

Despite the complaints about his 'intolerable' life in Bangalore, Churchill learned a great deal about the conduct of military operations in India, which stood him in good stead for the Malakand campaign. Decades of experience of fighting small colonial wars in inhospitable climes had helped the British army to refine the field uniforms worn by soldiers and officers on active service. Winston described the field uniforms as 'cool and comfortable khaki kit'. The dress code for officers allowed for the uniforms to be fitted loosely so that warm clothing could be worn underneath if necessary in cold weather. The uniform frock, or jacket, had five small brass buttons down the front and chain-mail epaulettes to deflect sword cuts from the enemy. A padded cloth spine protector could be buttoned on to the back to shield its wearer from the sun. Campaign ribbons, of which there were many, were worn above the left chest pocket.

More than a century of almost continuous fighting against the tribes of the North-West Frontier had generated no fewer than eighteen campaign medals, some issued for single battles or campaigns, others for longer periods, which had bars or clasps added to the medal ribbon in recognition of service in certain campaigns or expeditions. The India General Service Medal (1854–95), for example, had twenty-four bars, including North-West Frontier, while the decoration for which Churchill qualified, the India Medal (1895–1902), had seven bars, all for campaigns on the North-West Frontier, a reflection of where the British forces were most active during the late nineteenth century. For trousers, officers were given a choice of khaki or brown cord riding breeches, and Churchill wore leather boots with gaiters wrapping his legs in leather from the ankles to just below the knees. All the Hussars wore detachable steel spurs, so they could dismount in a hurry if they were required to fight on foot, which happened frequently amid the rugged terrain of the North-West Frontier. The uniform was topped off with a colonial 'pith' helmet made of cork and covered with a khaki cloth. Apart from their swords officers carried small pistols, and during his service in India Churchill carried a .455-inch model 1892 Webley-Wilkinson revolver that he had bought in London.

In preparation for active service on the frontier, Churchill had taken part in a demanding fifteen-day field exercise earlier in the year under the command of Kincaid-Smith. Winston suffered severe sunburn on more than one occasion, prompting him to complain to his mother that his skin had 'assumed a deep mulberry hue'. But he was delighted when asked to replace his friend Reggie Barnes, who was away on a training course, to perform the duties of regimental adjutant. This meant Churchill served as the operations officer and chief staff officer to the unit commander – Kincaid-Smith – with responsibility for record keeping, personnel and military discipline issues, preparation of the duty rosters and distribution of the commander's order of the day. This was a great opportunity for a young lieutenant, and recognition of the early promise Churchill had shown. Winston relished the extra responsibility as he participated in a series of mock battles, where he spent his time 'chasing or being chased by the native cavalry'. While he found that 'the discomforts all the time have been great and the days very long', he was proud of the fact that 'I have had for the first time in my military experience responsibility and have discharged it not altogether without success'.[4] Two weeks after the regiment returned to its barracks in Bangalore, Churchill set off on yet another five-day training mission in 'long reconnaissance', which included chart and compass practice. For this exercise Churchill was given another temporary promotion to the rank of brigade major, 'a most important duty', he told Jennie, 'and one which in England could never have been obtained in under 14 or 15 years service'.[5]

Winston's enthusiasm for field work made an impression on his superior officers. When Lieutenant Colonel Ramsay, his regimental officer, agreed to write a letter of recommendation to support Churchill's attempt to be posted for service to the Sudan, he noted that Churchill 'was a good rider, a very smart cavalry officer and knew my work in the field thoroughly', attributes that would serve him well on the North-West Frontier.[6] Sergeant Hallaway, Churchill's troop-sergeant, remembered Winston as a conscientious officer who was always eager to learn, even if it meant inconveniencing his fellow officers:

> After a field day Mr Churchill would arrive at stables with rolls of foolscap and lots of lead pencils of all colours, and tackle me on the movements we had done at the exercise. We were nearly always short of stable men, and there were a lot of spare horses to be attended to, so it was quite a hindrance to me. If I was not paying much attention to Mr Churchill's drawings of the manoeuvres he would roll the paper up and say, 'All right, you are bad-tempered today!'

I was not bad-tempered really, but I was a busy man, and
I had not time for tactics.[7]

Hallaway recalled that Churchill had an impressive knowledge of musketry. When they attended a musketry course, to
the sergeant's astonishment Churchill delivered a masterly lecture on the subject and passed out top of his class.[8] This was
just as well for, owing to the discomfort Winston suffered from
his dislocated shoulder, he often had to take to the field with his
arm strapped to his side, which meant that, rather than using
his sword in combat, he had to rely solely on his trusty pistol.
Whatever other qualities Winston might have lacked, courage
was not among them.

Churchill broke his long train journey at Rawalpindi, the
main military base for the Indian frontier. Staying with a
subaltern friend with the Fourth Dragoon Guards, he found
there was 'a certain stir in Rawalpindi', although it was hundreds of miles from the front. The whole garrison anticipated
being sent north, all leave had been stopped 'and the Dragoon
Guards were expecting to be ordered any day to grind their
swords', the standard preparation for cavalrymen about to enter
battle. From Rawalpindi he made the last stage of his railway
odyssey, crossing the mighty River Indus for the first time, on
his way to Nowshera, the main railhead for Britain's military
operations on the North-West Frontier, arriving six days after
he had left Bangalore. For the remaining fifty miles of the
journey to Malakand he travelled in a tonga, a small cart drawn
by relays of galloping ponies, which ferried him across the dusty
plains in the blazing heat of the Indian summer. This was the
route Blood had taken two years previously when organizing the
relief of Chitral, and along which the relief force for Malakand
and Chakdara had passed only a month earlier in its race to
save the British garrisons from wholesale slaughter. Churchill
recalled that the journey took seven hours and involved 'much

beating of galled and dilapidated ponies. Everywhere are the tracks of an army. A gang of prisoners chained hand to hand, escorted by a few Sikhs, marched sullenly by in the blazing heat. Suspicious characters, I am informed, being deported across the frontier into British territory until things are more settled. Some dead transport animals lay by the roadside, their throats hurriedly cut.'[9] After the relief of Malakand, Blood had established his headquarters at the Malakand fort, and had three fully equipped fighting brigades at his disposal. Winston bounced around in his little cart through the sweltering plain, before commencing the sharp climb to Malakand through the foothills of the Hindu Kush. Finally, on 2 September, Winston arrived at Malakand and, 'yellow with dust I presented myself at the Staff Office'.[10]

On arrival Churchill still did not know whether he would see action, but that did not diminish his enthusiasm to get to the front. If he only covered the campaign as a war correspondent, it would still provide him with good copy, and help to enhance his reputation as a journalist. Getting himself noticed was what really mattered to Winston, whether as a writer or a fighter. He wanted to enter politics, and the more he made a name for himself, the better would be his chances of selection for a parliamentary seat. Randolph Churchill's biography tells how he made his political ambitions known to his fellow officers in Bangalore before setting off for the frontier. A fellow officer recalled how Winston, 'in the course of conversation, said that he had no intention of serving indefinitely in the army and that he proposed eventually to go into Parliament and added that one day he would be Prime Minister'.[11] All the time Churchill expounded on his life plan to the startled officer, he smoked a cigar.

*

Churchill had not given up hope that he would be involved in the fighting. In the year of the Queen-Empress's Diamond

Jubilee, Winston was not the only cavalry subaltern who longed to win medals and clasps to pin upon his tunic. His desire to see action intensified, moreover, when he discovered that Viscount Fincastle, his rival for journalistic and military accolades, had already distinguished himself under fire during a skirmish at Landakai, in the Swat Valley, two weeks previously, and was likely to win a Victoria Cross for his valour. In *The Story of the Malakand Field Force*, Winston lets his resentment get the better of him when he is less than complimentary about Fincastle's exploits. Under the title 'A Disastrous Incident', Churchill writes that, while the event 'afforded an opportunity for a splendid act of courage', it 'involved an unnecessary loss of life, and must be called disastrous'.[12] There is rarely much love lost between rival journalists competing for a scoop in some remote war zone. More than thirty years later, writing in *My Early Life*, Churchill took a more generous view of Fincastle's award, stating that he won the VC 'in circumstances of peculiar valour'.[13]

Fincastle, who was reporting on the conflict for *The Times* and had been attached to the Corps of Guides cavalry, had joined Blood's first punitive military campaign, which took place in the Swat Valley against the Pashtun tribesmen who had taken part in the attacks against Chakdara and Malakand. Although the Pashtuns and their allies had suffered in excess of 2,000 dead in the failed assaults, this was not deemed punishment enough. The British response to any act of defiance of the *Pax Britannica* was to exact a terrible revenge on those who had taken up arms, together with their families and villages. Valleys were entered in force, entire villages laid waste and their crops destroyed while the tribesmen's primitive fortifications were blown up by teams of British sappers. Having retreated to their homes in the Swat Valley, the tribesmen, according to Fincastle's account, were 'under the delusion that, owing to the distance and difficulties of marching troops at this time of year, they would escape punishment and enjoy a well-earned rest until a more favourable opportunity should arise for exterminating the infidel'.[14]

Blood, however, had other plans. The British commander had a sizeable force at his disposal, comprising 6,800 infantry troops, 700 cavalry troopers and 24 field guns, and he had no intention of letting the tribesmen rest easily in their homes. The force was a typical mix of British and Indian units, with the 1st Battalion Royal West Kent Regiment and the 1st Battalion East Kent Regiment (the Buffs) forming the main British infantry contribution. These were the 'Tommy Atkinses' immortalized in Kipling's poem 'Tommy', which had been published to great acclaim in 1892. Churchill, who in his own distinctive way was following in Kipling's footsteps as a journalist on the North-West Frontier, admired the Victorian writer, and would have recognized Kipling's empathetic description of the 'single men in barricks', recruited from the slums, hard drinking, hard living, rejected as a match in marriage by respectable families but officered by the upper middle class – in the cavalry often by the upper class – to which Winston himself belonged. The rest of the Indian army, the sepoys, were drawn from the military castes of the empire – Rajputs, Sikhs, Punjabis and Mussulmans. The darlings of their officers, the high-caste sepoys held the mass of India's millions in disdain. Even so, British soldiers, always mindful of the treachery of the Indian Mutiny, rarely accepted Indians as their equals, and were suspicious that they might desert their posts in a crisis, while the British held their ground.

Blood set off from Malakand in mid-August with two brigades, while a third brigade was held in reserve at Malakand. Blood's force made rapid progress through the Swat Valley, which was still littered with the decomposing corpses of Pashtun tribesmen who had been abandoned by the retreating rebels. 'This advance into Upper Swat was extremely interesting,' Blood recalled in his memoirs, 'as that country had not been visited by a white man, so far as we knew, since Alexander sent an army that way when he invaded India.'[15] As they moved through the valley the British received reports that Mullah

Sadullah, who was said to have been wounded, or even killed, during the fighting at Malakand, was very much alive and active in the Swat Valley. There he hoped to persuade the local Bunerwals to rise up against the British and join his jihad against the infidels.

According to the intelligence reports received by Major Harold Deane, the political officer for the North-West Frontier, the 'Mad Mullah' and hundreds of Hindustani fanatics, the followers of the extreme Wahhabi sect, were gathering on a ridge close to Landakai. Blood's force moved steadily towards the rebellious gathering, until 400–500 of the enemy were spotted on a nearby ridge with fifteen standards. 'Our appearance was greeted with a fusillade, and from their shouting and light-hearted expenditure of ammunition, it was evident that larger numbers of them were in rear of their position,' Fincastle reported.[16] Blood devised a standard plan of attack to drive the enemy from their position, known locally as the 'Gate of Swat', which the tribesmen considered impregnable in summer when the Swat river was in full flood from the melting snow. Undeterred by this obstacle, Blood resolved 'to occupy the enemy well in front with artillery and infantry fire and then to attack their left vigorously and advance in front at the same time'.[17]

The attack was delayed for a few days by bad weather, and eventually began at 6.30 on the morning of 17 August, with the Guides cavalry leading the attack, followed by the 1st Battalion Royal West Kents, two mountain batteries, three battalions of native infantry and sappers. The West Kents quickly cleared and occupied the lower approaches to the ridge. The remainder of the force, in a bold flanking movement, then undertook a 'stiff climb' in the fierce morning heat to the top of the main ridge, where, Blood recalled, the 'quite unexpected appearance there of the three battalions and the mountain battery, which opened fire at once, caused great confusion among the enemy, who had made up their minds that I was fool enough to undertake a frontal attack on the formidable part of their position!'[18] The assault succeeded in driving the tribesmen from their well-fortified positions towards Landakai. At one point the British had to fend off a charge by a handful of Ghazis, who, desperate for martyrdom and entry to paradise, 'rushed down the hill on to the bayonets of the 24th Punjab Light Infantry, there to meet the death they so eagerly sought'.[19] The 'Gate of Swat' was taken with the loss of eleven men wounded out of an attacking force of around 5,000, while the tribesmen's losses were several hundred killed or wounded. Churchill, who was still marooned at Bangalore when the attack took place, gives Blood all the credit for the mission's success: 'That so strong a position should have been captured with so little loss is due, firstly, to the dispositions of the general and secondly, to the power of the artillery which he had concentrated.'[20]

During the subsequent mopping-up operation, Fincastle joined in a cavalry charge against a group of Pashtun tribesmen who were spotted trying to escape the British advance through the Landakai plain. Together with Lieutenant Robert Greaves, twenty-seven, of the Lancashire Fusiliers, who was acting as a war correspondent for the *Times of India*, he joined a squadron of Guides cavalry as they gave chase across muddy rice fields. Churchill's criticism was that Fincastle and the other members of the party had given little thought to the perils they faced. 'Carried away by the excitement of the pursuit, and despising the enemy for their slight resistance, they dashed impetuously forward in the hope of catching them before they could reach the hills,' he wrote.[21]

In the melee that ensued some of the party, including Greaves, became separated from the squadron, and suddenly they found themselves surrounded by a crowd of hostile tribesmen. As one officer tried to fend off the assailants with his sword, Greaves was shot and fell to the ground, whereupon the enemy closed around him and began hacking at him with their swords. Fincastle and other members of the squadron, realizing the beleaguered group were all about to be massacred, dashed to their rescue. The tribesmen responded with a heavy volley of fire, and Fincastle's horse was shot, knocking him to the ground. Fincastle continued fighting and, with the help of two other officers, recovered the badly wounded Greaves and tried to lift him onto a horse. As they did so, Greaves was hit by a second bullet, which killed him instantly. Another officer, Lieutenant Hector Maclean, twenty-six, of the Guides cavalry, who had also ridden to the rescue, was shot through both thighs while trying to rescue Greaves, causing him mortal injury. In spite of the constant fire raining down on them from the tribesmen, Fincastle and the surviving members of the party managed to rescue the bodies of Greaves and Maclean, as well as two other wounded officers, and bring them to safety. As a result of their courageous actions that day three Guides officers received the Victoria Cross – Fincastle, Lieutenant Colonel Robert Adams, the commander, and Maclean, who received a posthumous award ten years later. As the official history of the Corps of Guides records, 'the probably unique historic record was established of three officers in one regiment earning the Victoria Cross on the same day'.[22]

The heroics of Fincastle and his fellow Guides officers typified the courage and daring that was routinely required of young British officers fighting on the Afghan border. The constant state of agitation that afflicted the Pashtun tribes meant that between 1858 and 1897 the British mounted thirty-four punitive expeditions against them. On each occasion the officers and soldiers serving their Queen-Empress lived with the constant risk that, at any moment, they might suddenly be overwhelmed in a surprise attack and cut to pieces. Recklessness inevitably played its part in these officers' quest for glory and honour for, as Churchill remarked, 'It is the spirit that loses the Empire many lives, but has gained it many battles.'[23] Despite his disapproval of Fincastle's conduct, Churchill still managed to mention his rival's heroism in his *Daily Telegraph* report.[24]

Fincastle's family were always surprised to hear about his

heroic exploits on the battlefield, for at home in England he always professed himself a coward. According to Sir Angus Stirling, Fincastle's grandson, he never said a great deal about his exploits as a soldier, and always made light of the valour that had won him the highest medal. Sir Angus recalls his grandfather as being 'an exceptionally soft-spoken person – the absolute opposite of macho'. Fincastle, who later succeeded to the family title, becoming the 8th Earl of Dunmore in 1907, would tell his grandchildren, 'I am really a terrible coward. If there is a noise in the house in the middle of the night, I go to the bottom of the bed and tell Grandma to go and investigate.' In fact Fincastle, who, like Churchill, was in his nineties when he died in 1962, was one of the most decorated soldiers of his generation. Fighting on the Western Front during the First World War, he was awarded the Distinguished Service Order during the Battle of the Somme, was mentioned in dispatches on four occasions and wounded twice. His only son, David, was killed fighting in France during the Second World War. After leaving the military, Fincastle pursued a career in politics, serving as a government whip in the House of Lords, where he would occasionally come across his erstwhile competitor for scoops and medals on the North-West Frontier. But Fincastle's family had the impression that 'he was never very keen on Churchill'.[25]

Churchill longed to emulate Fincastle's achievements, even if it meant risking his own life. Writing to his mother from Malakand in early September, an air of fatalism for the first time entered Winston's outlook, no doubt spurred by the graphic accounts of the recent fighting he had heard from his fellow officers. Fincastle's exploits and recommendation for a Victoria Cross had certainly raised the stakes for Winston, who accepted that 'I am bound for many reasons to risk something ... I mean to play this game out and if I lose it is obvious that I never could have won any other. The unpleasant contingency is of course a wound which would leave permanent effects and would while leaving me life – deprive me of all that makes life worth living. But all games have forfeits. Fortunately the odds are good.'[26]

*

Blood was still fighting in the Swat Valley when Churchill arrived at Malakand, and Winston had to wait until the force returned to learn whether he would join the military operations. In the meantime he received a telegram from his mother that the *Daily Telegraph* had agreed to publish a number of his articles. Winston told her that he still expected to be paid 'not less' than £10 per letter, unaware that Lawson had already insisted that he would pay no more than £5 per contribution. As to the content of Churchill's dispatches, Lawson's only advice was, 'Tell him to post picturesque forcible letters.' Of more concern to Churchill, though, was whether or not the articles would have a byline. His articles from Cuba for the *Daily Graphic* and the *Saturday Review* had been signed 'WSC', and Winston told Jennie that, 'I am myself very much in favour of signing – as otherwise I get no credit for the letters. It may help me politically to come before the public in this way.'[27] If Winston was going to risk his life, he wanted everyone in Britain to know about it.

The late-Victorian age had seen a rapid expansion of best-selling national newspapers, which intensified competition among the titles to publish exclusive stories. Several decades before Evelyn Waugh satirized the haphazard nature of war reporting in his novel *Scoop*, Fleet Street editors were looking for inexpensive ways to cover small wars in remote corners of the empire. The sheer size of the British Empire – upon which the sun never set – meant that at any given time there was usually some conflict or other that required coverage. In the 1890s conflicts arose on a regular basis in Africa, India and the Far East, and the challenge for Britain's press barons was to find a cost-effective way of covering important events in faraway lands. One way of cutting costs was to commission educated young officers who knew how to file war dispatches at the same time that they were fighting. Some notable writers of the period had learned their trade by combining military duty with literary endeavour.

Fred Burnaby, one of Churchill's boyhood heroes, had reported for *The Times* on General Gordon's expedition to Khartoum before writing the best-selling *A Ride to Khiva*, based on his travels in Central Asia, which he finished while fulfilling his duties as the commanding officer of the Royal Horse Guards. From an editor's point of view, there were solid advantages to employing officers as makeshift foreign correspondents: they understood the technicalities of warfare and, as part of the army, they did not need to be fed or transported at the newspaper's expense. And if anything happened to them, the government, not the newspaper, was responsible. The senior officers had no objection, as they thought it far preferable to have one of their officers reporting their military operations than civilian corres- pondents, or 'drunken swabs' as Lord Kitchener called them. Kitchener would later change his mind when he read Churchill's dispatches, but Blood had no qualms about Churchill joining his campaign as a press correspondent.

Churchill was well aware of the risks he was taking in joining the Malakand Field Force in an ex officio capacity. Reflect- ing on the contrasting fortunes of Fincastle, who had won the Victoria Cross, and Greaves, who had lost his life, Churchill noted:

> Neither officer was employed officially with the force. Both had travelled up at their own expense, evading and over- coming all obstacles in the endeavour to see something of war. Knights of pen and sword, they had nothing to offer but their lives, no troops to lead, no duties to perform, no watchful commanding officer to report their conduct. They played for high stakes, and Fortune, never so capricious as on the field of battle, dealt to one the greatest honour that

a soldier can hope for, as some think, the greatest gift of the Crown, and to the other Death.[28]

Churchill's desire to become a 'knight of pen and sword' was motivated as much by the need to make money as the desire for fame. Now that he was posted overseas his salary had risen to around £300 a year (around £25,000 today). But to maintain the upkeep of his horses and cover his mess bills, Winston needed another £500 a year. He was forever asking his mother to supplement his income, but Jennie had her own problems and could ill-afford her son's extravagance. Money worries constantly preyed on Churchill's mind, and when his friend and housemate Hugo Baring received only a small settlement on the death of a relative, Winston complained, 'Poor Hugo – has been left with only two hundred a year! Awful! He talks of leaving the regiment.' It was a matter of honour that cavalry officers covered their debts: failure to do so risked social ostracism or worse. Winston fretted about his ability to pay his bills even as he set off for Malakand, hoping that a loan had been paid into his London bank account to cover a number of cheques he had signed, 'as the consequences would in any case be odious and might be serious'.[29]

Churchill needed to cover the costs of travelling to the North-West Frontier so, while waiting for Blood to return, he wrote the first of his dispatches for the *Daily Telegraph*. The article was datelined 'Malakund, Sept. 3', and signed 'By A Young Officer', the format used for all his war reports from the North-West Frontier. Under the headline 'On the Indian Frontier', it appeared in the edition of 6 October 1897, and is a personal account of the tortuous journey from Bangalore to Nowshera, in which Churchill struggles to fulfil Lawson's requirement for 'picturesque forcible letters'. It starts with a description of the womenfolk of the 6th Madras Infantry saying a tearful farewell to their husbands and sons as they leave for the front. His next observation concerns how the camels used to transport equipment are tethered tightly when they are loaded onto the railway trucks so as to prevent them suddenly raising their heads during transit and being decapitated when the train enters a tunnel. 'Sometimes, I am told, curiosity, or ambition, or restlessness, or some other cause induced a camel to break his bonds and stand up, and as there are several tunnels on the line, the spectacle of the headless "oont" (a camel in local dialect) is sometimes to be seen when the train arrives at Rawalpindi.'

Churchill was not impressed with Rawalpindi, the main military supply base for the North-West Frontier. 'When I recall the dusty roads, the burnt-up grass, the intense heat, and the deserted barracks, I am unable to recommend it as a resting-place for either the sybarite, the invalid, or the artist.' At Nowshera he visited the field hospital which 'presents the unpleasing and sombre side of the campaign. Fever, dysentery, and bullets have accumulated more than three hundred poor fellows in the different wards, and the daily deaths mark the progress of what tacticians and strategists have called "the waste of war".' It concludes with an account of his tiresome journey by tonga and his arrival at Malakand, where, 'the slopes are dotted with white tents, perches on platforms cut in the side of the hill. On one of these platforms my own is now pitched.'

From his vantage point overlooking the scene of the desperate battle that had taken place on those same slopes only a month previously, Churchill digresses into a personal critique of the Indian government's conduct of the campaign to date. He is critical of the decision to curtail General Blood's operations in the Swat Valley while large numbers of rebellious tribesmen are still at large. 'Forbearance is construed by the natives as fear,' he warns. He is more heartened, though, by the prospect of the forthcoming campaign against the neighbouring Mohmand tribe, which had opened a new front in the widespread Pashtun rebellion against the British by attacking territory to the north of Peshawar, another British garrison town. Churchill writes indignantly:

It should be remembered that this powerful tribe 'deliberately made an unprovoked attack on a British post, and, without cause or warning, committed a violation of the Imperial territory. I rejoice to be able to end this letter with the news that such audacity is no longer to remain unchastised, and that movements are now contemplated which indicate the adoption of a policy agreeable to expert opinion and suited to the dignity of empire. Of the progress of those movements, of the resistance that may be encountered, of the incidents that occur, I hope to give some account in my subsequent letters, and, if possible, to draw for the every-day reader at his breakfast-table in 'comfortable England', something of a picture of the vivid open-air scenes which are presented by the war in the Indian Highlands.'[30]

Churchill's stay at Malakand waiting for Blood to return was not all spent in high-minded endeavour. As he relates in *My Early Life*, it was at Malakand that he discovered his lifelong love of whisky and soda. Prior to his arrival at Malakand he had disliked the flavour of whisky intensely. 'I liked wine, both red and white, and especially champagne; and on very special occasions I could even drink a small glass of brandy. But this smoky-tasting whisky I had never been able to face.' Whisky, moreover, was out of favour in fashionable England. 'My father for instance could never have drunk whisky except when shooting on a moor or in some very dull chilly place.' But stuck in Malakand for five days in stifling heat and with nothing else to drink, Churchill overcame his aversion. 'Once one got the knack of it, the very repulsion from the flavour developed an attraction of its own; and to this day, although I have always practised true temperance, I have never shrunk when occasion warranted it from the main basic standing refreshment of the white officer in the East.'[31]

Churchill needed to make sure he had all the right equipment, just in case the opportunity arose for him to join Blood's force in a fighting capacity, rather than as a correspondent. To serve as a cavalry officer, he needed to buy two good horses, hire a military groom 'and complete my martial wardrobe in many particulars'. This he achieved by attending an auction held to sell the effects of several young officers who had been killed shortly before his arrival. In accordance with the Anglo-Indian campaigning custom, the dead officers' effects, including their uniforms, were sold by the camp auctioneer once their funerals had been held. 'In this way I soon acquired a complete outfit,' Churchill wrote. 'It struck me as rather grim to see the intimate belongings of one's comrade of the day before – his coat, his shirt, his boots, his water-bottle, his revolver, his blanket, his cooking-pot thus unceremoniously distributed among strangers. But after all it was quite logical and in accordance with the highest principles of economics.' Even so, Churchill did feel a pang when, a few weeks later, 'I first slung round my shoulder the lanyard of a gallant friend I had seen killed the day before.'[32] It was at the auction that Churchill bought a grey horse, whose previous owner had been killed in action.

The anxious wait at Malakand ended when Blood, fresh from his campaign to pacify the Bunerwals, returned to camp. Churchill was immensely grateful to Blood for allowing him to stay at Malakand in the first place, and held Blood in high regard. To Winston, Blood, a veteran of numerous campaigns on the North-West Frontier, 'was a striking figure in these savage mountains and among these wild rifle-armed clansmen. He looked very much more formidable in his uniform, mounted, with his standard-bearer and cavalcade, than he had done when I had seen him in safe and comfortable England.'[33] The general's personal stature among his men reached new heights during the campaign in the Swat Valley when a tribesman, part of a peace delegation, had suddenly whipped out a knife and rushed at Blood from about eight yards. Blood drew his revolver and shot his assailant dead at two yards.

The British, like the Pashtuns, gave little quarter on the field of battle. But once the fighting was over they applied the same amount of energy to making peace with the tribes and ending the conflict. Political officers such as Major Deane, who reported directly to the civilian authorities in Calcutta, were always in attendance, and were regarded with suspicion by the soldiers, who believed their civilian colleagues were more interested in talking to the tribal elders than fighting them. When military intervention was required, political officers like Deane, who wore white tabs on their collars to denote their civilian status, accompanied the force, maintaining a constant dialogue with the local maliks, mullahs and other local notables in the hope of bringing the conflict to a speedy and satisfactory conclusion. It was often the case that British interests were better served by playing one tribe off against another, paying a handsome stipend to those who supported the imperial cause, than by launching costly military campaigns.

A form of this divide-and-rule policy was pursued by the US-led coalition in Afghanistan following the September 11 attacks. Rather than launch a wholesale invasion of the country, Washington and its allies enlisted the support of the Northern Alliance established by Ahmad Shah Massoud, the 'Lion of Panjshir'. Massoud had worked closely with the CIA during the Soviet occupation of 1979–89 when, with American military assistance, he organized a highly effective resistance campaign against the Russians. Massoud's mujahedin fighters formed close ties with the Americans during the conflict that became known as 'Charlie Wilson's War', after the Texas congressman who lobbied on behalf of the Afghan resistance.[34] Massoud was murdered by Taliban sympathizers prior to the September 11 attacks, but his followers helped the US-led coalition to over-throw the Taliban government in Kabul in late 2001, driving them back to their traditional tribal territories on the Afghan border with Pakistan. By getting the Northern Alliance to do the fighting for them, the coalition was spared the necessity of deploying a full-strength invasion force to Afghanistan.

The British had tried to play a similar game on the North-West Frontier over a century earlier, the political officers working hard to enlist the support of pro-British tribes to maintain the balance of power in the tribal areas in Britain's favour. If young officers like Fincastle rejoiced at the slaughter of the tribesmen, calling them 'a horde of wild barbarians' thirsting for British blood,[35] the political officers took a more pragmatic view. Blood's campaign in the Swat Valley had claimed the lives of another 1,000 or so Pashtun tribesmen (precise figures were hard to come by), thereby bringing the total number killed since the start of the assault on Malakand and Chakdara to around 4,000. With their vastly superior manpower and equipment, the British could have continued the slaughter indefinitely. Young cavalry officers of Churchill's generation viewed these military operations in the same way they did hunting foxes or big game. With their immaculately groomed steeds, fine tunics and exemplary horsemanship, they liked nothing more than to demonstrate their martial prowess, and paid little consideration to the consequences of their dashing gallops through the foothills of the Himalayas. As with hunting, their participation was not without risk, and the cemeteries of the North-West Frontier are filled with the names of those who perished in these military campaigns, as well as those who lost their lives pig-sticking and tiger-shooting. In the mess, officers spoke of taking part in the next 'show', demonstrating that they were more interested in the theatre of warfare than the human cost of its destructive force.

Many years later NATO commanders in Afghanistan were to learn the limitations of military force. No matter how many Taliban fighters were killed as part of NATO's campaign to stabilize the country, peace remained elusive so long as coalition forces put more emphasis on fighting the Taliban rather than talking to them. The British had similar concerns in the 1890s, when they accepted that killing for killing's sake was counterproductive. If they wanted to protect India's northern border, they needed to reach an understanding with the local tribes, and this was unlikely to happen so long as British soldiers were engaged in the indiscriminate slaughter of the native population. The political officers recognized this fact, even if the soldiers did not. Churchill no doubt spoke for the majority of his fellow officers when he described the unpopularity of political officers like Major Deane: 'Just when we were looking forward to having a splendid fight and all the guns were loaded and everyone keyed up, this Major Deane would come along and put a stop to it all. Apparently all these savage chiefs were his old friends and almost his blood relations. Nothing disturbed their friendship. In between the fights, they talked as man to man and pal to pal, just as they talked to our General as robber to robber.'[36]

As a veteran of several campaigns on the North-West Frontier, Blood was more inclined to listen to the advice of his political officers than his gung-ho soldiers. Thus, while the soldiers were keen to continue with the campaign against the tribes of the Swat Valley, Blood was disposed to heed the advice of the government officers to sue for peace and return to Malakand. Churchill did not approve of the decision. Reports that the British had decided to withdraw 'spread like wildfire along the frontier, and revived the spirits of the tribes. They fancied they detected a sign of weakness. Nor were they altogether wrong. But the weakness was moral rather than physical.'[37] Blood was less concerned about the decision, as he had acquired grudging respect for the Pashtuns' warrior spirit. 'He liked these wild tribesmen and understood the way to talk to them,' wrote Churchill. Blood had learned from many years of campaigning how to negotiate with the Pashtun tribes, an attribute Churchill put down to the fact that Blood 'regarded the attempted stealing of the Crown Jewels by his ancestor as the most glorious event in his family history, and in consequence he had warm sympathy with the Pashtun tribes on the

Indian frontier, all of whom would have completely understood the incident in all its bearings, and would have bestowed unstinted and discriminating applause upon all parties'.[38]

Churchill's delight at being reunited with Blood was reciprocated by the general. 'When I returned from Upper Swat at the end of August,' Blood recalled in his memoirs, 'I had found my young friend (in his early twenties then) Winston Churchill, of the 4th Queen's Own Hussars, who joined me as an extra A. D. C. – and a right good one he was!'[39] With the uprising in the Swat Valley coming to an end, Blood turned his attention to the valleys of the neighbouring Bajaur region to the north-west of Malakand, where a number of Pashtun tribes had also joined in the revolt against British rule.

*

That summer, almost the entire length of the Afghan border had been affected by the tribal rebellion. There had been an anti-British uprising in nearby Waziristan earlier in the year which, in common with the others, had been caused by the Durand Line's arbitrary division of ancient tribal lands. The British blamed the Talib-ul-ilms for inciting the revolt of the Waziri tribes, and the attacks had continued throughout the summer. The British responded by launching raids, confiscating livestock and burning crops. But the unrest continued to spread to neighbouring districts, prompting one official to inform the Viceroy: 'Tribes generally are rising.' From the British perspective, the most serious attack had been the raid by tribesmen from the Mohmand Valley on the frontier village close to the British fort at Peshawar. The Mohmand revolt was deemed by the British to be far more serious than the uprisings in Waziristan and Swat because it constituted an attack against the 'settled areas' – i.e. British India itself. An urgent telegram was sent to the Indian government which described the raid as the 'most open and audacious violation of British territory which has occurred in the Peshawar District, or indeed in any Frontier district for many years'. Blood was ordered to end operations in the Swat Valley and to concentrate his efforts on subduing the Mohmands, and Churchill was invited to join him for the operation.

The Mohmands are a Pashtun tribe who can trace their origins in the mountainous border region to the fifth century BC. Based around Peshawar and the Khyber Pass area, they were one of the tribes that had been most affected by the establishment of the Durand Line, which divided their ancestral lands between Afghanistan and the North-West Frontier. They briefly attracted attention in the 1980s when Abdul Ahad Mohmand, a Mohmand tribesman from Ghazni, became Afghanistan's first astronaut after he spent nine days aboard the Soviet Union's Mir space station, also becoming the first Muslim to take a copy of the Koran into space. Like the other Pashtun tribes, they were angered by the disruption caused by the Durand Line, and the mullahs, with the encouragement of the Afghan amir, had little difficulty inciting the Mohmands to take up arms against the British.

On this occasion the uprising was led by the Hadda Mullah, and seventy-two British and Indian soldiers were killed or wounded in the Mohmand attack on British forts around the border town of Peshawar. The British force at Peshawar eventually succeeded in dispersing around 6,000 hostile tribesmen, but the Indian government could not tolerate an attack so close to its frontier. As Churchill remarked, 'That such an outrage, as the deliberate violation of British territory by these savages, should remain unpunished, Forward Policy or no Forward Policy, was of course impossible.'[40] Blood resolved to send half of the Malakand Field Force west towards the Mohmand Valley, which was located only a few miles from the newly designated border with Afghanistan. The general agreed that Churchill should accompany him, and from early September Winston was officially attached to Blood's staff. This meant he had freedom of movement within the entire area of operations, a privilege denied to other officers. Winston was excited at the prospect of finally seeing action, and in his last letter to his mother before setting off with Blood's force he wrote, 'We march tomorrow, and before a week is out there will be a battle – probably the biggest yet fought on the frontier this year.'[41] Not all Churchill's contemporaries approved of the preferential treatment he received. They were critical of his regiment for allowing him to join the Malakand campaign in the first place. They blamed Blood for giving an inexperienced officer like Churchill too much latitude. And they attributed the special treatment Churchill received to his family connections. Colonel Lionel James, a war correspondent for *The Times*, observed: 'He was a rather tempestuous youth with a ready tongue that was much given to laying down the law. Soldiers smiled at him, and said that he had been spoiled by the Colonel of his regiment, who had given him more rope than was good for a subaltern.'[42]

Spoiled or not, Churchill was determined to make the best of his opportunity. Fellow officers may have envied his indulgent treatment, but here was a young man, still only twenty-two, who had recently suffered the emotional misfortune of losing both his father and his beloved nanny, Mrs Everest, and whose family was locked in a constant battle against penury. Churchill may have been born into the Marlborough dynasty at Blenheim Palace, but he had no chance of succeeding to the title. While he was serving on the North-West Frontier, John Spencer-Churchill, the future 10th Duke of Marlborough, was born on 18 September 1897, providing his cousin Sunny, the 9th Duke, with an heir, thereby ending Winston's lingering inheritance prospects. More than ever the need to make his fortune rested on the young subaltern's slender shoulders.

Before setting off with Blood, Churchill worked hard to master his military and journalistic briefs. Despite knowing little about frontier life, he tried to acquire a basic understanding of the local tribes, with their bewildering network of alliances and hatreds. He concluded they were united by two common bonds: their Muslim faith and their opposition to British control. They saw the British as infidels, and were easily persuaded by their mullahs to drive the invaders from their valleys and preserve their traditional way of life. Churchill believed the conflict represented a fundamental clash between the values of Islam and those of the West. In one of his more thoughtful articles for the *Daily Telegraph*, dated 12 September, he observed that, on the North-West Frontier, 'civilisation is face to face with militant Mohammedanism'. In another, he said that, given the 'moral and material forces' arrayed against each other, 'there need be no fear of the ultimate issue'.[43] He had no respect for the mullahs and their exploitation of the superstition-prone tribesmen, but he respected the tribesmen's fighting prowess, which made them formidable foes. He remarked that, 'The Swatis, Bunerwals, Mohmands, and other frontier tribes with whom the Malakand Field Force is at present engaged are brave and warlike. Their courage has been abundantly displayed in the present campaign.'[44]

On the eve of the campaign, Churchill took a moment to reflect on the magnificence of the setting where he was about to do battle. The layout of the Malakand camp was typical of Anglo-Indian bivouacs used on active service. The infantry and artillery were formed in a large defensive square with the cavalry squadrons, pack animals, supplies and tents set within. The tents were formed in orderly rows, making a remarkable spectacle as night fell. 'To view the scene by moonlight is alone an experience which would repay much travelling,' wrote the young knight of sword and pen. 'The fires have sunk to red, glowing specks. The bayonets glisten in a regular line of blue-white points. The silence of weariness is broken by the incessant and uneasy shuffling of the horses. All the valley is plunged in gloom and the mountains rise high and black around. Far up their sides, the twinkling watch-fires of the tribesmen can be seen. Overhead is the starry sky, behind the pale radiance of the moon. It is a spectacle that may inspire the philosopher no less than the artist.'[45]

CHAPTER SEVEN

HIGH STAKES

'I am more ambitious for a reputation for personal
courage than anything else in the world.'
Winston S. Churchill, 2 December 1897

At 5 a.m. on 5 September 1897, Lieutenant Winston S. Churchill of the 4th Hussars rode out with the Malakand Field Force for
his first experience of military combat. Blood's force comprised
two brigades of British and Indian regiments, and its mission
was to tackle the revolt by the Mohmand tribes on the Indian
Empire's northern border. To suppress the revolt, the plan was
for Blood's force to move west from Malakand while another
two brigades based at Peshawar, less than a hundred miles away,
would move in a pincer movement to link up with Blood's force,
thereby completing the operation to occupy and subdue the
rebellious Mohmand territory. Although the British enjoyed military superiority, they expected a tough fight, not least because
they were entering uncharted terrain. 'Nothing was known of
the configurations of the country, of which no maps existed; nor
of the supplies of food, forage and water available by the way,'
Churchill noted.[1]

The first obstacle was the crossing of the Panjkora river, the
gateway to the Bajaur district where the Mohmands were based.
The local tribesmen had already tried to seize control of the
only river crossing, a makeshift bridge built by the British, but
they had been beaten off. To secure the passage, 12-pounder
guns had been placed at commanding positions around the
crossing to protect Blood's force. Moving a large army through

hostile terrain is a time-consuming business at the best of times, and in the late nineteenth century, when the only transportation available was pack animals such as mules and camels, progress was painstakingly slow. Every day the routine of the march was the same. It started at 5 a.m. with the troops standing to, and the march beginning before dawn so as to avoid the midday heat. After a stop for breakfast, the force reached the next bivouac around noon, having covered anywhere from eight to fourteen miles before the heat made further progress impossible.

Churchill travelled to the Panjkora crossing as a member of Blood's staff, taking the road from Malakand to Chakdara, the scene of the recent fighting, before arriving at Sarai, having passed through the summit of the Catgalla Pass. According to Winston, 'Catgalla' means 'Cut-throat' and, drawing on his imaginative powers, he remarked that: 'It is not hard to believe that this gloomy defile has been the scene of dark and horrid deeds.' The Sarai Valley is two miles wide with mountains rising steeply on each side. At certain points during the journey Blood and his entourage had to leave the road 'to avoid the long line of mules and marching men who toiled along it'. On the second night of the march Churchill camped with Blood's 2nd Brigade, resuming the journey to Bajaur the next morning 'while the stars were still shining'. Eventually the force arrived at the Panjkora bridge, 'a frail structure, supported on wire ropes'. Nothing of the bridge survives today after it was swept away during the fierce flooding the North-West Frontier suffered in the summer of 2010. But the stone abutments remain, a testament to the Royal Engineers' nineteenth-century endeavours.

Beneath the bridge the river flowed swiftly, plunging into a narrow cleft about a mile below before disappearing among the mountains. As Churchill camped nearby, two gunners 'lost their lives by falling in, and being carried down. Indeed,' he noted, 'watching the dead bodies of several camels being swept along, swirled around, and buffeted against the rocks, it was not hard to understand these accidents.'[2] Blood's force negotiated the

bridge without incident and advanced to Ghosam, where it set
up camp for three days while Major Deane, the ubiquitous
political officer, parleyed with the local chieftains, hoping for a
better understanding of their grievances and to encourage them
to end the revolt. Churchill, in common with most junior
officers, resented the political officers, and he argued that
Deane's interference had prevented Blood's force from making
a decisive strike against the tribesmen, thereby bringing the
campaign to a swift conclusion, 'probably at far less cost in lives
than was afterwards incurred'. The political officers, though,
were under orders to find a peaceful resolution to any dispute
with the frontier tribes, and Deane arranged a series of *jirgas*, or
tribal gatherings, hoping to persuade the rebels to lay down
their arms. 'All day they kept arriving and squatting in rows
before Major Deane's tent, to hear the Government's terms,'
Churchill recorded.[3] The chief condition was the surrender of
the tribesmen's rifles, the number of which the British calculated
according to the wealth and size of each clan.

As this laborious process continued, Blood sent his cavalry
squadrons on regular scouting patrols to assess the strength of
the enemy, and to gain a better understanding of the terrain.
Always restless for adventure, Winston set aside his misgivings
about Deane's activities and, on 10 September, accompanied
two squadrons of the 11th Bengal Lancers as they escorted the
political officer to meet a number of tribal leaders in the upper
Jandol Valley, just ten or so miles from the border with
Afghanistan. Viscount Fincastle, Winston's great rival, was also
in the party. Winston believed Jandol was typical of the Afghan
valleys in the area. Seven separate castles formed the strongholds
of seven separate khans, some of whom had been implicated in
the original attack on Malakand. Only four days previously
these same tribes had been massing for an attack against the
British. Now they said they wanted to sue for peace. Winston
related that, 'as we approached the first fortified village the
sovereign and his army rode out to meet us, and with many

protestations of fidelity, expressed his joy at our safe arrival'.
Churchill witnessed at first hand the extraordinary ritual of the
British negotiating with Afghan tribesmen who had a few days
ago been their sworn enemies, but now declared they wanted to
be their friends.

In his account of the meeting, Churchill gives full rein to his
descriptive powers. The local khan was

> a fine-looking man and sat well on a stamping road stallion.
> His dress was imposing. A waistcoat of gorgeous crimson,
> thickly covered with gold lace, displayed flowing sleeves
> of white linen, buttoned at the wrist. Long, loose, baggy,
> linen trousers, also fastened above the ankle, and curi-
> ously pointed shoes clothed his nether limbs. This striking
> costume was completed by a small skull-cap, richly em-
> broidered, and an ornamental sabre. He sprang from his
> horse with grace and agility, to offer his sword to Major
> Deane, who bade him mount and ride with him. The
> army, four or five rascally looking men on shaggy ponies,
> and armed with rifles of widely different patterns, followed
> at a distance.[4]

This scene would be as familiar today for soldiers serving in
Afghanistan as it was in Churchill's day.

Once inside the khan's mud-walled fort, Major Deane proceeded to reproach the tribesmen for their participation in the
attack on Malakand the month before. But rather than deny
their involvement as Churchill had expected, they readily
admitted to their role in the uprising. According to Churchill's
record of the conversation, ' "Well, why not?", said they, "There
was a good fair fight." ' With the fighting over, they wanted to
make peace. They bore no malice, so why should the British?
Throughout the visit the Pashtun tribesmen seemed to regard
the whole affair as nothing more than an elaborate game. When
Deane asked them about the rifles they were supposed to
surrender as part of the peace terms, 'They looked blank. There

were no rifles. There never had been any rifles,' wrote Churchill. 'Let the soldiers search the fort and see for themselves.' Depriving the tribesmen of their guns, particularly the home-made version of the breech-loading Martini-Henry rifles, was considered vital to the security of British forces on the frontier. Pashtun men are taught to shoot at infancy, and are renowned for their marksmanship. Equipped with long-range rifles, they had the ability to inflict serious damage on British forces, both men and animals. The British therefore insisted that the tribesmen surrender their weapons as part of the peace terms. When no guns were forthcoming, Deane ordered that a search be made of the fort, but no rifles were found, as the tribesmen, anticipating Deane's visit, had already hidden them away. But Deane was not prepared to allow the tribesmen to go unpunished, and as the meeting came to an end he announced that the tribal leaders were to be taken prisoner. 'Yet,' said Churchill, 'they behaved with Oriental composure and calmly accepted the inevitable. They ordered their ponies and, mounting, rode behind us under escort.'[5]

The British continued in similar vein along the valley, meeting all the tribal chiefs. For Churchill, the highlight of the day was their visit to Barwa Sagar, a fort at the head of the valley, the former fiefdom of Umra Khan, the Pashtun chief of the Jandol Valley who had instigated the original revolt against Chitral in 1895. Two British lieutenants had been taken hostage at the fort during the Chitral siege, and Churchill was impressed when he was shown the room in which they had been held. The room 'opened on a balcony, whence a fine view of the valley could be obtained. There are many worse places of durance.'[6] Umra Khan was no longer in residence, having fled across the border to Afghanistan, and the fort was now occupied by a pro-British chieftain whose treachery had made him deeply unpopular with his Pashtun neighbours. He thus had no choice but to maintain his loyalty to the British Crown. This was typical of the way political officers like Deane played one tribe off against another. There were some tribal leaders, like the Khan of Dir, who received handsome stipends from the government in Calcutta, and whose loyalty the British could generally rely upon. Taking the British shilling, though, made these tribal leaders vulnerable to attack by their fellow tribesmen, who resented foreign interference in their affairs. This meant that they had to stay close to their British protectors. Their very survival depended upon it.

Eager to impress his British paymasters, the new resident at Barwa Sagar offered his visitors a healthy breakfast. The British officers sat on carpet-covered charpoys (bedsteads) in the shade of beautiful chenar trees, and Churchill tells how 'a long row of men appeared, each laden with food. Some carried fruit, apples or pears; others piles of chupatties, or dishes of *pillau*. Nor were our troopers forgotten. The Mahommedans among them eagerly accepted the proffered food. But the Sikhs maintained a resourceful silence and declined it. They could not eat what had been prepared by Mussulman hands, and so they sat gazing wistfully at the appetising dishes, and contented themselves with a little fruit.'[7] There was no love lost between the Indian Sikhs and the Muslims of the North-West Frontier, a tension evident today in the residual hostility between India and Pakistan. On the field of battle neither side showed their foe any mercy. The Muslim Pashtuns vengefully hacked captured Sikhs to pieces, while the Sikhs rarely spared the lives of captured Pashtuns. During the fighting at Malakand, for example, Winston heard that the Sikh soldiers had put a wounded Muslim 'into the cinerator and burned him alive. This was hushed up.'[8] At Barwa, the innate antipathy between the Muslims and Sikhs was too deep for either group to want to break bread with the other.

Churchill's story of the Malakand campaign contains many of the qualities of good travel writing. By comparison, the contemporaneous account published by his great rival Fincastle is rather prosaic. In his account Fincastle makes no mention of his fellow cavalryman, while Churchill makes several references to Fincastle when it is relevant to his narrative. Perhaps Fincastle thought Churchill, who was younger by five years and his inferior in rank, experience and class (Fincastle succeeded to a title, Winston did not), was not worth mentioning. Alternatively he may have felt there was no need to grant the publicity-seeking young subaltern any further exposure to the public eye. But whatever advantages Fincastle enjoyed over Churchill, he could not compete with the descriptive force of the younger man's prose. Fincastle joined Churchill on the same expedition to the Jandol Valley, but while the visit inspired Churchill's descriptive powers, Fincastle's only observation was that the tribes 'entertained us in the most hospitable manner . . . It was still very hot here during the day, but the nights were rapidly getting cooler, and the health of the troops was excellent.'[9] In the writing stakes, there was little doubt which officer was the better wordsmith.

*

A week into the campaign Churchill was still a knight of the pen, rather than one of the sword, so he concentrated his energy on finding good copy for his *Daily Telegraph* dispatches, getting scoops at the expense of Fincastle of *The Times*. He kept himself busy by accompanying the daily reconnaissance patrols, and observing their map-making efforts. As he told his friend Reggie Barnes, he spent most days with the 11th Bengal Lancers – 'such nice fellows' – and the evenings in the general's mess. 'Sir Bindon is a fine fellow to serve with. Always confident and amiable, civil and kind to every one and up to all the tricks.' When out riding with the Lancers, Churchill was always on the lookout for action, but had little luck. 'I take every opportunity and have accompanied solitary patrols into virgin valleys and ridden through villages and forts full of armed men – looking furious – but without any adventure occurring. It is a strange war. One moment people are your friends and the next they are shooting. The value of life is so little that they do not bear any grudge for being shot at.' On 12 September the camp came under sniper fire, the first time Churchill had been shot at since Cuba. Churchill was having dinner with Blood when 'a bullet hummed by over head'. The incident strengthened Churchill's view that the Mohmands needed to be dealt with. As he told Barnes, 'After today we begin to burn villages. Every one. And all who resist will be killed without quarter. The Mohmands need a lesson, and there is no doubt we are a very cruel people.' Such action was vital, Churchill argued, because the Pashtuns 'recognise superiority of race'.[10]

On the 13th, Blood dispatched two squadrons from the 11th Bengal Lancers to scout the north of the Mohmand Valley, the focus of the tribes' anti-British revolt. The Lancers set fire to one village and, as they withdrew, came under fire from tribesmen hidden on the surrounding hillsides. It was a minor skirmish, with no British casualties, but it was a harbinger of the more serious fighting to come. Churchill was at the camp to welcome the Lancers on their return, and noted, with a degree of envy, 'They were vastly pleased with themselves. Nothing in life is so exhilarating as to be shot at without result.'[11]

Churchill's galloping around with the Lancers provided good material for his *Daily Telegraph* dispatches. From Blood's camp at Ghosam, Churchill sent three articles to London, where they appeared on consecutive days in the editions of 7–9 October under the same heading, 'The War in the Indian Highlands'. All the articles were signed 'By A Young Officer', and Churchill did his best to post 'picturesque forcible letters', as Lawson had demanded, even when he had not seen a great deal. His dispatch of 5 September gives an account of Blood's journey to the Panjkora bridge. Like all good reporters, Churchill is careful not to reveal his source, even though his report clearly draws heavily on the conversations he has had with the general while travelling with his entourage. At Chakdara, the only activity of note was 'a group of Kharki-clad [*sic*] figures, playing desultory football' close to 'the smooth grass of the polo pitch'. Churchill was able to explore the area where fierce fighting had taken place during the siege, and his dispatch pays tribute to the bravery of the Pashtuns. 'Their swordsmanship, neglecting guards, concerns itself only with cuts and, careless of what injury they may receive, they devote themselves to the destruction of their opponents.' But he is less well disposed to the mullahs who incited the violence in the first place, and is appalled by their habit of trading their womenfolk to buy rifles. 'This degradation of mind is unrelieved by a single elevated sentiment,' he writes. 'Their religion is the most miserable fanaticism, in which cruelty, credulity, and immorality are equally represented. Their holy men – the Mullahs – prize as their chief privilege a sort of "droit de seigneur". It is impossible to imagine a lower type of beings or a more dreadful state of barbarism.'[12]

Churchill's next article, written on 9 September, opens with the somewhat pitiful observation, 'I cannot recall any incident that occurred' – hardly the kind of insightful journalism that wins Pulitzers. He justifies this less-than-compelling remark by reminding his readers that, to obtain a clear idea of a soldier's life on active service, they 'must mentally share the fatigues of the march and the monotony of the camp'.[13] In the final article written from Ghosam on 12 September, Churchill explains the challenge of marching in the heat of an Indian summer, noting, 'The soldiers of India naturally feel the effects of the climate less than those from cooler lands. This, of course, the British infantryman will not admit. The dominant race resent the slightest suggestion of inferiority.'[14] Continuing in this jingoistic vein, he tells how he meets soldiers from the Queen's Regiment after they have completed a fourteen-mile march carrying their arms and ammunition. 'Not one had fallen by the way. They looked strained and weary, but nothing would induce them to admit it. "An easy march," they said. "Should have been here long ago if the native troops had not kept halting." This is the material for empire-building.' Churchill was simply reflecting the view of his imperial contemporaries that British officers such as himself were superior to the Indians who served under them. 'Nothing is so remarkable as the ascendancy which the British officer maintains over the native soldier. The dark Sowars [Indian cavalrymen] follow the young English subaltern who commands them with a strange devotion. He is their "butcha" – the best in the regiment – as brave as a lion. None ride so straight as he; no one is so confident.' In this dispatch Churchill sets aside his rivalry with Fincastle, and uses the incident at Landakai, where *The Times* correspondent won the Victoria Cross, to support his argument. 'It is an excellent instance of the actions by which the ascendancy of the British officer is maintained over the gallant Asiatics he commands,' Churchill writes. 'The example of these men calmly endeavouring to rescue their brother officers within fifty yards of a hundred rifles, and surrounded by a ferocious mob of swordsmen, probably does more to preserve the loyalty of the Indian soldier than all the speeches of Westminster.'[15]

On 14 September Churchill moved seven miles west to Nawagai with the 3rd Brigade and Blood's divisional headquarters, while the 2nd Brigade marched towards the Rambat Pass, aiming to cross it the following day. But as the 2nd Brigade, commanded by Brigadier General Patrick Jeffreys, a highly decorated soldier who had fought in the Zulu Wars and Burma, established camp at Markhanai, eleven miles south of the pass, it came under sustained attack. Blood ordered Jeffreys to move against the tribesmen the next day. The following morning Jeffreys began moving up the Mohmand Valley with three columns, but he was met with strong resistance from the local Pashtun tribesmen, forcing him to withdraw. As darkness fell, the general and his small escort found themselves cut off, and defended themselves with some difficulty until relief arrived. The action resulted in the British sustaining nearly 150 dead and wounded, some of them subalterns no older than Churchill. As Blood later recalled in his memoirs, 'As soon as I heard of General Jeffreys' mishap, I sent for Churchill and suggested his joining the General in order to see a little fighting. He was all for it, so I sent him over at once and he saw more fighting than I expected, and very hard fighting too.'[16] The knight of the pen had become a knight of the sword.

*

The 2nd Brigade was the standard mix of British and Indian regiments. The main British contingent was the East Kent Regiment, 3rd of Foot, more commonly known as the Buffs, one of Britain's oldest and most famous infantry regiments, which had fought with the Duke of Wellington during the Peninsular campaign, as well as in Crimea and Afghanistan. The rest of the brigade was made up of Indian regiments: the 35th Sikhs, 38th Dogras, the Corps of Guides infantry, as well as a company of native sappers and No. 7 Mountain Battery. Blood cancelled the orders for the brigade to cross the Rambat Pass, and instead instructed Jeffreys to enter the Mohmand Valley 'and thoroughly chastise the tribesmen'.[17] Churchill accepted Blood's offer to join the 2nd Brigade without hesitation, and set off immediately for the ten-mile ride to the brigade's new base at Inayat Kila, which the soldiers called 'Fort Grant'. He was allowed to join an escort of Bengal Lancers for the journey, and hurriedly packed a few items in his saddle, 'of which the most important were a cloak, some chocolate and a tooth-brush'.[18] They travelled through a network of deep ravines, taking care to avoid the hostile tribesmen lurking in the surrounding hills.

Eventually they emerged onto the plain, where they saw a 'long brown streak' – the troops of the 2nd Brigade, who were marching from Markhanai to the entrance of the Mohmand Valley. 'The smoke of five burning villages rose in a tall column into the air – blue against the mountains, brown against the sky,' Churchill wrote. When his party eventually caught up with the brigade, he found his fellow officers still reeling from the events of the previous night. 'You were lucky to be out of it,' they told him. 'There's plenty more coming.' Churchill continued on his journey to the main camp at Inayat Kila, and on arrival he found the cavalry returning from their pursuit of the fleeing tribesmen, the points of their spears covered with dark smears. He asked how many tribesmen had been killed, to which the officer replied 'Twenty-one. But they're full of fight.' The Buffs, who had been sent by Blood to occupy the Rambat Pass, came into the camp at sunset having received new orders to march all the way back again. As evening fell, the soldiers settled down for some well-earned rest, hoping that they would not be subjected to another night-time attack. The enemy was also exhausted and had no interest in launching an assault. Instead they sent a few snipers, who fired into the camp until about 2 a.m., thereby denying the British their precious sleep. Churchill, wrapped in a blanket, lay awake until the early hours contemplating the night sky, 'those imperial stars which shine as calmly on Piccadilly Circus as they do on Inayat Kila'.[19] The following day, 16 September, he would experience the action he so desperately sought, as well as having one of the most danger-filled days of his life.

Churchill was conspicuous riding a grey charger when the 2nd Brigade moved out from Inayat Kila at 6 a.m. and headed for the Mohmand Valley. Winston had bought his horse at an auction of the effects of a fellow junior officer who had been killed earlier in the campaign. His choice of a grey may well have been inspired by his previous experience in Cuba, when he had been impressed by General Valdés, the Chief of Staff of the Spanish force, who had ridden a grey charger while wearing a white and golden uniform, thereby drawing a great deal of enemy fire. By choosing to ride a grey as he travelled with the Bengal Lancers, Churchill was making sure that no one could fail to notice his endeavours were he to find himself in the thick of the action.

The Mohmand Valley, located to the south-east of the Afghan border, is a fan-shaped cul-de-sac about ten miles in length from north to south. It begins in a mile-wide opening at its southern end and is about six miles wide at its broadest point. The centre of the valley is dominated by the Watelai river, and on each side terraced fields rise from the valley floor with more than two dozen villages dotting the terrain from the banks of the river up to the steep hillsides that form its walls. The valley has traditionally been controlled by tribes that jealously guard their independence, and later became a renowned stronghold for the Taliban. (It was at Salala in the Mohmand Valley that, on 26 November 2011, US aircraft killed twenty-four Pakistani troops during a cross-border raid that was supposed to target Taliban insurgents. The incident caused a serious diplomatic rift between Washington and Islamabad, and the Pakistan government retaliated by closing NATO's vital supply routes into Afghanistan, including the Khyber Pass.)

At the time 2nd Brigade entered the Mohmand Valley, very little was known 'concerning either the inhabitants or their country', as the official history states.[20] The tribes of the Mohmand Valley were victims of the Durand Line's arbitrary division of their land. Those living on the Afghan side of the boundary remained the subjects of the amir, Abdur Rahman, while the rest fell within Britain's sphere of influence. At the lower end of the valley, where the British had their camp at Inayat Kila, the tribes came under the jurisdiction of the pro-British Khan of Nawagai, to whom they paid taxes and owed nominal allegiance. The Khan of Nawagai, like other local potentates such as the neighbouring Khan of Dir, depended on British support for his survival. They therefore found it in their interests to support the British campaign that targeted their enemies. Further along the valley, the British found 'the inhabitants of the valley were absolutely independent of every one',[21] making them susceptible to the amir's plots to incite a tribal rebellion against the British.

Umra Khan, a close ally of the Afghan amir who had instigated the original attack on Chitral in 1895, was, the British discovered, active in the Afghan-controlled region of the Mohmand Valley, and had sent 'certain retainers' to link up with the tribes and encourage them to revolt against the British. The British found that, 'Their numbers gradually increased until, at the time of our operations in the valley, they numbered some 80 men, all armed with breech-loading rifles and possessing large amounts of ammunition which was said to be constantly reaching them from Kabul.'[22] Churchill, in common with his fellow officers, was well aware of the Afghan amir's double-dealing. With Umra Khan living 'in exile' in Kabul, Abdur Rahman used him as a 'trump card' against the British when the occasion arose. The British soon found that they were not only fighting against the local tribes of the Mohmand Valley: they were waging a proxy war against the amir of Afghanistan.

The 2nd Brigade's mission was to 'chastise' the local tribes by burning crops, destroying reservoirs and blowing up fortified buildings in the village. Within the context of Blood's broader campaign to restore order to the North-West Frontier, this was a routine operation designed to curtail the threat posed by one group of particularly troublesome tribesmen. In his account of events Churchill is at pains to stress that 'the reader must make allowances for what I have called the personal perspective. Throughout he must remember, how small is the scale of operations. The panorama is not filled with masses of troops. He will not hear the thunder of a hundred guns. No cavalry brigades whirl by with flashing swords. No infantry divisions are applied at critical points.'[23] It was, in effect, the standard British response to tribal unrest on the Afghan border, but it was not without risk, as the mounting casualty toll in Blood's force testified.

As they set off to tackle the Mohmands, the British were buoyed by the knowledge that they enjoyed a significant advantage, in terms of both the numbers of men deployed and the equipment available to them. Churchill was particularly impressed with the new Lee-Metford rifle, the first repeat-fire rifle to be used by the British infantry and the forerunner of the better-known Lee-Enfield weapon. With a range accurate up to 500 yards, it enabled the British soldier to counter the accuracy of the breech-loading *jezails* used by Afghan sharpshooters, as well as enabling them to fire up to ten rounds in rapid succession. The weapon's effectiveness was greatly augmented by the introduction of the exploding dum-dum bullet, which Churchill regarded as being 'of the greatest value', as 'its stopping power is all that could be desired'. As Churchill noted, the bullet 'is not explosive, but expansive' and 'the result is a wonderful and from the technical point of view a beautiful machine. On striking a bone this causes the bullet to "set up" or spread out, and it then tears and splinters everything before it, causing wounds which in the body must be generally mortal and in any limb necessitate amputation.'[24] Not long afterwards use of the dum-dum bullet in armed conflicts was banned by international law on account of the appalling injury it inflicts on the victim, a prohibition that exists to this day.

The Afghans had learned, over many decades of fighting, that they were no match for the British in set-piece battles. Instead they relied on classic guerrilla tactics, withdrawing when confronted by a superior force, and then launching highly effective ambushes against any weak point they found in the British positions. Churchill rode out with a force comprising around 1,000 fighting men, which was divided into three columns so that it could cover as much of the Mohmand Valley as possible in a single day. For that day's action Churchill was attached to the centre column commanded by Lieutenant Colonel Thomas Goldney of the 35th Sikhs, and the column included infantry units from the Buffs and the 35th Sikhs, as well as a cavalry squadron from the 11th Bengal Lancers, a half-company of sappers and four artillery pieces from No. 7 Mountain Battery.[25] The objective of Goldney's column was to destroy two villages at the far end of the valley, Badelai and Shahi-Tangi. By 7.30 a.m. the Lancers had reached the end of the valley, dismounted and engaged a group of tribesmen spotted on a conical hill, who returned their fire. By the time this preliminary skirmish ended an hour later, the infantry had arrived. Goldney decided that the best plan of attack was for a company of Sikhs to move on Shahi-Tangi, while the Buffs attacked Badelai to the right.

Churchill joined the Sikhs for their attack on Shahi-Tangi. Seventy-five men from the Sikhs were detached from the main force to take the conical hill between the two villages while another company of around eighty-five men, including Churchill, were ordered to advance up the long, rocky spur that led to Shahi-Tangi. Churchill dismounted and advanced on foot for the final mile-long climb up to the village with the Sikh contingent. It was hard going, taking them two and a half hours to reach the village, and they arrived at around 11 a.m. The party met with little resistance on the way up, except for some intermittent sniping. 'Everybody condemned their pusillanimity in making off without a fight,' Churchill wrote of the tribesmen.

Having satisfied themselves that the village was deserted, the soldiers set fire to whatever would burn before being ordered to withdraw after fifteen minutes. But in their haste to reach the village, the Sikhs had inadvertently strayed beyond the safety of the cover provided by the mountain guns. They were now, as one officer noted drily, 'rather far from their supports'. This was just the kind of opportunity the tribesmen, who had taken a keen interest in the Sikhs' ascent to the village, thrived upon. The British force suddenly found itself isolated, and the tribes-men gathered to attack. As Winston and the other soldiers rested from the exertion of their morning climb, they found the eeriness of the deserted village disconcerting. 'We are rather in the air here,' remarked one of Winston's fellow officers. When Goldney eventually gave the order to retire, the enemy began to collect on all sides, and 'thereupon promptly attacked in force, and the Sikhs were driven back about a mile, to the foot of the spur', as the official account later recorded.[26] While Churchill and the Sikhs were fighting their way back to safety, another large group of tribesmen moved to the foot of the hills with the aim of cutting off their retreat. All of a sudden, Winston and his party found themselves in a position of the utmost peril. As he recalled in *My Early Life*, 'Like most young fools, I was looking for trouble, and only hoped that something exciting would happen. It did!'[27]

The tribesmen had kept themselves well concealed as the Sikhs made their advance towards Shahi-Tangi, but now they emerged in force to attack the retreating British:

> Suddenly the mountain-side sprang to life. Swords flashed from behind rocks, bright flags waved here and there. A dozen widely scattered smoke-puffs broke from the rugged face in front of us. Loud explosions resounded close at hand. From high up on the crag, one thousand, two thousand, three thousand feet above us, white or blue figures appeared, dropping down the mountain-side from ledge to ledge like monkeys down the branches of a tall tree. A shrill crying rose from many points. Yi! Yi! Yi! Bang! Bang! Bang! The whole hillside began to be spotted with smoke, and tiny figures descended nearer to us.[28]

The spur along which the British force was retreating consisted of three interconnected knolls. One group of Sikhs served as the rearguard and provided covering fire as the rest of their comrades withdrew from the village to the first knoll. Once this had been accomplished they in turn provided cover as the rearguard left the village to join them. The first manoeuvre was accomplished without incident, but as the Sikhs sought to repeat the ploy by moving to the second knoll they came under intense fire.

Churchill, another officer and eight sepoys were left to hold the second knoll and provide cover as the rest of the unit withdrew to the third knoll below. But when the turn came for Churchill's group to retire, they came under heavy fire from the advancing tribesmen, who had already seized the first knoll vacated by the retreating British. Up until this moment Churchill, unaware of the impending danger, had spent around five minutes taking what he called 'casual pot-shots' at the tribesmen from his protected position at the second knoll. Before leaving, he even insisted on picking up some unspent cartridges lying on the ground beside him, thereby observing the standing rule of the British army to let no ammunition fall into the hands of the tribesmen. Then, as Churchill's ten-strong group rose to complete their withdrawal to the third knoll, they were met with a well-aimed volley of fire from the tribesmen, which killed two, including Churchill's fellow officer, and wounded three others. As Churchill recalled,

> The rest of our party got up and turned to retreat. There was a ragged volley from the rocks: shouts, exclamations, and a scream. I thought for a moment that five or six of our men had lain down again. So they had: two killed and three wounded. One man shot through the breast and pouring with blood, another lay on his back kicking and twisting. The British officer was spinning round just behind me, his face a mass of blood, his right eye cut out. Yes, it was certainly an adventure.[29]

Winston and the other uninjured members of the party desperately tried to pull the wounded back to safety, but found they had no covering fire to protect them. Even so, as Churchill observed, 'It is a point of honour on the Indian frontier not to leave wounded men behind. Death by inches and hideous mutilation are the invariable measure meted out to all who fall in battle into the hands of the Pashtun tribesmen.'[30] The adjutant of the 35th Sikhs, Lieutenant Victor Hughes, hurried to the scene with a number of sepoys to assist with the recovery of the dead and injured, but was himself shot. Churchill and the other survivors continued to drag and carry the casualties down the hill, passing through a group of deserted houses on the way, with the tribesmen in hot pursuit. All the while the enemy continued to fire at the retreating British. 'The bullets passed in the air with a curious sucking noise, like that produced by drawing the air between the lips,' Churchill observed.[31] One of the Sikhs helping to carry the wounded along the spur was shot through the calf, causing him to shout out in pain. 'His turban fell off,' Churchill recorded, 'and his long black hair streamed over his shoulders – a tragic golliwog.' Now Churchill and another soldier tried to drag the injured Sikh to safety, but they treated him so roughly, dragging him across sharp rocks, that he pleaded to be allowed to go alone. 'He hopped and crawled and staggered and stumbled, but made a good pace. Thus he escaped.'[32]

Amid the heat of battle, Churchill reacted with blind fury when he caught sight of a group of Pashtuns about to launch a murderous assault on the injured adjutant and his rescuers. Four soldiers were trying to carry Hughes to safety when they were suddenly attacked by half a dozen Pashtun swordsmen. The bearers immediately dropped the adjutant and rushed for their lives. Churchill was aghast as 'the body sprawled upon the ground. A tall man in dirty white linen pounced down upon it with a curved sword. It was a horrible sight.'[33] Churchill could not bear to see his injured comrade hacked to death by the fanatical tribesman. As he recalls in *My Early Life*,

> I forgot everything else at this moment except a desire to kill this man. I wore my long cavalry sword well-sharpened. After all, I had won the Public Schools fencing medal. I resolved on personal combat *a l'arme blanche*. The savage saw me coming. I was not more than twenty yards away. He picked up a big stone and hurled it at me with his left hand, and then awaited me, brandishing his sword. There were others waiting not far behind him. I changed my mind about the cold steel. I pulled out my revolver, took, as I thought, most careful aim, and fired. No result. I fired again. No result. I fired again. Whether I hit him or not, I cannot tell. At any rate he ran back two or three yards and plumped down behind a rock. The fusillade was con-

tinuous. I looked around. I was alone with the enemy. Not
a friend was to be seen. I ran as fast as I could. There were
bullets everywhere.[34]

One reason Churchill thought it more prudent to use his
revolver than rely on his fencing skills was that, because of the
problem with his dislocated shoulder, he found himself at a distinct disadvantage during close combat. Churchill managed to
make good his escape, and scrambled his way down to the bottom
knoll, where a group of Sikhs was waiting to receive him.

Churchill's stirring account of his bravery on the field of
battle, written more than thirty years later, illustrates just how
close the young subaltern came to losing his own life or, at the
very least, suffering serious injury in his fierce encounter with
the Pashtun tribesmen of the North-West Frontier. Neither side
gave any quarter. In Churchill's more contemporaneous account
of the fighting in *The Story of the Malakand Field Force*, he concedes
that, 'Had the swordsmen charged home, they would have cut
everybody down. But they did not. These wild men of the
mountains were afraid of closing. The retirement continued.'[35]
The Pashtun fighters were skilled in the art of hit-and-run
attacks, but were less confident in taking the fight to the enemy.
At Shahi-Tangi, the failure to press home their superiority when
'they had the whole advantage of ground' enabled the survivors
of the British raiding party to reach the bottom of the spur and
regroup. Even so, the British sustained significant casualties. Of
the eighty-five or so men who had set off for Shahi-Tangi earlier
that morning, eight of the wounded were carried back to the
bottom of the spur, while the bodies of Lieutenant Hughes and
the other dead or wounded – estimated at a dozen – were left
to be cut to pieces by the tribesmen on the spur. Nearly one in
four of Churchill's unit had been killed or wounded during the
first hours of fighting against the Mohmands.

After the withdrawal from the spur had been completed,
the British position still remained perilous. The squadron of
Bengal Lancers was unable to come to the rescue, as it was

fighting the enemy further along the valley. The Buffs, meanwhile, who had been sent to attack the neighbouring village of
Badelai, were nearly a mile away. The Sikh ranks, which had
borne the brunt of the fighting at Shahi-Tangi, were becoming
increasingly agitated, despite the reinforcement of their numbers by another company that had been held in reserve.
Churchill noted that, as a 200–300-strong force of tribesmen
gathered in a wide and spreading half-moon around the British
flanks, the 'white officers' struggled to get the Sikhs to hold
their formation. There was a distinct possibility that the Sikhs
might break ranks and flee, leaving Churchill and his fellow
officers to their fate.

Fearing a mutiny, Goldney ordered Churchill to ride over to
the Buffs 'and tell them to hurry or we shall all be wiped out'.
Churchill was about to set off on his grey charger when he had
second thoughts: 'I saw in imagination the company overwhelmed and wiped out, and myself, an Orderly Officer to the
Divisional General, arriving the sole survivor, breathless, at top
speed, with tidings of disaster and appeals for help.' Fearful that
his personal courage would be questioned if the rest of the force
was destroyed, Churchill demanded to have the order in writing.
The colonel, taken aback by this unusual request, fumbled in
his tunic looking for his pocket-book. In the event, the note was
not required, for the British captain commanding the Sikhs
succeeded in restoring order to the ranks. At this point some-
body ordered the bugler to sound the charge. 'Every one began
to shout,' Churchill recorded. 'The officers waved their swords
frantically. Then the Sikhs commenced to move slowly forward
towards the enemy, cheering. It was a supreme moment. The
tribesmen turned, and began to retreat. Instantly the soldiers
opened a steady fire, shooting down their late persecutors with
savage energy.'[36]

Soon afterwards the Buffs arrived to lend their support to
the Sikhs. Goldney then took the decision to restore regimental
prestige by marching back along the spur to Shahi-Tangi and,

under the supporting fire of the mountain battery, recover the bodies of the slain adjutant and his comrades. It took another two hours to climb the spur and, when the Buffs reached the village at three o'clock, they destroyed all the remaining buildings and structures. Repeating their tactics of the morning, the tribesmen pressed heavily as the British made their second withdrawal from the village, but this time the Buffs put their Lee-Metford rifles to good use to keep them at bay, and the withdrawal was completed without further incident by a quarter to five.

Another company of the 35th Sikhs arrived to link up with Goldney's force. They had spent the day fighting on a mountain to the north-east of Churchill's party, and had suffered even greater casualties, sustaining around a dozen wounded 'and leaving several officers and about fifteen soldiers to be devoured by the wolves'. With the shadows of the evening starting to fall across the valley, the troops set off on the eight-mile return journey to camp at Inayat Kila, with Churchill joining the Buffs and the 'much-mauled' 35th Sikhs for the homeward march. It was a miserable end to what had been an exhausting day. Officers who fought with the Buffs that day recalled

> Thunder rolled overhead, and for a while, aided by the lightning that flashed continually, the enemy pressed on in small numbers, but no concerted effort was made to charge home. By 8 p.m. the troops were left to trudge wearily on to camp, the officers carrying men's rifles, and every available horse and mule bearing an exhausted British or Indian soldier. Since 6 a.m. the men had been marching and fighting with no more to eat than their early morning biscuit; utterly worn out the battalion reached camp at 9 p.m. just as there broke a violent storm of rain which turned the lines into a sea of mud.[37]

The action at Shahi-Tangi on 16 September 1897 provided Churchill with the front-line experience he had craved for so long. But it proved costly for the 2nd Brigade, which had suffered the highest casualty rate for an Anglo-Indian force in many years. Several officers around Churchill's age were killed or seriously wounded, while the 1,000-strong force that had set off to tackle the Mohmands that morning suffered around 150 casualties. The total number of tribesmen killed was estimated at 200. Shahi-Tangi was one of several skirmishes fought on 16 September, and Churchill found himself involved in fierce combat on several occasions, demonstrating courage and resolve in the face of a determined enemy, qualities he would display on many more occasions during his long and eventful life.

*

Three days after the fighting at Shahi-Tangi Churchill wrote to his mother from Inayat Kila providing a vivid account of his role in the skirmish. 'When the retirement began I remained till the last and here I was perhaps very near my end . . . this retirement was an awful rout in which the wounded were left to be cut up horribly by these wild beasts.' He recounted his role in trying to save 'poor Hughes's body', and how the fighting was so close at times that the tribesmen were able to throw stones at the retreating British. But his most important concern was for his conduct to have been noticed by his senior officers, so that he might receive 'some notice' – i.e. a decoration – particularly for his role in rescuing the wounded sepoy. 'My pants are still stained with the man's blood . . . I felt no excitement and very little fear. All the excitement went out when things became really deadly.' It was, said Winston, 'the biggest thing in India since Afghan war', and he hoped he would be suitably rewarded for his efforts.[38]

Churchill derived no great thrill from the experience of combat, but regarded it as a necessary part of fulfilling his ambition to pursue a career in politics. It was therefore essential that the commanders took note of his exploits, and to this end 'I rode my grey pony all along the skirmish line where everyone else was lying down in cover. Foolish perhaps but I play for high stakes and given an audience there is no act too daring or too noble. Without the gallery things are different.' After so many of his fellow officers were killed or seriously wounded, Churchill understood the risk he was taking, and cautioned his mother that, if he were to perish in his quest for glory, 'know my life has been a pleasant one, quality not quantity is after all what we should strive for. Still I would like to come back and wear my medals at some big dinner or some other function.'[39]

As Churchill had been assigned to Blood's divisional staff, the least he could expect was to receive the India Medal, which was awarded to all those who saw action on the subcontinent, though mainly for service on the North-West Frontier. But winning a decoration was another matter, and depended to a certain extent on being in the right place at the right time. The three Victoria Crosses awarded after Fincastle's adventure in the Swat Valley the previous month had been made for rescuing wounded men under fire. Churchill had demonstrated similar courage during the withdrawal from Shahi-Tangi. His problem, though, was that the skirmishing around Shahi-Tangi was not part of the main campaign undertaken by Jeffreys in the Mohmand Valley, and so would not receive official recognition. Fincastle's account of the fighting at Shahi-Tangi, for example, makes no mention of Churchill's involvement, merely recording that two companies 'got somewhat too far ahead of their support, and were attacked by the enemy in such large numbers that they were forced to retire about a mile. This movement was carried out under great difficulties. Hampered by their wounded, many of our men were unable to return the fire of the tribesmen, who swarmed round, pouring in heavy and disastrous fire at close quarters.'[40] And the only reference to Churchill in the official account of the operation relates to his role in informing his commanding officer of the heavy losses suffered by the 35th Sikhs during the withdrawal from Shahi-Tangi.[41] Because Jeffreys and other senior officers were occupied with operations elsewhere in the Mohmand Valley, it was Churchill's misfortune that there was no 'gallery' of senior officers to observe his display of courage under fire, and make the appropriate recommendation for an award.

A number of decorations were awarded for acts of valour on 16 September, but they mainly went to soldiers who accompanied Jeffreys. These were made for the dangerous moment when Jeffreys and his small group of Buffs became separated from the main force when a violent thunderstorm erupted as they were making their way back to Inayat Kila. Jeffreys, with a group of just under fifty men, was forced to seek refuge in the village of Bilot, which itself was still burning after the British had torched it earlier in the day. The tribesmen, seeing the British contingent in difficulty, launched a sustained attack on the village, at times firing at them from ranges of five to twenty yards. The Mohmands also hurled large stones from the rooftops, and Jeffreys himself received a severe blow from a stone which cut open the back of his head. The British were fighting for their lives until their absence was eventually noted by their comrades at Inayat Kila, and a relief column dispatched to drive off the tribesmen. Four of the ten British officers at Bilot were wounded in the fighting, including one who had his left hand smashed and another who was shot through both legs. 'Their faces, drawn by pain and anxiety, looked ghastly in the pale light of the early morning,' Churchill recorded. 'The brigadier, his khaki coat stained with the blood from a wound on his head, was talking to his only staff-officer, whose helmet displayed a bullet hole.'[42] In the space of twenty-four hours Churchill had received a crash course in the reality of frontier warfare. 'I saw for the first time the anxieties, stresses and perplexities of war,' he wrote many years later. 'It was not apparently all a gay adventure.'[43]

The fighting at Bilot resulted in the award of three Victoria Crosses, two Distinguished Service Orders and four Distinguished Conduct Medals, as well as a number of Indian Orders of Merit. The valour shown by the officers and men fighting alongside their brigade commander was no different from that displayed by Churchill at Shahi-Tangi. But while Jeffreys could see with his own eyes the heroism of the men fighting alongside him in the besieged village, Churchill's own acts of courage had taken place on a remote mountainside far from his commander's gaze.

Churchill's conduct at Shahi-Tangi did not altogether go unnoticed, however. In the dispatch written by Major General Sir Bindon Blood on the action of 16 September, which contained a report of the action from Brigadier General Jeffreys, it was noted that Jeffreys 'has praised the courage and resolution of Lieutenant W. L. S. Churchill, 4th Hussars, the correspondent of the *Pioneer* newspaper with the force who made himself useful at a crucial moment'.[44] In his memoirs, Blood is even more praiseworthy: 'He was personally engaged in some very serious work in retirement, and did excellent work with a party of Sikhs to which he carried an order, using a rifle from a severely injured man.'[45] Churchill may have missed out on a decoration, but he had received a mention in dispatches, which ranks just below a medal. As Churchill himself wrote when he received news of the coveted mention in dispatches a few weeks later, 'I am more ambitious for a reputation for personal courage than anything else in the world. A young man should worship a young man's ideals.'[46]

After the exertions of the 16th, the brigade spent the following day catching up on much-needed rest. Churchill took advantage of the respite to deal with correspondence and write his next batch of articles for the *Daily Telegraph*. Churchill sent two more letters from Inayat Kila, which appeared in consecutive editions of the newspaper on 14 and 15 October. Both articles were again published under the headline 'War in the Indian Highlands', with the byline 'By A Young Officer'. The first article, datelined 'Camp Inayat Kili [*sic*], Sept. 17', recounts the Mohmands' initial attack on Jeffreys's 2nd Brigade, and how

it prompted Blood to order the punitive expedition in the
Mohmand Valley. Churchill's account of his participation in
the fighting appears in the second dispatch, which was written
at Inayat Kila on 18 September. It reads almost like a draft
version of *The Story of the Malakand Field Force*, with parts of the
article, such as the description of a tribesman in 'dirty-white
linen' hacking the unfortunate Hughes to death, being repeated
verbatim in the book. It also contains a gripping account of
the fighting at Shahi-Tangi, which was no doubt well received
by the newspaper's readers as they digested the report of the
unnamed 'young officer' over their breakfast tables back home
in Britain.

Having risked his life on the North-West Frontier, Churchill
succeeded in fulfilling many of his youthful ambitions. First and
foremost, he had demonstrated to himself and his peers that he
possessed the all-important virtue of courage to the extent that,
in times of peril, he was prepared to sacrifice his life in the
service of others. As Randolph S. Churchill remarked, 'All his
life Churchill thought that military service was an essential
ingredient of a political career,'[47] and proving to himself that he
had the courage to confront danger was an enormous consolation for someone who had set his heart on a political, rather
than a military, career. The man who would become one of the
world's greatest wartime leaders had looked death squarely in
the eye, and lived to tell the tale. His mention in dispatches,
while not equal to decorations like the Victoria Cross, nevertheless secured his reputation for bravery. At the very least he was
guaranteed a campaign medal, and perhaps even a couple of
clasps. And through his vivid articles for the *Daily Telegraph* he
had displayed a talent for descriptive prose and observation that
set him apart from the other ambitious young officers of his
generation. While Winston complained that his columns bore
no signature, by dint of Jennie's relentless social networking no
one of any consequence in London high society was left in any
doubt as to the true identity of the anonymous 'young officer'

responsible for the colourful dispatches adorning the *Telegraph*'s columns.

Any sense of personal triumph Churchill may have felt about his own performance under fire, though, was tempered by the knowledge that others had not been so fortunate. The following day he attended the funerals of the soldiers and men who had lost their lives on the 16th – those, that is, whose bodies could be recovered. The remains of Lieutenant Hughes, for example, were never returned, and his sacrifice is today commemorated in a simple memorial at St Thomas the Martyr Church, Oxford, located only a few miles from where Churchill himself is buried at St Martin's in Bladon. The inscription reads, 'To the glory of God and in loving memory of Lieutenant Victor Hughes ... killed in action at Shahi-Tang whilst leading his men against the Mamunds on the frontier of India, 16th Sept. 1897.' Back at Inayat Kila, Churchill found the simple service for those whose bodies were recovered deeply moving. 'There were no Union Jacks to cover the bodies, nor were volleys fired over the graves, lest the wounded should be disturbed ... Looking at these shapeless forms, coffined in a regulation blanket, the price of race, the pomp of empire, the glory of war appeared as the faint insubstantial fabric of a dream, and I could not help realising with Burke: "What shadows we are and what shadows we pursue".'[48]

CHAPTER EIGHT

A SPLENDID EPISODE

'Unfortunately all fighting must be attended with loss of life.'
Winston S. Churchill, 2 November 1897

After the mauling the 2nd Brigade received at the hands of the Mohmands, Blood sent orders that the force was to stay put in the valley and, in Churchill's words, 'lay it waste with fire and sword in vengeance'.[1] The British, who had known little about the occupants of this remote region prior to the engagement, had seriously underestimated the strength of the enemy, in terms of both their numbers and the effectiveness of their weaponry. Many of the tribesmen were equipped with breech-loading Martini-Henry rifles, which had either been captured from British soldiers in battle or supplied by agents working for the duplicitous Afghan amir in Kabul. Although inferior to the new Lee-Metfords supplied to the British infantry, they were none-theless highly effective in the hands of expert Afghan snipers, and well suited to their tactic of firing at British positions from their protected sanctuary in the surrounding hills. The tribes-men had acquired another twenty-two of these highly prized weapons following the intense fighting of 16 September, and the British made it one of their primary objectives to recover all the captured weapons and ammunition.

Before the 2nd Brigade could begin the next phase of operations, the soldiers needed time to recover from their exertions, and come to terms with the full extent of their losses. The tribesmen were clearly better organized and posed more of a threat than the British had reckoned, and subduing the tribes would be no easy feat. 'No one knew . . . that these tribesmen were as well-armed as the troops, or that they were the brave and formidable adversaries they proved themselves,' remarked Churchill.[2]

The campaign against the Mohmands recommenced on the morning of 18 September, and continued for two weeks as the 2nd Brigade moved methodically through the valley, burning crops, levelling houses, destroying wells and reservoirs and blowing up fortifications. Churchill participated in a number of these actions, accompanying either the Buffs or the Guides cavalry, and returning each evening to Inayat Kila, where he spent his time writing further dispatches for the *Daily Telegraph*. The routine was much the same each day. Units from the brigade would move out at 5.30 a.m. and, employing a combined force of cavalry, infantry and artillery, would capture and destroy a village before returning to camp at Inayat Kila by nightfall. The campaign resumed with an attack on Damadola on 18 September, followed by assaults on Zagai on the 20th, Dag on the 22nd and Tangi on the 23rd.

For the attack on Damadola, the entire brigade was deployed so as not to repeat the mistakes of the 16th, when the troops had been too thinly spread. The Guides led the assault on the village itself, which was entered without a fight. The sappers and miners then moved in, followed by 400 transport mules. While the pack animals were loaded with the grain the villagers had stored for the winter, the sappers busied themselves preparing the towers and village defences for destruction. The Buffs, meanwhile, remained in the open fields south of the village, ready to prevent the enemy from trying to intervene in any way. When a group of tribesmen was spotted gathering on a nearby hill, the artillery opened fire. At about midday, when all the pack mules had been loaded up and safely withdrawn from the village, the sappers detonated their explosives. 'A great cloud of thick brown-red dust sprang suddenly into the air, bulging in all directions,' Churchill recorded. 'The tower broke in half and toppled over. A series of muffled bangs followed. The dust-cloud cleared away, and nothing but a few ruins remained.'[3]

At this moment the tribesmen appeared in force on the surrounding hills, and started to attack the British positions. But a few rounds from the mountain battery soon put them to flight before the Guides climbed up the face of the mountain to make sure it had been cleared of the enemy. Churchill joined a Guides company during this operation and came across the body of a tribesman who had been killed during the fighting.

> We found him sitting by a little pool, propped against a stone. He had been an ugly man originally, but now that the bones of his jaw and face were broken by pieces of bullet, he was hideous to look upon. His only garment was a ragged blue linen cloak fastened at the waist. There he sat – a typical tribesman, ignorant, degraded and squalid, yet brave and warlike; his only property, his weapon, and that his countrymen had carried off. I could not help contrasting his intrinsic value as a social organism, with that of the officers who had been killed during the week.[4]

In contrast to their tactics on the 16th, the British now undertook a well-organized and orderly withdrawal from the village, with the retirement of each company covered by the fire of others, thereby denying the tribesmen the opportunity to outflank the retiring troops, and by 1.30 p.m. the force was safely back at Inayat Kila. On this occasion the casualties were few, with the British force suffering just two dead and six wounded.

For the next few days the campaign proceeded in similar vein, with the brigade moving out in force each morning against a designated target, rather than trying to take on too much at once. On the 19th the British attacked the villages around Bilot, where Jeffreys's force had been besieged on the night of the 16th, although they met little resistance. At Bilot they discovered that the tribesmen had disinterred the bodies of the Muslims who had fought with the British, and mutilated them. Throughout these operations the political officers kept a wary eye out for the brown-clad 'retainers', or followers, of Umra Khan, the agent of the Afghan amir who was constantly inciting the local tribes to continue their rebellion against the British. Deane and the other political officers were particularly concerned with Umra Khan's fighters, who were all armed with Martini-Henry rifles and wore brown cloaks to distinguish themselves from the local fighters. Their presence at Zagai at the head of the valley, from where they smuggled weapons and supplies to the tribesmen from Afghanistan, was deemed vital to sustaining the revolt, as some of the less fanatical tribes were keen to sue for peace, particularly after the British began laying waste to their villages. A tribal delegation approached the British, saying they were prepared to make an unconditional surrender if their villages were spared. The British responded that they would only negotiate if a *jirga* of all the tribes was convened, and demanded the immediate return of the twenty-two Martini-Henry rifles captured on the 16th as a demonstration of the tribes' goodwill.

The British approach to pacifying militant Pashtun tribesmen in the 1890s had many similarities to the counter-terrorism strategy for Afghanistan set out by US President Barack Obama in his address to the West Point Military Academy in December 2009. By applying intense military pressure against the Taliban fighters, Obama believed that the 'surge' strategy would result in the Taliban losing interest in fighting the Americans and their NATO allies, and entering into negotiations to resolve Afghanistan's long-running civil war. Lieutenant General Sir Graeme Lamb, a British officer attached to US General Stanley McChrystal, the commander of the NATO force, said the purpose of NATO's military operation was to hit the Taliban 'till their eyes bleed', so that they were forced to come to the negotiating table.[5] During the next two years the Taliban suffered thousands of casualties as NATO maintained the military pressure against their fighters, but persuading them to come to the negotiating table to discuss ending the conflict proved to be more problematic.

While the moderate tribal leaders of the Mohmand Valley sought to persuade their kinsmen to comply with the British demands, Jeffreys maintained the military pressure by launching an attack against Zagai, nine miles from Inayat Kila. The cavalry protected the flanks while the brigade marched straight up the valley until it came to within a mile and a half of Zagai, which, like Damadola, lay on the lower slopes of a high hill. By making skilful use of the brigade units, the attack was successful and the entire village was destroyed. Furthermore, the tribesmen suffered significant losses when they tried to attack the retreating soldiers. On the return march to Inayat Kila, the brigade paused to destroy a fort that Umra Khan's followers had used to support the uprising. Churchill was convinced members of the amir's army had crossed the Durand Line from Afghanistan to act as military advisers to the Mohmands, as 'numerous figures in khaki uniform' were spotted on the slopes around Zagai, and appeared to be directing the movements of the tribesmen.

The involvement of so many outside parties made it difficult for the local tribes to sue for peace, as the amir continued to offer money and arms to any tribesman who was prepared to fight the British. As Churchill noted, 'Their valley was in our hands; their villages and crops were at our mercy; but their allies [i.e. the Afghans], who suffered none of these things, were eager to continue the struggle.'[6] These 'allies', moreover, had the Martini-Henry rifles whose immediate return the British demanded, as maintaining the prestige of the empire dictated that the British continued with their military operations until all the rifles were recovered. In an attempt to end the fighting, the British persuaded a friendly tribal elder to arrange a meeting with the hostile Mohmand tribes. The message came back that, while they were interested in holding a peace *jirga*, it was difficult

17. Sir Bindon Blood posing with his senior officers during the Malakand campaign.

18. A British cavalry unit crossing the Swat river at the start of the campaign.

19. Frontier tribesmen laid in wait to launch their attacks on British soldiers passing through narrow gorges.

20. The Fort at Chakdara, which guarded a key crossing point at the Swat river, was besieged for several days at the start of the Malakand rebellion.

21. Major Edmund Hobday's sketch of the relief of Chakdara. Churchill was deeply irritated that his great rival Viscount Fincastle secured Hobday's sketches for his own account of the Malakand campaign.

22. Colonel William Meiklejohn and the officers who organized the successful defence of Malakand Fort in August 1897.

23. British officers
attached to the
Malakand Field Force
in relaxed mode.

24. A group of native
soldiers take up defensive
positions in readiness for
the tribesmen's attack.

25. Camels and mules transporting vital supplies through the daunting terrain of the North-West Frontier.

26. Hobday's sketch of tribesmen firing at the British camp under cover of darkness.

27. 'To encourage their friends': Hobday's depiction of the tribesmen waving their banners as they launch an attack on British positions.

28. A family portrait of Viscount Fincastle, Churchill's great rival for military honours and journalistic scoops. (Kindly provided by Sir Angus Stirling, his grandson.)

29. Most of the engagements between British soldiers and the tribesmen were fought at close quarters.

30. The sign outside Churchill's room at Malakand Fort where he wrote his first *Daily Telegraph* dispatches, with his name spelt incorrectly.

Part

I have already described the Indian service camp and the "sniping" with out which no night across the frontier could be complete. I shall therefore only notice two points which were previously omitted as they looked suspiciously technical. As the night firing is sometimes varied by more serious attacks and even actual assaults & sword makes, it is thought advisable to have the ditch of the entrenchment towards the enemy. Modern weapons notwithstanding the ultimate appeal is to the bayonet and the advantage of being on the higher ground is then considerable.

When a battery forms part of the line ⑥ round a camp, infantry soldiers should be placed between the guns. Artillery officers do not like this; but, though they are very good fellows, there are some things in which it is not well to give way to them. Everyone is prone to over-estimate the power of his arm.

In the Mamund valley all the fighting occurred in capturing villages which lay in rocky and broken ground in the hollows of the mountains and were defended by a swarm of active riflemen. Against the quickly moving figures of the enemy it proved almost useless to fire volleys. The tribesmen would dart from rock to rock exposing themselves only for an instant, and before the attention of a section could be directed to them & the rifles aimed, the chance & the tribesman would have vanished together. Better results were obtained by picking out good shots and giving them permission to fire when they saw their opportunity without waiting for the word of command. But speaking generally infantry should push on to the attack with the bayonet without wasting much time in firing, which can only result in their being delayed under the fire to arrange so long as the British continued to mount daily attacks against them. To break the impasse, Blood agreed to a forty-eight-hour armistice, which he hoped would allow the tribes enough time for their *jirga*.

Both sides used the break in hostilities to take stock. For the British, the main priority was to reinforce the 2nd Brigade, which had suffered serious losses during the first week of campaigning against the Mohmands. The Buffs, 'who were full of fever', and the 35th Sikhs, who had borne the brunt of the casualties, were withdrawn and replaced with 1,000 reinforcements from the Royal West Kent Regiment and the 31st Punjab Infantry. Churchill took advantage of the break to catch up with his correspondence and write some more articles for the *Daily Telegraph*. With the reorganization of the 2nd Brigade he was now attached to the 31st Punjabis as an emergency measure. The Punjabis, who had themselves been involved in heavy fighting, had suffered significant losses and, besides their colonel, had only three white officers left. Blood writes in his memoirs that the Punjabis' colonel specifically requested Churchill to replace an officer who had been invalided out of the campaign through injury. 'He was most useful for several weeks,' Blood recalled, 'though he only knew a few words of the language. The Sikhs took to him at once, recognising immediately that his heart was in the right place.'[7] Many years later Churchill remembered that, of all the military units he served with in Asia, Africa and Europe, 'this Punjab Infantry business' was the oddest experience because of the language barrier. 'I had to proceed almost entirely by signals and dumbcrambo. To these I added three words, "Maro" (kill), "Chalo" (get on) and Tally Ho! Which speaks for itself. However, in one way or another we got through without mishap three or four skirmishes ... There was no doubt they liked to have a white officer among them when fighting, and they watched him carefully to see how things were going. If you grinned, they grinned. So I grinned industriously.'[8]

At Inayat Kila, Churchill made a lasting impression on some of his fellow officers. Captain Ernest Maconchy, of the East Yorkshire Regiment, recalled that Winston provided him with a detailed account of the mauling the 35th Sikhs had suffered on the 16th.[9] Another officer, Lieutenant Donald A. D. McVean of the Manchester Regiment, recorded in his diary entry for 25 September 1897: 'Churchill, son of Late Randolph Churchill who is with Blood arrived from front and shares my tent for the night on his way down as his leave is finished.' McVean later recalled that Churchill was 'quite fearless in going about in the considerable action seen by the Malakand Field Force and that the only thing Churchill was frightened of was getting wounded in the mouth so that he could not talk'.[10]

As they rested, the troops received a message from Queen Victoria expressing her sympathy at the sufferings of the wounded and satisfaction at the conduct of the troops, which was warmly received by all concerned. Churchill, like all the other soldiers participating in the operations of the Malakand Field Force, had been surprised by the intensity of the fighting and the high casualty toll. For example, the mountain battery, which had supported the 2nd Brigade's attacks on the Mohmand villages, had been reduced to four guns, having lost half its officers, a third of its mules and a quarter of its men in just a week of fighting. Thus the Queen's message provided a timely fillip for all concerned, 'but particularly to the native soldiers, who heard with pride and exultation that their deeds and dangers were not unnoticed by that august Sovereign before whom they know all their princes bow', Churchill recorded.

*

The next batch of *Daily Telegraph* articles, also written at Inayat Kila, continues Winston's narrative of the 2nd Brigade's operations against the Mohmands. Because of the difficulty of getting his copy to London from a remote corner of the North-West Frontier, these articles were not published in chronological order, but rather as they arrived at Lawson's Fleet Street office. The next dispatch, which was published on 2 November 1897, was written on 23 September and is datelined 'The Camp, Inayat Kila'. It describes the relief of Jeffreys's force after the fighting at the village of Bilot on the night of the 16th. As with Churchill's other accounts of the fighting, much of the detail later appears in *The Story of the Malakand Field Force*. Even so, Churchill demonstrates his precocious talent for war reporting, reassuring his readers:

> The situation here need cause no anxiety at home. There are difficulties and dangers on the Indian frontier, as in many parts of the British Empire. These difficulties and dangers are being faced with skill, courage and composure. Unfortunately all fighting must be attended with loss of life. But the ultimate issue is certain, and Continental Powers who watch with jealous elation the obstacles with which England is confronted in India may be assured that the strong and vigorous spirit that conquered an Empire in the past will be sufficient to maintain it in the future.[11]

The next article in the series, published on 6 November, was written on 12 September, when Winston was travelling with Blood and had not yet been assigned to the 2nd Brigade. Under the heading 'The Imperial Question', it analyses the events leading up to Britain's involvement in the North-West Frontier, in which he argues the British had no alternative other than to pursue the Forward Policy so as to prevent the Russians from occupying the 'No-man's land' of the border region. So far as Winston is concerned, 'It is very doubtful whether it was ever possible to avoid it. The frontier policy makes itself, and is dictated by circumstances rather than by men.'[12] In the last of this batch of articles, written at Inayat Kila on 28 September, Churchill details the 2nd Brigade's raids against a number of Mohmand villages in the run-up to the ceasefire, noting, 'As long as things are going on all right, as long as Fortune smiles and discipline prevails, few people are killed. But a slip, an omission, an accident swiftly expands the casualty list to a very different proportion.' He reserves particular praise for the Buffs, and the accuracy of their firepower as they covered the with-drawal of British forces from one of the destroyed villages: 'At the bottom of the hill the Buffs took up the duty of rear-guard, and the deliberate care with which the fire of that terrible weapon the Lee-Metford, with its more terrible dum-dum bullet, was directed effectually checked any pursuit.' In this article Churchill expresses his disgust at the tribesmen for disinterring the bodies of Muslim soldiers who had fought for the British at Bilot:

> These tribesmen are among the most miserable and brutal creatures on earth. Their intelligence only enables them to be more cruel, more dangerous, more destructive than the wild beasts. Their religion – fanatic though they are – is only respected when it incites to bloodshed and murder. Their habits are filthy, their morals cannot be alluded to. With every feeling of respect for that wide sentiment of human sympathy which characterises a Christian civilisa-tion, I find it impossible to come to any other conclusion than that, in proportion as these valleys are purged from the pernicious vermin that infest them, so will the happiness of humanity be increased, and the progress of mankind accelerated.[13]

Despite his loathing for the tribesmen's conduct, Churchill was uneasy about Britain's policy of subjecting the tribes to collective punishment, and he took issue with government min-isters who made misleading statements whenever the issue of village-burning was raised in the Commons. Some politicians, fearful of a public outcry, were reluctant to confirm that entire villages had been laid waste, and instead claimed that only those properties belonging to rebellious tribesmen were destroyed. Churchill himself had no qualms about destroying the tribesmen's property, for he saw it as the only remedy open to the British in a conflict where the enemy regularly retired into the hills, making it impossible to follow them. 'Of course it is cruel and barbarous, as is everything else in war, but it is only an unphilosophic mind that will hold it legitimate to take a man's life, and illegitimate to destroy his property.' What irked him, though, was the government's deliberate attempt to deceive the public about its policy, which Churchill believed led to misconceptions and 'extraordinary ignorance' among the British people about what was really taking place. To Churchill's mind, 'The people of our islands only require to have the matter put fairly before them to arrive at sound, practical conclusions.' [14]

The Mohmands, meanwhile, took advantage of the break in the fighting to put their own affairs in order. It soon became apparent to the British that the tribal leaders, for all their protestations to the contrary, had no real interest in striking a deal. The British continued to insist that, before peace talks could commence, the tribes must first hand over fifty guns 'in proof of their earnest desire for peace'. Delegations from the tribes came and went from Inayat Kila saying that they needed more time, and pointing out the many difficulties that were involved in organizing a *jirga*. As British patience began to wear thin, a group of tribesmen arrived with '50 old and useless *jezails*', but when they were told they must provide weapons that were in current use, they continued to procrastinate. Deane and the political officers soon received intelligence reports that the Mohmands, rather than organizing the *jirga*, were using the time to prepare for an attack on Inayat Kila. To this end they devoted most of their time moving property from their villages to the hills, so that it would survive the next round of fighting. Other tribesmen, meanwhile, took advantage of the truce to sow as much land as possible, 'for if their sowing operations were delayed much longer, no spring crops could have been obtained'.[15]

On 29 September the British finally lost patience and

Jeffreys, making full use of the 2nd Brigade's newly arrived reinforcements, resumed operations against the Mohmands. A dozen villages in the centre of the valley were destroyed, and more than thirty forts belonging to the local tribes blown up. On each occasion stores of grain, wood and other supplies were removed and sent to Inayat Kila before the sappers detonated their charges. On the first day of operations the brigade suffered no serious casualties, but on the 30th it experienced stiffer resistance when it moved to attack the villages of Agrah and Gat, eight miles to the north of Inayat Kila. 'These two villages occupied a very strong position on the lower slopes of the great spur which divides the head of the valley,' the British report stated. 'Long rocky spurs strewn with enormous boulders guarded the flanks of the two villages, while between them is a small rugged spur with precipitous sides, covered with large rocks.'[16] The villages were located within a few miles of the Afghan border and, as the British began to advance through terraced fields at around 8.45 a.m., they were confronted by thousands of tribesmen who had taken up defensive positions around the villages. The Guides cavalry assumed a holding position in the fields, while the Guides infantry, supported by the Royal West Kents and Churchill's unit from the 31st Punjabis, continued to advance.

From his position with the 31st Punjabis, Churchill had an uninterrupted view of the fighting, which quickly became the fiercest engagement the British had experienced since 16 September. The tribesmen were well protected in their *sangars*, small dugouts fortified with piles of stones and rocks, and the Guides infantry, which led the assault, came under intense fire as they made a brisk approach on the village. 'The bullets kicked up the dust in all directions, and whistled viciously through the air,' Churchill observed. The Guides quickly closed in on the enemy positions and, when they got to within a hundred yards, fixed bayonets and prepared to storm the *sangars*. Locally raised companies of Afridi and Pashtun Guides, 'uttering shrill cries of exultation, culminating in an extraordinary yell, dashed forward, climbed the hill as only hillmen can climb, and cleared the crest'. The tribesmen fled in the face of the sustained assault, and many were shot down before they could find shelter, 'their fall greeted by strange little yells of pleasure from the native soldiers'.[17]

After this initial success, the fighting took a more serious turn when the West Kents arrived at the village outskirts, and encountered stiff resistance. Very soon they were fighting at close quarters with the tribesmen, and even when the West Kents were joined by the 31st Punjabis, they still struggled to keep the tribesmen at bay. The mountain battery tried to relieve the pressure by firing at the slopes above the village from where the enemy was pouring fire on the attacking force, but it soon became apparent that the British were outnumbered and in danger of being overrun. At one point a company that had stormed a *sangar* on the outskirts of the village suddenly found itself surrounded by the enemy, whose fire was accurate and intense. With four or five of those caught in the *sangar* either killed or wounded, the company was ordered to retire. It was at this point that Second Lieutenant William Browne-Clayton, who had become close friends with Churchill during the campaign, tried to organize the withdrawal, including the dead and injured, and was the last to leave. As he did so he was shot dead, the bullet severing the blood vessels in his heart. Churchill, who was involved in a furious fight of his own with the 31st Punjabis, was powerless to intervene as comrades of the mortally wounded Browne-Clayton tried to prevent his body being hacked to pieces by the vengeful tribesmen. As the soldiers tried to pass his body over a rock wall, they were charged by a group of thirty Ghazis, forcing them to abandon Browne-Clayton's body and escape down the hill.

The West Kents then dispatched a reserve company to retrieve Browne-Clayton's corpse, and they succeeded in clearing away the enemy, although they sustained a further five or six injured in the process. The 31st Punjabis, meanwhile, where Churchill was stationed, also came under heavy fire, with the tribesmen venturing at times to within a hundred yards of the British positions. The Punjabis directed their attack on a great mass of boulders that were being tenaciously held by the enemy. Lieutenant Colonel James O'Bryen, a forty-three-year-old frontier veteran who had fought in the Second Afghan War in 1879 and in Burma, as well as the 1895 Chitral campaign, supervised the assault, and impressed Churchill by leading from the front: 'Moving swiftly from point to point, he directed the fire and animated the spirit of the men, who were devoted to him.' But O'Bryen's inspired leadership soon caught the attention of the enemy's marksmen, and, having escaped a number of near misses, he was eventually 'shot through the body and carried mortally from the action'.[18] By this time both villages had been set ablaze by the British troops and, finding his force under continuous enemy fire, Jeffreys gave the order to withdraw, which was undertaken under the cover of shrapnel shells fired by the guns of the mountain battery. Not wishing to risk their luck against the cavalry squadrons that were covering the retreat, the tribesmen did not follow up and decided to hold their ground. The attack on the two villages cost the British dear: two officers and two men killed, six officers and twenty men wounded. Among the Indian contingent, seven were killed and twenty-three wounded.

Churchill, who spent five hours under fire, emerged unscathed, but he was deeply affected by the experience, particularly the death of his friend Browne-Clayton. In *The Story of the Malakand Field Force* he gives a matter-of-fact account of his friend's death. But several months after the fighting, when recalling the incident in a frank letter to his mother, he writes how he broke down in tears when he saw Browne-Clayton's body being returned to camp on the back of a mule. 'I cried when I met the Royal West Kents on the 30th Sept and saw the men really unsteady under fire and tired of the game, and that poor young officer Browne-Clayton, literally cut to pieces on a stretcher,' he confided to Jennie.[19] The horrific nature of warfare made a deep impression on Churchill during the two weeks he spent fighting the Pashtuns on the North-West Frontier, one that was to remain with him for the rest of his life. Having survived the fierce fighting on 16 September, he was equally fortunate not to suffer serious injury on the 30th. Of the 1,200 men who fought with the Malakand Field Force, 245 were killed or wounded – including twenty-five officers. 'This has been the hardest fighting on the frontier for forty years,' Churchill wrote to his mother from Inayat Kila on 2 October. 'The danger and difficulty of attacking these hill men is extreme. They can get up the hills twice as fast as we can – and shoot wonderfully well with Martini-Henry rifles. It is war without quarter.'[20]

Riding back to Inayat Kila, Churchill passed a convoy carrying the dead and injured back to camp. The dead were strapped to mules, with their heads on one side of the animal and their legs on the other. 'The long black hair of the Sikhs, which streamed down to the ground, and was draggled with blood and dust, imparted a hideous aspect to these figures . . . At the entrance to the camp a large group of surgeons – their sleeves rolled up – awaited the wounded. The operating tables, made of medical boxes, and covered with waterproof sheets, were also prepared. There is a side to warfare browner than khaki.'[21] The loss of so many of his fellow officers and comrades caused Churchill to reflect on the risks inherent to a military career. In other callings, such as politics, business or the arts, a person who conducted themselves properly and worked hard could look forward to advancement, while successful pursuit of a military career depended to a large extent on luck. It did not matter how many times a soldier had been under fire, each time he took to the field his chances of being killed were the same. He was saddened by the death of Colonel O'Bryen, a career officer with a record of distinguished service who had been destined for further promotion. But his career was cut short when he met, as Churchill remarked, 'as fine an end as a soldier can desire' fighting the Mohmands. The life of O'Bryen, who was buried with full military honours at Peshawar, is now commemorated by a simple, brass plaque erected by his fellow officers at St John's Church, Peshawar, while the body of Browne-Clayton rests in the overgrown cemetery on the out-skirts of the old British fort at Malakand. This is where Churchill himself may well have been laid to rest had fate taken a different course.

*

The fighting at Agrah and Gat was Churchill's final involvement in the campaign against the Mohmands, and soon afterwards both the campaign and Churchill's involvement in it began to wind down. The operations in the Mohmand Valley were part of Blood's wider campaign to pacify all the rebellious tribes to the north of Peshawar. While Jeffreys concentrated on subduing the Mohmands, Blood focused his attention on the tribes of the neighbouring Swat and Bajaur districts, to make sure they did not provide support for the Mohmand revolt. Although the Swat tribes, which had initiated the attack on Malakand, agreed to renounce violence, Blood did not trust them, and feared they might switch allegiance at any moment. The tribes of the adjoining Bajaur district, meanwhile, were being encouraged by the Hadda Mullah, another fanatical Muslim cleric, to rise up against the British. Desperately short of forces, Blood opted to remain at the strategically important town of Nawagai, thereby making sure the local Khan of Nawagai remained pro-British, and that the Hadda Mullah's followers were unable to link up with the Mohmands.*

---

* Nawagai, which is now located on Pakistan's border with Afghanistan, has retained its strategic importance to this day. After the September 11 attacks, Nawagai became the centre of intense fighting between the Pakistani security forces and al-Qaeda sympathizers who had sought refuge in the village after

Blood's decision to remain at Nawagai until the arrival of reinforcements from Peshawar attracted the attention of the local tribes, who started to gather at the Bedmanai Pass, eight miles from Nawagai, with a view to launching an attack. Hundreds of followers of the Hadda Mullah started to arrive, and they were soon joined by a number of Afghan fighters, who had been sent to support the attack by the amir.[22] The tribesmen calculated that if Blood's troops could be forced out of Nawagai, then Jeffreys's 2nd Brigade in the Mohmand Valley would find itself isolated and outflanked, and in serious jeopardy of being destroyed. Churchill says the Hadda Mullah incited his followers to attack the British by promising that no bullet would harm them if they attacked, and that they would always be honoured and respected for their part in defeating the infidel. The Taliban makes similar promises to persuade today's young Afghans and Pakistanis to become suicide bombers.

A 4,000-strong enemy force soon assembled on the outskirts of Nawagai, and the British received intelligence that they planned to attack on the night of 20 September. Blood recalled, 'As it got dark about 8 p.m., we dined early so we had everything ready for the enemy.'[23] The attack duly commenced at around 9 p.m., with some of the tribesmen firing into the camp from the surrounding hills while the mass of the enemy attempted to storm the camp. 'Determined and vigorous sword charges' took place all around the camp, Churchill reported, but the superior firepower of the defenders, together with their discipline, meant they were able to hold off the attackers, who suffered a heavy defeat and 'retired to their hills in gloom and disorder'.[24] Blood's casualties amounted to one killed and thirty-one wounded, while estimates of the enemy dead stood at around 330.

Blood's rout of the Hadda Mullah's followers enabled him

---

they were driven from Afghanistan. There were also a number of clashes with the Taliban that involved both the Pakistani military and US drone strikes.

to reassess his priorities, especially when long-awaited reinforcements arrived from Peshawar the following morning. The failure of the tribesmen's assault at Nawagai, one British official concluded, 'had a most beneficial effect all over the country', as the Hadda Mullah's followers realized they were no match for the firepower of the British guns, and rapidly dispersed to the neighbouring hills.[25] Those who had travelled from Afghanistan to support the uprising – the 'trans-frontier men' as the British called them – fled back across the border to Kunar. Blood sent a force to clear the remnants of Hadda Mullah's followers from the Bedmanai Pass, before deciding to join up with Jeffreys with the intention of bringing the Mohmand operations to a successful conclusion. Blood arrived at Inayat Kila on 2 October determined to finish the job, having wired the government, 'I am now crowding every man and gun on the decisive point, and if no unforeseen complications arise, I hope there will be an end of the Mamund difficulty in a few days.'[26]

Blood maintained the brigade's offensive, destroying the village of Badelai, which had been the scene of the intense fighting on the 16th. Even at this late stage in the campaign the Pashtuns continued their defiance, and a 3,000-strong force of tribesmen attempted to cut off the withdrawal of Blood's force from the village. The British responded with heavy fire, including the use of two batteries firing shrapnel shells – a forerunner of the modern-day cluster bomb – which fired hundreds of bullets at the enemy on impact. Even so the attack on Badelai cost the British twenty men killed and wounded. Blood was making the final preparations to return to Agrah and Gat, which had been only partially destroyed during the fierce fighting of the 30th, when the tribes, realizing that more British reinforcements were on the way, 'recognised that Government were determined to insist on their complete submission and that therefore continued opposition on their part would merely bring upon them further loss and heavier punishment'.[27] The operations of the Malakand Field Force were at an end and the business of negotiating a settlement with the tribes could now begin in earnest.

Major Deane arrived at Inayat Kila on 4 October to oversee the talks, having previously concluded an agreement with the tribes of the Swat Valley. As part of the surrender terms, the 'Swatis', as the British called them, agreed to return the sword of Lieutenant Robert Greaves, the *Times of India* correspondent who had been killed fighting alongside Fincastle. Realizing the game was up, the leaders of the Mohmand tribes approached the pro-British Khan of Nawagai, asking him to obtain peace on the most favourable terms. Other local khans also agreed to join the negotiations, and for the next few days military operations ceased in order to give the peace talks a chance of success.

While Deane immersed himself in the negotiations, Churchill continued with his regimental duties during early October, as well as catching up on correspondence and writing another batch of newspaper articles. Despite the suspension of military operations, there remained the possibility that they might resume if the talks failed and, as a precaution, the cavalry continued to undertake daily reconnaissance missions. Churchill joined the cavalry squadrons on some of their patrols, which on occasion came under sporadic fire from disgruntled frontiersmen. Churchill, a cavalryman through and through, was deeply impressed by the professionalism of his comrades as they collected valuable information about this remote corner of the North-West Frontier. Indeed, his admiration for the cavalry was such that he devoted a whole chapter of *The Story of the Malakand Field Force* to extolling what he calls 'The Work of the Cavalry', in which he urges the government to appreciate the value of maintaining a significant number of cavalry regiments. At times the chapter reads like a recruiting brochure when he writes, 'To the young man who wants to enjoy himself, to spend a few years agreeably in a military companionship, to have an occupation – the British cavalry will be suited.'[28]

When not on patrol Churchill spent his spare time writing

war reports for the *Daily Telegraph*. In an article published on 26 October 1897 and datelined 'Inayat Kila, Oct. 2', he provides a full account of the fierce fighting at Agrah on 30 September. Its most noteworthy passage concerns Churchill's accusation that the Afghan amir, Abdur Rahman, was personally responsible for inciting the tribes to rise against the British. 'I cannot refrain from suggesting that the proximity of the Afghan frontier and of this Afghan army may perhaps explain how it was that the defenders of an obscure village were numbered by thousands, and the weapons of a poverty-stricken tribe were excellent Martini-Henry rifles.'[29] Another dispatch, published on 13 November and datelined 'Inayat Kila, Oct. 6', sees Churchill taking issue with those 'so foolish to imagine that the day of the cavalry is over', and rehearses many of the arguments in defence of the cavalry that were soon to appear in his book of the campaign.[30]

Churchill's first war was drawing to a close. As Deane negotiated with the Mohmands, Winston went down with a fever and a temperature of '103 and an awful head'. Even so he still maintained his demanding writing schedule. Writing to his mother on 2 October, he confided that the campaign had been a war without quarter. 'They kill and mutilate everyone they catch,' he wrote of the Pashtuns, while the British 'do not hesitate to finish their wounded off'. He continued, 'I have seen several things which have not been very pretty since I have been up here – but as you will believe I have not soiled my hands with any dirty work – though I recognise the necessity of some things.'[31] During his stay on the North-West Frontier he had been under fire several times, and had made a good impression on Blood, who wrote to Colonel Brabazon, Churchill's former mentor in the 4th Hussars: 'I have put him in as he was the only spare officer within reach, and he is working away equal to two ordinary subalterns. He has been mentioned in despatches already, and if he gets a chance will have the VC or a DSO – and here such chances have sometimes gone begging.'[32] To which Brabazon commented, 'I am sure there's *grit* in that boy.' Brabazon, who owned a large Irish estate and had himself fought with distinction in the Second Afghan War, was very much in favour of continuing the campaign until the resistance of the tribes had been totally crushed. 'I do hope we are not going to make idiots of ourselves, let these fellows off easily,' he wrote to Winston's mother. 'They will cause us endless trouble unless we grind them to dust and disarm every man Jack of them. Personally I should destroy their crops and burn their villages and let them die of starvation and cold.'[33]

This was not the view held by Deane and the other officials of the Indian government, whose primary concern was to ensure peace and stability on the North-West Frontier. As Deane explained to the tribal elders during the preliminary meetings to discuss a settlement, he believed the tribesmen had suffered quite enough already. They should be allowed to rebuild their lives so long as they agreed to submit to British rule and surrendered the requisite number of guns. The last shots in the operations of the Malakand Field Force were fired on 6 October, when a cavalry patrol had a small brush with a group of Pashtun tribesmen, which resulted in one Indian trooper being slightly wounded. After that, all efforts were concentrated on the peace *jirga*, which duly took place at Nawa Kila, half a mile from the main camp, at 3 p.m. on 11 October. The *jirga* opened with the rebellious tribal leaders making their formal submission to Blood, who was accompanied by Deane as well as a number of pro-British khans from the locality. After much arguing, the tribes agreed to return the twenty-two Martini-Henry rifles captured during the fighting on 16 September. They also returned two officers' swords and a lance.

The negotiations slowly moved towards a conclusion. The tribesmen expressed their regret for the uprising and declared that they now desired a lasting peace. They acknowledged that they had lost very heavily in killed and wounded, but argued that they would never have taken up arms in the first place had they not feared the British were planning to annex their territory. To allay their fears, the British delegation agreed to give them a written undertaking that they had 'no desire' to annex their country, so long as the tribes behaved themselves. The elders then raised their familiar complaint about the Durand Line, which they argued, with some justification, 'cut their country in half'. Blood was less willing to be drawn on the Durand Line issue, stating that this was 'an imperial question' and one that was not open for discussion. The general's only comment was that the British would never tolerate Afghan interference on the British side of the border. This reassured the Pashtun participants at the *jirga*, who resented the constant meddling in their affairs by Umra Khan and the amir's other agents. All the parties agreed that Umra Khan's 'gang' should be sent back across the border to Afghanistan, never again to return to Mohmand territory. 'With uplifted hands the whole *jirga* then rose and swore with acclamations to abide by their agreement,' a British official present at the meeting recorded. 'Thus the durbar, which merely lasted for some fifteen minutes, brought to a conclusion the operations against the Mamunds, whose undeniable bravery and good fighting qualities had much impressed every British officer opposed to them.'[34]

With the conclusion of the negotiations, Umra Khan and his followers returned across the border to Afghanistan, where they continued to enjoy the patronage of the amir, and persisted with their attempts to incite the tribes to launch fresh revolts against the British until Umra's death in 1903. Today his flag is proudly displayed in the fort which is now home to the Chitral Scouts, one of the paramilitary units responsible for keeping the peace on the Afghan border. Umra Khan's descendants, meanwhile, are now located in the frontier town of Dir, where they set up the local Taliban movement. Umra Khan himself is not regarded with any great fondness among the Chitralis, as he is remembered as an invader whose only concern was to further his own interests. 'He invaded Chitral to occupy the area, enslave the people and annex the region to his own fiefdom,' explained a professor at the Chitral Academy. 'He was an agent of the Afghan amir, which is why the local people didn't trust him. He was always writing letters to the British asking for money and weapons, offering his obedience to the British in return.'[35]

Churchill's brief participation in the Malakand Field Force was at an end. The conflict had been hard and brutal. During the course of the month-long campaign the 2nd Brigade alone had suffered nearly three hundred killed or wounded – around 20 per cent of the combat force – while the total number of tribesmen killed or seriously injured was in the thousands. Before the negotiations finished Churchill had already been informed that his presence was no longer required, as his regiment desired him to return to Bangalore to resume his normal duties. Being Winston, the idea of returning to sleepy Bangalore after all the excitement he had experienced on the North-West Frontier filled him with dread. Once the Malakand campaign was wound up, another expedition was to be organized to tackle the tribes in the Tirah region west of Peshawar, where the Afridi tribesmen were in revolt. The Tirah Expeditionary Force was to be led by General Sir William Lockhart, another veteran of the North-West Frontier, and Churchill strained every sinew to get himself attached to Lockhart's force, rather than return to the torpor of Bangalore. Blood had no objection to his young protégé joining the Tirah force, but his application did not meet with the approval of the military establishment in Calcutta and Churchill's regiment in Bangalore, which believed he had enjoyed his fair share of excitement and should knuckle down to his regimental duties rather than indulging his indomitable passion for fame and glory. Lockhart declined Churchill's request to join his force with the result that, on 9 October, Winston began the long and tedious journey back to Bangalore.

*

Churchill left Inayat Kila with a convoy of the sick and wounded which was escorted by the Royal West Kents. The party crossed

the Panjkora river on the 11th, and Churchill then rode to the
rail terminal at Nowshera. He arrived the following day and
then had to wait for five days before boarding the train to
Bangalore. While waiting for his train, he summed up his
experiences on the North-West Frontier in a letter to his mother:
'I have seen two or three sharp skirmishes and have now been
10 complete times under fire. Quite a foundation for political
life.' He revealed that he was planning to write a book and
would need her help to get it published: 'I know the ground, the
men, and the facts. It is a fine idea . . . I have earned my medal
and clasp fully. Blood says not one in a hundred have seen as
much fighting as I have – and mind you – not from the staff or
a distance but from the last company of the rearguard every
time. A splendid episode.'[36]

At Nowshera Churchill wrote the last batch of his fifteen
articles for the *Daily Telegraph*, which were published on 19
November and 3 and 6 December. The first is an account of his
journey from Inayat Kila to Nowshera with the sick and
wounded, while the second provides a more detailed consideration of the military tactics the British employed during the
Malakand campaign. He meditates on the superiority of mule
transport over camel transport, because 'the mule moves faster,
and can traverse more difficult ground. He is also more hardy,
and keeps in better condition.' He gives a detailed analysis of
the difficulties British troops encounter when withdrawing under
enemy fire, praises the introduction of the 'tremendous' dum-
dum bullet, and criticizes the effectiveness of the artillery 'which
did very little execution'.[37] The series of articles concludes with
an assessment of 'the old frontier policy', where he argues the
British have no alternative than to persist with their occupation
of the tribal belt. 'It is unfortunate for the tribesmen that our
spheres of influence clash with their sphere of influence,' he
writes. But 'it is impossible to go back. Indeed, bearing in mind
the unrest in India, the hostility in Afghanistan, the irritation
of the frontier tribes, and the possibility of further Russian

encroachments, it seems that retrocession is made impossible by the sheer force of solid, concrete, materialised facts. We must therefore go on.'[38]

Churchill arrived back at Bangalore to a civil, if somewhat cool, reception from his regiment. 'I found a very general opinion that I had had enough leave and should now do a steady spell of routine duty.' He immediately sat down at his writing table in his old room to write a more detailed account of the Malakand campaign while it was still fresh in his mind. 'I saw a great many people killed and wounded,' he told his mother, 'and heard many bullets strike all round or whistle by – so many that had I counted them you would not perhaps believe me.' He vented his anger at the military authorities for not allowing him to join the Tirah expedition, complaining that 'they had been very disagreeable indeed to me' by deliberately blocking his attempts to join the force. After six weeks fighting on the frontier, he had become a firm supporter of the Tories' Forward Policy, which he believed would ultimately result in the annexation of the tribal lands. The sentiments he expressed to Jennie were the same as those in his final *Daily Telegraph* article: 'Now we are started we can't go back and must go on . . . Financially it is ruinous. Morally it is wicked. Militarily it is an open question, and politically it is a blunder. But we can't pull up now. Annexation is the word which the B.P. [British Public] will have ultimately to swallow, and the sooner they do it, the sooner things will begin to mend.'[39]

Back in Bangalore, Churchill found it hard to settle into the mundane routine of regimental life. Soon after his return the regiment set off for its autumn training schedule, where Winston took part in 'sham' fights firing blank cartridges, when only a few weeks previously he had been fighting for his life. 'It seemed very odd to hear the cracking rifles on all sides, and nobody taking cover or bobbing their heads.'[40] Nor was his mood improved when the cuttings of his dispatches for the *Daily Telegraph* arrived, and he discovered they had been published

without his name attached. 'I will not conceal my disappoint-
ment at their not being signed,' he told Jennie when the cuttings
arrived. 'I had written them with the design, a design which
took form as the correspondence advanced, of bringing my
personality before the electorate. I had hoped that some political
advantage might have accrued.' Churchill was furious that all
his hard work had been in vain, and that the amount the 'stingy
pinchers' at the *Telegraph* were offering to pay barely covered his
travelling costs. Quoting Dr Johnson's aphorism 'No one but a
blockhead ever wrote except for money', he told his mother
that, rather than accept the £75 'old Lawson' was offering
for the fifteen articles, she should hold out for £150. He also
expressed his irritation that glaring misprints had occurred,
which was not surprising, given the difficulties of getting dispatches from the North-West Frontier to Fleet Street. In one
article, for example, the word 'frequent' had appeared where he
had written 'pregnant', and in another 'exterminate' was printed
instead of 'extricate'. He further complained that ten lines were
cut from one of his dispatches to enable it to fit into a single
column, thereby spoiling the balance of the concluding sentence.
The novice journalist had all the makings of a literary prima
donna, and Churchill did not lack for confidence so far as his
own writing ability was concerned. He told Jennie some of the
dispatches were 'the best things I have ever written', and he was
anxious to hear what someone with a good literary education
thought of them. 'I feel plenty of confidence in myself now and
am certain that I shall do something in the world – if physical
injury does not befall me.'[41]

Churchill was keen to capitalize on his month-long adventure fighting the Mohmands. He had risked his life to gain
public recognition and lay the foundations for a career in
politics. As his *Daily Telegraph* articles were unsigned, he decided
the best way to bring his exploits to the public's attention was
by writing a book, which he believed 'would of course sell well
and might do me good'. The only drawback was that, prior to

leaving for Malakand, he had already started work on something else, a novel called *Savrola*, which was eventually published in 1900. Very much a young man's novel, the allegorical tale features a dictator, President Antonio Molara, who is challenged by Savrola, a man of the people. Savrola leads a democratic effort to restore political liberties and enlists the help of Molara's beautiful wife, Lucile, a character clearly inspired by his own mother. 'She had arrived at that age of life when, to the attractions of a maiden's beauty, are added those of a woman's wit. Her perfect features were the mirror of her mind, and displayed with every emotion and every mood that vivacity of expression which is the greatest of woman's charms.'[42] *Savrola* ends with Molara being killed during a violent revolution, allowing the hero and Lucile to be united in love.

Churchill was torn between continuing work on *Savrola*, which he considered was 'full of promise', or starting work on an entirely new book. In the end he decided to write an account of the Malakand Field Force, not least because he hoped it might earn him some much-needed cash. Money concerns continued to plague both Winston and his mother, and when he heard that another young officer, who had written an account of the 1895 Chitral campaign, had 'made a large sum of money by his book', he resolved to do the same. 'I do not see why I should not make an account of the much more severe fighting we experienced equally interesting.' It was, he conceded, a 'great wrench' to shelve *Savrola*, but he believed his new project, which was to be called 'The Story of the Malakand Field Force' and dedicated to Sir Bindon Blood, needed to be published at the earliest opportunity while the subject was still fresh in the minds of the public. He even decided on the quotation from Lord Salisbury, the Tory prime minister, he wanted printed on the front cover, to the effect that frontier wars are 'but the surf that marks the edge and the advance of the wave of civilisation'. Writing the book was a means of 'repairing the non signature of my letters' for the *Daily Telegraph*. And it would establish his reputation, as he believed it 'will yield substantial results in every way, financially, politically, and even, though do I care a damn, militarily'.[43]

Churchill began work on the book on 10 November, and embraced the challenge with his customary enthusiasm. His mother was given responsibility for soliciting the views of all the key participants – politicians, diplomats, soldiers – in London so that he could understand the broader context of the campaign. From Bangalore he wrote to all the colonels and political officers he knew on the North-West Frontier asking them to provide their own views on the conflict. In a sustained burst of activity, he wrote from three to eight hours a day in the scorching heat of Bangalore while his fellow officers napped or played cards. Previously he had spent a great deal of his spare time in Bangalore reading and writing, but he found the task of writing a proper book was far from easy. 'Quite a hole is worn in my second finger by it,' he complained. Putting together a comprehensive account of the campaign was a laborious process, requiring 'hard labour and frequent polishing'. He was inspired to even greater effort by the unwelcome news that his rival Viscount Fincastle had decided to write a book of his own about the campaign. Winston regarded this as 'a great nuisance', because the subject matter was 'so small that there is not room for two books on it'. Fincastle further annoyed him by persuading Major Edmund Hobday, a skilful artist who had witnessed all the operations, to illustrate his book, when Winston had hoped to secure the sketches for his own work. 'Fincastle has not altogether treated me civilly in the matter and he has neither answered my letters nor informed me of his intention to write an account. With many qualities he is not a good sort. I shall not give way.'[44] It now became a race against time between the two soldier-authors to see which account was published first. Winston aimed to have his manuscript completed by the end of the year, and told Jennie that it must then be published at once. He was ambitious for something 'better than the railway bookstalls. However I daresay I take an inflated view of everything.'

*

Authorship was not the only activity that occupied Churchill's time during this frenetic period. His regimental duties continued to make demands on his time, especially the annual inspection of the regiment undertaken by Lieutenant General Sir Mansfield Clarke, commander of the troops in Madras. Clarke made his inspection of the 4th Hussars in late October, and reported that the horses were in a creditable state and that much effort had been undertaken 'to get the saddlery into proper order'.[45] Winston took an active role in the regimental polo team, and took part in a tournament at Hyderabad in December where he played well and scored eleven of the sixteen goals, even though he complained afterwards about the inconvenience of participating when he was so busy with other matters. Nor did his confinement at Bangalore in any way dim his desire to enter politics. One of his first remarks to Jennie after returning to Bangalore was to lament the fact that he had not been available to contest a vacancy in a Lancashire constituency because he was away fighting. He pestered Jennie to find him a seat, even expressing an interest to stand for his father's old Paddington constituency if it became vacant.

In the absence of any political openings, Churchill continued lobbying to be allowed to join the Tirah campaign against the Afridi tribesmen around Peshawar. Failing that, he revived his campaign to go to Egypt and join Kitchener's expedition in the Sudan. 'I do not feel justified in neglecting any opportunity of adding to my experience,' he told Jennie shortly after celebrating his twenty-third birthday in Bangalore. '"Fame" sneered at, melodramatised, degraded, is still the finest thing on earth. Nelson's Life should be a lesson to the youth of England. I shall devote my life to the preservation of this great Empire and to trying to maintain the progress of the English people.'[46]

For all these distractions, Churchill managed to complete the book in less than two months, posting the manuscript to his mother on 31 December 1897. He asked Jennie to find him a publisher, which she was only too happy to do. She had already made sure that everyone in London high society knew the identity of the anonymous author of the *Daily Telegraph* dispatches, including Arthur Balfour, George Curzon and the Prince of Wales, people whom she believed might be helpful to Winston in later life. Balfour, the man Churchill had earlier that year dismissed as a 'languid, lazy, lackadaisical cynic',[47] helped to introduce Jennie to the literary agent A. P. Watt in January 1898. Watt had read Churchill's *Daily Telegraph* dispatches, and was impressed by the 'conspicuous ability' of his prose. Within a week Watt had placed the book with the publisher Longman, who aimed to publish it at the earliest opportunity. To save time, Churchill asked his mother to request her brother-in-law, Moreton Frewen, to review the proofs, rather than having them sent out to India. He hoped the book would make him around £300, which would ease his financial difficulties considerably. He was still seething over the *Daily Telegraph*'s refusal to increase the fee for his Malakand articles, and was angered further when he finally received a cheque for Rs1,238 – about £80 – in early January. 'I think they are most mean – and that the reward is altogether inadequate to the value or interest of the letters.'[48] He took consolation from the knowledge that some of the dispatches had been printed on the paper's front page. Now he hoped his book would raise his public profile and launch his career in politics.

The Story of the Malakand Field Force: An Episode of Frontier War, which was dedicated to Sir Bindon Blood with a handsome portrait of the general on the frontispiece, was published in mid-March 1898, at about the same time that Fincastle's own effort on the subject was made available by Methuen. Fincastle's account also contained a frontispiece of the general and was simply dedicated 'To Blood'. Churchill, who resented Fincastle's encroachment on a subject he wanted exclusively to himself, was dismissive of his rival's contribution. 'I don't think Lord Fincastle has taken much trouble over his book,' he told Jennie. 'Some people have written one chapter, some another. Slipshod. But he never takes life seriously.'[49] Churchill's own approach to authorship was hardly a model of professionalism. The draft manuscript of the book, parts of which are now held at the Churchill Archive in Cambridge, show that, between passages written in his neat handwriting, he simply pasted portions of his *Daily Telegraph* articles. It was a formula he retained for the rest of his writing life, regularly recycling in his books passages he had written in newspaper articles and even, on occasion, reusing them for articles in other publications. Writing would become Churchill's most profitable occupation in the course of his long life, earning him much more than he received for his political activities.

Thanks to Jennie's assiduous courting of Fleet Street's leading editors, the book was favourably received, even if Churchill, who from the outset of his literary career took a meticulous interest in the editing process, was appalled at the number of basic errors contained in the final manuscript. Moreton Frewen had made a terrible hash of correcting the proofs, allowing many errors of spelling, punctuation and poor word choice, prompting Winston to nickname him 'Mortal Ruin'. Churchill, stuck in Bangalore, was furious about the number of 'gross and fearful blunders' that had appeared in the printed edition, although they do not seem to have affected its reception by the reviewers. The *Athenaeum* noted in its review: '*The Story of the Malakand Field Force* needs only a little correction of each page to make its second edition a military classic.' *The Times* called the book 'an extremely interesting and well-written account' and noted, 'The author shows a keen insight into frontier questions and his outspoken comments frequently go straight to the mark.'[50]

In terms of sales, the book fulfilled Churchill's expectations, earning him a handy sum. In addition to the initial advance of

£50, the equivalent of £3,000 in 2012, he received an additional £100 for every 2,000 copies sold. The print run amounted to 6,500 copies in the course of the first year, which meant that, taken together with his earnings from the *Daily Telegraph* and *Allahabad Pioneer*, he had a healthy bank balance for the first time in his life.

The money was useful, but it was not Churchill's primary reason for writing the book. Winston's priority was to advance his political prospects, so he was gratified to receive a number of favourable letters from people of influence, including George Curzon, who was soon to become Viceroy of India, and the Prince of Wales, whom Churchill had already engaged in personal correspondence from Bangalore. The future King Edward VII read Churchill's accounts in the *Daily Telegraph* and wrote Winston a fulsome letter of praise: 'I cannot resist writing a few lines to congratulate you on the success of your book. I have read it with the greatest possible interest and I think the descriptions and the language are generally excellent. Everybody is reading it, and I only hear it spoken of with praise.'[51]

Churchill was delighted with the book's reception. Its success meant that his daring gamble of getting Blood to take him to fight on the North-West Frontier had paid off. The book, the newspaper articles, his mention in dispatches; all helped to confirm Churchill's position as one of the most promising young officers of his generation. It meant his name was firmly planted in the national consciousness, which would be an enormous benefit when the time came for him to enter politics. He could also look forward to the prospect of a lucrative literary career, for within weeks of publication of *The Story of the Malakand Field Force* he received offers to write a biography of his father, and another about his great ancestor, the Duke of Marlborough, both of which he accomplished later in life. 'I have faith in my pen,' he confided in Jennie. 'I believe the thoughts I can put on paper will interest and be popular with the public.'[52]

CHAPTER NINE

A ROUGH HARD JOB

'I took every chance and displayed myself with ostentation
wherever there was danger.'
Winston S. Churchill, 2 December 1897

Churchill had mixed feelings about the outcome of the Malakand campaign. On a personal level, it had been a great success.
He had achieved his goal of building his reputation with the
British public, and it enabled him to undertake further military
adventures in Africa. But he had also experienced at first hand
the brutality of modern warfare and had seen many friends
and colleagues killed. The cruel death of Browne-Clayton had
moved him to tears, and he was under no illusion that, despite
their military superiority, the British campaign could hardly be
deemed a success. The tribesmen, he concluded, 'have been
punished, not subdued; rendered hostile, but not harmless. Their
fanaticism remains unshaken . . . the riddle of the frontier is still
unresolved.'[1]

There have been many changes in the hundred or so years
since Churchill fought on the Afghan border, but the 'riddle of
the frontier' remains as problematic for the modern generation
of soldiers fighting the Pashtun tribesmen on the North-West
Frontier as it was in the 1890s. In Pakistan it is no longer known
as the North-West Frontier, but has been renamed Khyber
Pakhtunkhwa, the Land of the Pashtuns of the Khyber. The
renaming was part of Pakistan's attempt to make the country's
Pashtun population feel more integrated, and to head off any
attempt by Pashtun nationalists to revive their calls for an

independent Pashtunistan state. But the tribal areas, a narrow belt of territory that occupies a significant proportion of Pakistan's border with Afghanistan, retained the semi-autonomous status that was granted to them by the British at the end of their military operations in the late 1890s.

George Curzon, the family friend of the Churchills who became Viceroy of India in 1899, did not subscribe to Churchill's claim that the Forward Policy was the only effective means of controlling the border. Churchill went so far as to argue that annexing the entire Pashtun area south of the Durand Line to India was the only viable solution. 'Military rule is the rule best suited to the character and comprehension of the tribesmen,' Churchill wrote in his conclusion to *The Story of the Malakand Field Force*. 'They will soon recognise the futility of resistance, and will gradually welcome the increase of wealth and comfort that will follow a stable government.'[2] Curzon, a thoughtful, if arrogant, administrator who confessed to being 'an imperialist heart and soul', was not persuaded by the views of a young subaltern with an eye for self-promotion. Even Churchill conceded that the cost of annexing the border area was prohibitive, and Curzon reasoned that the presence of thousands of British troops in the tribal belt was at the same time a provocation to the tribes and a liability to the government of India, which had to pay for their upkeep. Curzon, who wrote a personal letter to Churchill congratulating him on the publication of his book, was determined to end what he called the 'infatuated nonsense' of the Forward Policy.

Curzon was the architect of the border policy that was to keep the peace on the frontier for a century or more. In exchange for agreements that were individually tailored to the tribes' needs, the British granted the Pashtuns a large degree of autonomy on the understanding that they agreed not to oppose or interfere with British interests. After all the toil and bloodshed Britain had expended in its attempts to bring peace and stability to the Afghan border, it was Curzon's blueprint that brought the unrest to an end, and reached an accommodation with the tribes that lasted until the American-led intervention in Afghanistan of 2001.

Curzon's first act, in 1901, was to create the North-West Frontier Province as a new administrative framework for the settled areas of northern India. He then proceeded to negotiate a series of treaties with individual tribes, granting them self-government in return for undertakings that they would not threaten British interests in India. Curzon, who felt he had a good understanding of the Pashtun tribes, travelled through the tribal belt and personally agreed terms with the leaders. He respected the Pashtuns, with whom he was already familiar from his travels through the frontier before becoming a minister in Lord Salisbury's government. 'They are brave as lions, wild as cats, docile as children,' Curzon wrote of the Pashtuns in 1900. 'You have to be very frank, very conciliatory, very firm, very generous, very fearless.' He believed he had the perfect formula for keeping them in their place. The key to keeping the peace with the Pashtun tribesman was 'to leave him alone where his country is not wanted for purposes of Indian defence; where it is, to enlist and employ him in looking after his own country, and after the roads and passes which it is necessary for us to keep open; to pay him and humour him when he behaves, but to lay him out flat when he does not'.[3]

Curzon's reforms succeeded in pacifying the region, as well as reducing significantly the cost of conducting expensive military operations against the tribes. Compared with the £4.5 million that had been spent on military operations on the frontier between 1894 and 1898, the total amount spent during Curzon's longer rule as Viceroy (1899–1905) was £250,000. Curzon's settlement with the frontier tribes survived virtually uninterrupted until the start of the twenty-first century. Apart from governing their own affairs, they were also given responsibility for administering justice according to the code set out in the Frontier Crimes Regulations that Curzon finalized in 1901. The Frontier Corps, comprising seven militias and scout units (one for each of the tribal areas) was established to keep the tribes in check, with famous regiments such as the Khyber Rifles given responsibility for guarding specific areas, such as the vital passes leading into Afghanistan.

The British had to deal with one brief uprising after the implementation of Curzon's reforms. The revolt was orchestrated by the new Afghan amir, Amanullah, at the end of the First World War. But the unrest was quickly suppressed, particularly after the newly formed Royal Air Force sent two Sopwith Camels to bomb the rebellious tribesmen, an early version of the drone strikes in use today. These primitive aircraft flew so low through the mountain passes that the tribesmen were able to shoot down on them from their vantage points. Relations between Britain and Afghanistan eventually stabilized after Nadir Shah established a new ruling dynasty in Kabul in 1929 that provided Afghanistan with a rare, forty-year period of peace and prosperity until the country was plunged into its most recent cycle of conflict and instability with the Soviet invasion of 1979.

The North-West Frontier and the tribal areas voted overwhelmingly to become part of Pakistan when the country won independence during the partition of the Indian Empire in 1947, but the new Pakistani government showed little interest in meddling with Curzon's arrangements. Dr Humayun Khan, a Cambridge-educated civil servant who served as Pakistan's political officer at Malakand in the late 1960s, explained that there was no appetite in Islamabad to change Curzon's frontier policy. 'There was something comfortable about the status quo concerning the tribal areas so we did very little to accelerate the process of change,' explained Dr Khan, who fulfilled the same role as that undertaken by Major Harold Deane in the 1890s. 'The tribals like having things their own way, and it is best not to disturb them unless you have to.'[4]

There were occasions when the authorities in Islamabad felt

compelled to intervene, such as during the 1960s when the Khan of Dir – a direct descendant of the tribal leader who had provided support for the Malakand campaign – was accused of conspiring with the Afghans against the Pakistani government. The Khan was deposed in 1961 and sent into exile in Lahore, where he eventually died. The other big change to the region was the Pakistan government's decision to annex the Swat Valley in 1969. But until the intervention of NATO forces in neighbouring Afghanistan in late 2001, the region was relatively calm. In 1961, during an official tour of Pakistan by the British royal family, the Queen paid a visit to the old British fort at Malakand, from where she sent a brief telegram to Sir Winston Churchill, who was then approaching his ninetieth birthday, offering her best wishes from the scene of one of his youthful triumphs. Prince Philip, meanwhile, spent the day duck shooting in the Swat Valley.

*

The tribal system set up by Curzon survived until 2004, when the Pakistani military, under pressure from Washington, began its own offensive to tackle the tribes, which were accused of supporting the Taliban in its resistance against the coalition forces in Afghanistan. Until that point, the Pashtun communities on the Pakistan side of the border had thrived, and the tribes had cleverly exploited their quasi-autonomous status, for example by not paying taxes, to make their fortunes. They have succeeded in both business and politics, too: modern Pakistan's road transportation industry is dominated by Pashtun-owned companies, and three of Pakistan's post-independence presidents have been Pashtuns. As one envious Pakistani government official remarked, 'With all the exemptions the Pashtuns enjoy they can make a lot of money. They are not subject to the laws of Pakistan like everyone else, so they have it pretty good. That is the real reason they are so reluctant to change the status quo.'[5]

When America launched its campaign to overthrow the Taliban government, Washington was, in effect, declaring war
on the Pashtun tribes who lived on both sides of the Afghan-
Pakistani border. In areas such as the Mohmand Valley, where
Churchill had fought, the tribes had still not come to terms with
the division of their lands by the Durand Line, and their interests
were affected as much by events taking place in Kabul as they
were by those in Islamabad. During the Taliban's rise to power
in Afghanistan in the 1990s, an estimated 10,000 tribesmen from
the Malakand area travelled across the border to Afghanistan to
fight alongside them. After the US-led intervention, an estimated
30,000 Taliban fighters were driven back across the border to
Pakistan's tribal belt, where they helped to incite a fresh frontier
rebellion against the regime of President Pervez Musharraf, the
dictator who was widely regarded in Pakistan as Washington's
stooge. Many Pakistanis resented American interference in their
affairs, and believed that Washington's insistence on confronting the tribal belt was a mistake. 'The British army never tried
to control the tribes,' explained an experienced Pakistani military officer. 'The Pakistan army had the same attitude, but the
Americans did not like our laissez-faire approach.'[6]

The Pakistani government responded to the Taliban's challenge by deploying 150,000 troops to restore order to the tribal
area, and all the old frontier forts, such as Malakand, were once
again brought into action to contain the first major tribal
rebellion on the frontier for a century. Many of the old British
cavalry regiments, such as the 15th and 19th Lancers which
today form part of the Pakistan army's Armoured Corps, found
themselves returning to their former battlefield haunts.

Malakand today is situated on the border between the
province of Khyber Pakhtunkhwa and the Federally Administered Tribal Agencies (FATA), and the old fort once again finds
itself located at the epicentre of the new campaign against the
frontier tribes. The structure of the fort at Malakand has not
changed much from Churchill's day, as I discovered when the

Pakistan military allowed me to visit the camp in the autumn of 2012. It took just three hours to drive from Rawalpindi to Malakand along the new M1 motorway, and as I made my way through the well-cultivated plains that lead to the foothills of the Hindu Kush I thought of Churchill sitting anxiously in his padded railway carriage wondering whether he would make it to the frontier in time to see some fighting. These days the British-built railway line has fallen into disuse, and the dusty road from Nowshera to Malakand is no longer filled with the plodding tongas that carried Winston on the final stage of his marathon journey to the front. The local Pashtun tribesmen now travel in noisy, three-wheeled motorized rickshaws known as Qingqis after the company set up to manufacture them 'with the sole objective to provide vehicles for everyone at [an] affordable price'.[7]

It was hard not to feel the same sense of foreboding that Churchill must have experienced as I embarked on the climb from Dargai, the last low-lying town in the settled area of the plain. The road to Malakand was blocked by a military check-point manned by heavily armed Pakistani troops, who carried out detailed searches of every vehicle and its contents. Just as when Churchill arrived at Malakand, the area remains a hotbed of anti-government violence, and travellers are frequently subjected to random kidnappings and the perils of roadside bombs. The journey must have been daunting for Churchill who, having undertaken a much more arduous expedition, faced the very real prospect of engaging in mortal combat when he finally arrived. To make the twenty-minute drive from Dargai to Malakand, the Pakistani military deemed it necessary to provide me with a heavily armed escort, as British visitors are rarely seen in this troubled part of the world. My guide, a lieutenant colonel in a Pakistani tank regiment, was friendly enough, and was intrigued when I explained the purpose of my mission. 'We have fond memories of the British Empire,' the officer remarked. 'It was the best empire in the history of the world. But when Mr

Churchill was here they always hesitated about taking on the tribesmen because they caused so much trouble.'⁸

When we eventually arrived I was greeted by a sign bearing the words, 'Malakand Fort 1896', and many of the buildings in the compound, which was under construction at the time of the Malakand Field Force, dated back to Churchill's era. In the colonial-style officers' quarters, which enjoy a panoramic view of the surrounding mountains and neatly cultivated valleys, a small plaque – with Churchill's name spelled incorrectly – has been placed outside the room where he wrote his first batch of *Daily Telegraph* articles.

The inscription reads: *Churchil Room: Sir Winston Churchil ex British prime minister stayed in this room during 1897 as a war correspondent.* But that is the extent of the British memorabilia. Inside the room, a neat and spacious accommodation with whitewashed walls and a disused fireplace, a copy of the Koran and prayer mat were tidily stored on the bed, the possessions of a Pakistani officer with the 1st Battalion, Free Kashmir Regiment. Elsewhere, the temple used by the Sikh sepoys who fought so heroically during the siege in August 1897 had been turned into a dormitory for Pakistani soldiers, while the display cabinets in the mess where Churchill first acquired a taste for whisky were filled with trophies commemorating the regiment's involvement in various military campaigns against India. There were a number of swords that had been used fighting the Indians in Kashmir in 1947, while the portraits of six Pakistani officers who had been killed in a more recent border skirmish had pride of place on the mess walls. The old polo field, meanwhile, had been converted into a training ground for Pakistani soldiers.

If Churchill might struggle to recognize the layout of the modern fort, the names of the tribes, villages and valleys involved in the latest uprising against the Pakistan government would be more familiar. As in 1897, the main rebellion in October 2007 against the central government in Islamabad began in the Swat Valley, and was led by a radical Islamic cleric, Maulana Fazullah. Fazullah, a former ski-lift attendant who was nicknamed 'The Radio Mullah' for his constant broadcast appearances, succeeded in persuading the tribes of the Swat Valley that they were the victims of a corrupt Pakistani government, and that their living conditions would be dramatically improved if they supported the Taliban's plan to establish Sharia law in their homeland.

Like the 'Mad Mullah' Sadullah of Churchill's day, Fazullah kept in touch with rebel tribesmen on the other side of the Afghan border. His father-in-law had been a keen supporter of the Taliban movement during its campaign to seize control of Afghanistan. The modern Taliban, when it first emerged in the early 1990s, was founded by veterans of the mujahedin movement that had fought the Russians following the Soviet invasion. The mujahedin were supported by both the CIA and Pakistan's ISI during its guerrilla war against the Soviets, and the Pakistani intelligence service maintained its links with the movement's leaders once the Soviets had withdrawn in 1989. Many of the ISI's senior officers are Pashtuns and, because of their tribal links, have tended to see the movement as a useful ally in securing Pakistan's border with Afghanistan.

The anti-Western fanaticism of the Taliban was so deeply ingrained that, when they finally seized control of Kabul in 1996, one of their first acts was to destroy the graves of the 150 or so British soldiers who had died fighting in the city during the colonial wars of the nineteenth century. The British military cemetery was restored following the overthrow of the Taliban in 2001, and the remnants of the headstones were placed in a commemorative plaque, which is set next to a new memorial to those who have lost their lives in the present conflict.

The arrival of tens of thousands of Taliban fighters in Pakistan's tribal areas at the end of 2001 led to the radicalization of the Pashtun tribes on the frontier. Fazullah made skilful use of the radio station he set up in the Swat Valley to preach his strong, anti-Western jihadi agenda, and by 2006 his movement had seized control of most of the valley's towns and villages. The following year the revolt – just as happened in 1897 – spread from the Swat Valley to the surrounding districts of Bajaur and Malakand, and by the spring of 2007 the Taliban had control of the town of Batkhela, which is just a ten minute drive from Malakand. As the revolt spread, Fazullah inflicted a reign of terror on the local population, banning music and dancing as 'unIslamic', preventing girls from attending school and even punishing barbers who cut the beards of their Muslim customers. The Taliban drove away Western aid agencies operating in the Swat Valley because they did not like the idea of 'infidels' in Muslim territory. Each night Fazullah would broadcast the names of those accused of violating Islamic law, and the next morning their decapitated bodies would be found by the roadside. Others who opposed his demands were hanged from lamp posts at roundabouts in the towns and villages in the Swat Valley under the Taliban's control.

Fazullah and his supporters eventually overplayed their hand when they used their power base in the Swat Valley to launch an attack on Pakistan's settled areas around Islamabad. At first the offensive was a success, and at one point the Taliban came within sixty miles of the city, prompting fears that the militants might be able to seize control of the country's nuclear weapons arsenal. The turning point came in December 2007, when the Taliban was implicated in the assassination of Benazir Bhutto, the charismatic leader of Pakistan's main opposition party, as she campaigned in Rawalpindi in the presidential election contest. Bhutto's death galvanized the Pakistani military into action, and the subsequent offensive – code-named 'Operation Black Thunderstorm' – resulted in Pakistan's armed forces fighting in exactly the same terrain where Blood's had fought in the 1890s.

The operation began with an attack on Lower Dir, before moving into the Swat Valley where the offensive was primarily directed against the Bunerwals. The fighting between the Taliban and the Pakistani military was every bit as brutal as the conflict between the British and the Pashtun tribesmen a hundred years before. For example in Malakand a local car mechanic who was suspected of being a Taliban sympathizer was detained by the ISI; the following day his badly beaten body was found in a ditch by the roadside.[9] Rumours abounded that the Pakistani military operated death squads, and that on at least one occasion they had shot pregnant women in cold blood. The Taliban were also accused of committing atrocities. A Pakistani general recounted how, in one particularly grisly incident, Taliban fighters had cut open the head of a Pakistani soldier, ripped out his brains and fed them to a dog.[10]

Further afield in Bajaur, close to the Mohmand Valley where Churchill had been based, the Pakistanis adopted similar tactics to those used by the British to punish rebellious tribes. The villages of tribesmen who had remained loyal to the Pakistani government were left untouched, but those associated with the rebels were completely destroyed. These included the border village of Damadola, where Churchill had fought on 18 September 1897. Damadola had been the scene of a failed attempt by the CIA to assassinate Ayman al-Zawahiri, who became the head of the al-Qaeda movement following bin Laden's death. In 2006 Zawahiri was reported to be hiding in a safe house in Damadola, which was targeted by a drone strike aimed at a group of men sitting down to dinner in the village. The strike killed only local villagers, and two weeks later Zawahiri released a videotape celebrating the fact he was still alive.[11] In 2010, the Pakistan military undertook an extensive military operation to drive the Taliban from the village, and once it had been completed all that remained was a network of abandoned caves that the fighters had carved into the surrounding mountains as a makeshift refuge.[12]

The Pakistani operation succeeded in recapturing the Swat Valley, and those Taliban fighters who were not killed or captured made their customary flight across the border to Afghanistan, which they then used as a base to maintain the anti-government insurgency in Pakistan. In the spring of 2011 Fazullah was accused of organizing a series of cross-border raids in Dir, Bajaur and Mohmand, where Churchill spent most of his time during the Malakand campaign and which today is one of the seven tribal agencies that form the FATA. At Shahi-Tangi, where Churchill so nearly lost his life, the local tribesmen, who had supported the Taliban when they first arrived from Afghanistan, held a tribal *jirga* at which they agreed to lay down their arms and have nothing more to do with the militant group. From Afghanistan, Fazullah continued to rally his supporters to maintain their campaign for Sharia law, and in October 2012 a Taliban gunman, acting on Fazullah's orders, provoked an international outcry by shooting a fourteen-year-old Pakistani schoolgirl, Malala Yousafzai, in the head. Malala was attacked because of her campaign for Pakistani girls to be allowed to attend school. She survived the shooting, and was airlifted to a Birmingham hospital for emergency treatment, where she was visited by William Hague, the British Foreign Secretary, a post formerly held by Lord Curzon. The shooting took place at Mingora, the main town located at the head of the Swat Valley, which is about four miles to the east of Landakai, where Viscount Fincastle won his Victoria Cross.

The Pakistani offensive in the tribal belt was supported by the NATO mission in Afghanistan, where, by the summer of 2010, more than 100,000 foreign troops – including a 10,000-strong British contingent – were based. The Americans had sent an extra 30,000 soldiers to support the Obama administration's 'surge strategy' against the Taliban. By increasing the military pressure on the Taliban leadership, Washington hoped to force them to the negotiating table. The US was particularly active in launching drone strikes against Taliban and al-Qaeda targets in the FATA, a strategy which for many years enjoyed the active support of the Pakistani military, although this was never publicly admitted. One of the early drone strikes in October 2006, against a suspected Taliban base in Chenagai, in Bajaur Province, killed an estimated eighty-two people, many of them students. The attack was authorized by the CIA after satellite spy cameras showed that a 3,000-strong crowd of protesters had gathered on the outskirts of the town, and were chanting slogans in praise of Osama bin Laden while denouncing the 'infidel' American invaders.

The number of drone strikes in Pakistan rose dramatically after President Obama took office in January 2009, prompting some officials to describe the campaign as a 'drone war'. The Pakistani authorities were more than happy to support the strikes, to the extent that General Ashfaq Parvez Kayani, Pakistan's army chief, requested that the Americans increase the number of attacks, and even allowed American drones to operate from Shamsi Air Base, in western Pakistan.[13] If the CIA produced a map of all its drone targets in the FATA area, it would be almost identical to the frontier territory where Churchill fought in the late 1890s. Locals in the tribal belt said they preferred the American drone strikes to bombing raids by the Pakistan Air Force, as the drones were more accurate in targeting rebel groups, while the air force tended to launch carpet-bombing raids that killed scores of civilians.[14]

The tacit cooperation between Washington and Islamabad ran into difficulty following the operation by American Special Forces in May 2011 that resulted in the death of Osama bin Laden at his compound in Abbottabad, the former British garrison town a hundred miles to the east of Malakand. The Americans did not inform their Pakistani counterparts about the mission because they feared that senior officers in the ISI, who were close to the Taliban, would raise the alarm. The bad feeling caused by the killing of bin Laden led the Pakistanis to scale down their cooperation with the Americans, particularly with regard to operations against the Taliban. Ordinary Pakistanis became resentful of the West's interference in their affairs. At Gilgit, for example, where the British adventurer George Hayward is buried, the slogan 'Go Home Britain and America' was painted on the perimeter wall at the local airport. The Pentagon responded by accusing the ISI of using the Haqqani network, a militant Pashtun group linked to the Taliban, to wage a 'proxy' war against coalition forces in Afghanistan. Tensions deepened when US forces mistakenly attacked a Pakistani military position at Salala, in the Mohmand Valley, in November 2011, killing twenty-four Pakistani soldiers. Pakistan retaliated by closing NATO's main supply routes into Afghanistan, as well as ordering the closure of the American drone base at Shamsi. Imran Khan, the Pashtun leader of Pakistan's Movement for Justice party, was one of the most vociferous critics of the drone strikes, and organized a protest rally in the North-West Frontier in October 2012, announcing he would order Pakistan's military to shoot down the drones if ever he were elected to office.

*

The longer the war against the Taliban continued, the more it seemed that history was repeating itself. At the height of the coalition effort in Afghanistan in 2011, the modern invaders followed the example set by the British in the nineteenth century by building their own self-contained fortress in the centre of Kabul to protect themselves against 'hostile elements' within the native population. The British had contented themselves with building a modest cantonment on the city outskirts, but the NATO coalition occupied an area of around one square mile in the city centre, which was fortified with 40-foot-high barricades, barbed wire and guard towers fitted with bulletproof glass, all designed to protect the NATO mission from attacks by the Afghans they had been sent to protect. The entire area was closed to the local population, who needed special passes and were required to undergo airport-style security checks before being allowed to enter.

Beyond the walls of this high-tech citadel, the rest of Afghanistan was deemed too dangerous for the thousands of soldiers, diplomats, officials and aid workers crowded inside the claustrophobic compound to venture into without a team of armed bodyguards to protect them. My request to visit the old Afghan fortress at Ghazni was denied on the grounds that the area was occupied by 'fanatics', an excuse that could just as easily have been made during General Roberts's occupation of the city in the 1880s. Rather than indulging the British passion for polo, the NATO soldiers occupied their spare time playing games of volleyball and football on the compound's helicopter pad, or relaxing in the 'Tora Bora' cafe, named after the site of bin Laden's final stand during the 2001 military campaign. Like the British before them, the NATO officers struggled to come to terms with the country's challenging terrain. 'Afghanistan is a country with lots of mountains and only a few roads which makes it very hard to secure,' one American officer complained to me. One of the biggest problems they faced in their attempts to rebuild the country was widespread illiteracy, because it was difficult to train as policemen Afghans who could not read a driving licence while carrying out identity checks. 'The terrain is horrendous and it is impossible to control the borders,' another American officer remarked, a lament as true today as it has been for centuries.

Nor did this new generation of invaders appear to have much understanding of the campaign's historical antecedents. When a young US Marine officer gave a slide presentation on the Taliban to a group of visiting diplomats, he showed pictures of mujahedin fighters from the 1980s, not realizing they had been America's allies in the war against the Soviets.[15] The latent hostility of the marine's attitude towards the mujahedin contrasted sharply with the Americans' attitude in 1989 when the Russians withdrew from Afghanistan, an event that was later credited with bringing about the end of the Cold War and the collapse of the Iron Curtain in central Europe. On that occasion the mujahedin were hailed as heroic warriors, and Robert Oakley, the US ambassador to Pakistan, and his wife Phyllis were the guests of honour when the Pashtun tribes staged a celebratory game of *buzkashi* at the frontier city of Peshawar. An intensely violent game, *buzkashi* is Afghanistan's national sport and consists of rival teams of Pashtun horsemen competing to carry a headless goat carcass from one end of the pitch to the other. Polo, Churchill's 'emperor of games', is *buzkashi*'s more refined offspring.

The most obvious difference between NATO's campaign in the twenty-first century and the British experience in the nineteenth was that, instead of Pashtun tribesmen crossing the border from Afghanistan to attack British positions on the North-West Frontier, they now travelled in the opposite direction from Pakistan to attack NATO forces in Afghanistan. After the arrival of the 'surge' troops in 2010, NATO waged a relentless campaign against the Taliban, using a combination of Special Forces and drone strikes to 'kill or capture' Taliban fighters. But despite the ferocity of the campaign, the Taliban showed little interest in seeking peace terms. As Taliban commanders were fond of telling Western visitors, 'You may have all the watches, but we have all the time.' Their disinclination to negotiate was, in part, due to President Obama's announcement in the summer of 2011 that all American combat troops would be withdrawn by the end of 2014. The Obama administration, like the British a century earlier, concluded that, for all the loss of life and the vast resources expended on trying to subdue the Pashtun tribes, it was ultimately a fruitless exercise that was unlikely to yield any long-term rewards. As one senior Obama administration official remarked, 'We have been in Afghanistan for ten years, suffered more than 30,000 casualties and spent around $1 trillion trying to sort out this mess. Enough is enough.'[16]

NATO's intervention did result in some modest improvements in the quality of life for ordinary Afghans. The main sports stadium in Kabul, which had been used by the Taliban to stage executions after Friday prayers, began hosting football matches, and a number of Afghan entrepreneurs grew wealthy from the vast amount of foreign currency that poured into the country to sustain the NATO mission. Large numbers of young Afghans were recruited into the armed forces and police service to enable the country to take care of its own security, rather than relying on outside help. Girls were allowed to go to school, and several Taliban commanders, who were supposed to enforce the movement's wholesale ban on female education, asked for their daughters to be privately educated so that they would not miss out.[17] Extensive geological surveys were undertaken that revealed the country had an estimated $3 trillion worth of mineral deposits, including copper, lithium, oil, gas and iron ore. If the country ever managed to enjoy peace and stability, its people might grow rich.

Despite these modest advances, the strength of the Taliban continued to grow, to the extent that General David Petraeus, the US commander of NATO forces, said he faced an insurgency on an industrial scale when he arrived in Kabul to take up his command in the summer of 2010. When British soldiers first deployed to southern Afghanistan as part of the NATO mission in the summer of 2006, the Taliban's fighting strength was estimated at around 5,000; by 2010 it had reached 50,000 as young Pashtun tribesmen responded to the call to jihad by their mullahs. Petraeus said he had studied the lessons of the British in Afghanistan in the nineteenth century as he sought to quell the revolt. 'Basically you cannot kill or capture your way out of an industrial-strength insurgency,' he explained. 'You have to do some of that, but you also need to include a political dimension.' It would also be unacceptable for modern NATO soldiers to employ the same tactics as those used in Churchill's day. 'What they did was not something you could do today,' said Petraeus. 'They undertook what we would call today a scorched-earth policy. Then they would wait for the tribes to come out of the hills and cut a deal. But undertaking a scorched-earth policy is not an option for us.'[18]

Back at Malakand, the defeat of the Taliban in the Swat

Valley left the Pakistani authorities with a novel humanitarian problem. Large numbers of children who had been caught fighting on the Taliban side had been radicalized and trained as suicide bombers. To help them learn the error of their ways the military set up a special school on the outskirts of Malakand called Sabaoon (which means 'First Light of Dawn' in Pashto). Teams of specialist Pakistani psychiatrists were brought in to reverse the brainwashing techniques the children had been exposed to at the Taliban's mosques and madrasas. The school's rehabilitation programme was so sensitive that its location was kept a secret, and the complex was protected by steel barricades and razor wire to prevent the Taliban from attacking the staff. The Taliban nevertheless succeeded in murdering Dr Mohammed Farooq Khan, one of the school's founders and a leading Pakistani intellectual, who was shot at his private clinic in Mardan, about fifty miles to the south of Malakand.

Persuading frontier tribesmen of all ages to renounce violence was one of the main strategies employed by the British throughout the course of their troubled engagement with the region in the nineteenth century. Rather than resort to military action, the political officers always preferred to strike a deal with the tribes. A similar approach was attempted both by leaders of the NATO alliance in Afghanistan and by the Pakistani government. To strike a deal with the Taliban in Afghanistan, NATO opened an office in the Gulf state of Qatar, in the expectation that a neutral location might help to break the impasse between the Taliban and the Afghan president Hamid Karzai, whose legitimacy to run the country the Taliban hotly disputed. In Pakistan, the government made several attempts to reach agreement with the Taliban's leadership, with mixed results: in the spring of 2008, for example, a ceasefire in the Swat Valley collapsed when the Taliban failed to surrender their weapons – just like the Mohmands and their *jezails* in the 1890s. Instead, they used the lull to strengthen their position, and when the fighting resumed later in the year, the Pakistani authorities concluded they had no alternative but to place the Swat Valley under military occupation.

Churchill would have approved of the Pakistani military's approach, for he argued in the concluding passage of *The Story of the Malakand Field Force* that 'the most desirable' policy was to mobilize 'a nice field force, and operate at leisure in the frontier valleys until they are as safe and civilised as Hyde Park'.[19] But it was Curzon, not Churchill, who solved the 'riddle of the frontier', and the deal he agreed with the border tribes was based on his conclusion that the less the outside world interfered with the affairs of the frontier tribes, the less inclined the frontier tribes would be to interfere with the outside world. Curzon's primary requirement was that, in return for leaving the tribes to run their own affairs, the Pashtuns must provide a solemn undertaking not to allow their territory to be used for attacks against the British. As Curzon's approach was the most successful of Britain's various attempts to stabilize the region, it was hardly surprising that the Obama administration adopted a similar tactic in its own attempts to reach a deal with the Taliban. It was surely no coincidence that the same tribes Churchill had fought against in the 1890s were now at the forefront of the insurgency against NATO and the Pakistani government. Whether it was the British, Americans, Russians, Pakistanis or even rival tribes from neighbouring valleys, they simply would not tolerate outsiders meddling in their affairs.

As the dominant power in the NATO alliance, whatever terms Washington set for a deal with the Taliban would most likely be accepted by other Western powers, such as Britain and France, that had made significant military contributions to the NATO war effort. And Washington's fundamental requirement for any peace deal with the Taliban was the undertaking that, irrespective of which political faction governed Kabul, Afghanistan must never again allow itself to become a safe haven for Islamist groups intent on attacking America and its allies. In essence, the deal America sought for ending its decade-long involvement in Afghanistan was little different from the assurances Curzon had demanded from the Pashtun tribesmen in the nineteenth century. The Americans had no desire to involve themselves in Afghan affairs, so long as Afghanistan no longer posed a threat to their well-being. As one of Obama's senior advisers remarked in early 2012, 'The best outcome is that the Americans and NATO go and never come back.'[20] David Cameron, the British prime minister, expressed similar sentiments in the summer of 2010 when setting out his government's policy for Afghanistan. 'Nobody wants British troops to be in Afghanistan a moment longer than is necessary.'

But Ryan Crocker, the US ambassador to Afghanistan, issued a public warning that, if NATO withdrew from the country without negotiating a peace deal with the Taliban, it would result in the return of Islamist terror groups. 'Al-Qaeda is still present in Afghanistan,' Crocker explained shortly before retiring from government service. 'If the West decides that 10 years in Afghanistan is too long then they will be back, and the next time it will not be New York or Washington, it will be another big Western city. We have killed all the slow and stupid ones. But that means the ones that are left are totally dedicated,' he said. 'We think we've won a campaign before our adversaries have even started to fight. They have patience, and they know that we are short on that.'[21]

*

If parallels can be drawn between Churchill's experience fighting on the North-West Frontier and the modern conflict, his own concern at the time was not so much with resolving the frontier question but to ensure that his own contribution, as both a soldier and writer, was utilized to further his career. He was proud of his literary contributions on the Malakand campaign, which, whatever their shortcomings, he hoped would help to build his public profile and further his political ambitions. As

Churchill quipped later in life, 'History will be kind to me because I intend to write it myself.'

Even as he awaited publication of *The Story of the Malakand Field Force*, Churchill agitated to see more front-line action. Throughout the winter and spring of 1898 he badgered his senior officers and his mother's social contacts to be granted permission to travel to Egypt, where Kitchener was making the final preparations for his campaign to crush the Mahdi's revolt in the Sudan. But he made little headway, not even after he persuaded Lord Roberts of Kandahar, the hero of the Second Afghan War, to intercede on his behalf by writing to Kitchener directly. General Sir Evelyn Wood, the army's Adjutant General who had won the Victoria Cross during the Indian Mutiny, was another of the Churchill family's contacts who wrote to Kitchener, suggesting that he take Churchill instead of Fincastle, who had been reported three times 'as below average of rank'.[22]

But Churchill's reputation for pushiness was starting to count against him. Many of his fellow subalterns had already come to regard him as a medal hunter devoted to his own self-promotion, a criticism against which Winston himself did not demur. Epithets such as 'self-advertiser', 'super-precocious' and 'insufferably bumptious' were frequently used by fellow sub-alterns to describe his conduct. The relative of an officer who served with Churchill at Malakand recalled his grandfather relating how 'Churchill could not pass a mirror without inspecting himself, or practising some speech or other'. But Churchill's self-knowledge was such that he freely admitted to his shortcomings. On hearing the news that he was to receive a mention in dispatches, he told his mother he fully deserved it because 'I took every chance and displayed myself with ostentation wherever there was danger.'[23] He told his younger brother Jack, moreover, that he needed to prove himself. 'Being in many ways a coward – particularly at school – there is no ambition I cherish so keenly as to gain a reputation of personal courage.'[24] And while his contemporaries mocked his vainglorious pursuit of medals and glory, Churchill was unrepentant: 'I know myself pretty well and am not blind to the tawdry and dismal side of my character but if there is one situation in which I do not feel ashamed of myself it is in the field.'[25]

In *My Early Life*, Churchill takes a more sanguine view of the 'disapproval and hostility' he attracted from his peers. 'It is melancholy to be forced to record these less amiable aspects of human nature, which by a most curious and indeed unacceptable coincidence have always seemed to present themselves in the wake of my innocent footsteps, and even sometimes across the path on which I wished to proceed.'[26] But suspicions that Churchill was more interested in self-promotion than defending the national interest dogged his political career for the rest of his life. This was particularly true during the 'gathering storm' of the 1930s, when his opposition to the Baldwin government's appeasement of Hitler caused many of his Tory colleagues to see him as a self-serving opportunist who was not to be trusted.

The refusal of the authorities in Calcutta to allow Churchill to join the Tirah force after the conclusion of the Malakand campaign should have been a warning to him not to overstep the mark. But rather than take the hint, he compounded his unpopularity by taking his Christmas leave in Calcutta, the winter seat of the Indian government, where he spent his time pestering the authorities for an audience with General Sir George White, the commander-in-chief, in the hope of securing permission to travel to Egypt. No meeting was forthcoming, nor permit to join Kitchener's force. But he did manage to stay at Government House, the Viceroy's official residence, where he was 'hospitably entertained' by none other than the Viceroy himself, Lord Elgin.

Jennie wrote directly to Kitchener in Cairo trying to secure her son a place with the Egyptian army, but the publication of Churchill's book made that prospect even more remote. In the eyes of Kitchener and the other senior officers, it was presumptuous in the extreme for a mere subaltern to publish an appraisal of his senior officers' conduct, and quite insufferable for his views to appear in the daily newspapers. Under the heading 'Military Observations', the penultimate chapter of *The Story of the Malakand Field Force*, Churchill gives a wide-ranging critique of the conduct of the military campaign, from the difficulties of fighting a guerrilla war of the type he had experienced in Cuba, to the need to provide the soldiers with proper provisions to carry with them into the field: 'Great efforts should be made to give the soldier a piece of chocolate, a small sausage, or something portable and nutritious . . . it is well to remember the stomach governs the world.'[27]

Kitchener and the rest of the top brass were not amused, and concluded that young Churchill needed to be kept firmly in his place, not given further opportunities for self-promotion. Churchill understood the reasons for the disinclination of the military establishment to allow him to travel to Egypt. 'The hybrid combination of a subaltern officer and a widely followed war correspondent was not unnaturally obnoxious to the military mind.'[28] But there was another reason Kitchener was so reluctant to allow Churchill to join his force. Frank Rhodes, the *Times* correspondent for the Egyptian campaign, spoke with Kitchener about Churchill, and later reported the conversation to Winston, who explained Kitchener's reasoning in a letter to Jennie: 'Kitchener said he had known I was not going to stay in the army – was only making a convenience of it; that he had disapproved of my coming in place of others whose professions were at stake.' Churchill was indignant when he heard Kitchener's reasoning. 'He may be a general – but never a gentleman.'[29]

Dismayed by his failure to persuade the 'gang of bureaucrats', as he called those responsible for administering India, to send him to Egypt, but buoyed by the success of his book, Churchill resolved to return to London in the summer of 1898, hoping to use his contacts to get himself posted to Egypt, and also to take the first steps towards making a career in politics. In late May he asked Jennie to arrange for him to address at least two public gatherings, suggesting the northern working city of Bradford as a possible venue. Before setting off for England, though, he managed to have one last experience of fighting on the North-West Frontier, when he finally managed to get himself posted to the Tirah force just as it was nearing the end of its operations against the Afridi tribesmen around the Khyber Pass.

Churchill spent the best part of a month between March and April 1898 with the Tirah Expeditionary Force, travelling as a guest of General Sir William Lockhart, the commander, and covering much of the hostile mountain terrain between Peshawar and the border with Afghanistan. On this occasion there is no record of Churchill coming under fire, but he made full use of the opportunity to extend his network of military contacts. 'I now know all the generals who are likely to have commands in the next few years,' he informed his mother. 'And I now have a great many friends in high places – as far as soldiering is concerned.'[30] Indeed, Churchill greatly enjoyed his last few days among the savage tribesmen of the North-West Frontier, even though it only served to harden his prejudices about their temperament. 'They are a fine race of fighting men and what I wrote in my book about their callousness is truer than I thought,' he concluded at the end of the campaign. 'They bear but little malice – would kill you if they could – but otherwise perfectly friendly. I confess I like them.'[31]

Captain Aylmer Haldane, who befriended Churchill during the Tirah expedition, recalled that, far from being 'super-precocious', 'insufferably bumptious' or any of the other unflattering descriptions applied at the time, Churchill was modest and attentive, and did not attempt to 'monopolise the conversation or thrust his opinions'. Instead Haldane, who later commanded British forces on the Western Front during the First World War, regarded Churchill 'at almost first sight as cut out on a vastly different pattern from any officer of his years that I had so far met'.[32]

Churchill wrote one final newspaper dispatch for *The Times*, as he still felt resentful of his treatment by the *Daily Telegraph*. In the article, which, to Winston's satisfaction, carried his byline, the observations he makes on the futility of waging war against the fierce tribesmen of the Afghan border are as valid today as they were during the final years of the nineteenth century. 'The peculiar difficulty which attends mountain warfare is that there are no general actions on a great scale, no brilliant successes, no important surrenders, no chance for *coups de théâtre*. It is just a rough hard job, which must be carried through. The war is one of small incidents. The victory must be looked for in the results . . . yet while the army receives the humble sub-mission of the most ferocious savages in Asia, we are assailed by taunts and reproaches from our countrymen at home.'[33]

As for the Tirah campaign itself, he thought it a dismal failure. 'The whole expedition was a mistake,' he informed Jennie, 'because its success depended on the tribesmen giving in when their country was invaded and their property destroyed. This they have not done. We have done them all the harm possible and many of them are still defiant.' Similar conclusions could be drawn from the more recent campaign against the Taliban. Churchill also contradicted the 'annexation' argument he had advanced during the Malakand campaign, when he argued that, as Britain had 'no real means, except by prolonged occupation, of putting the screw on these tribesmen and making them give in . . . it was a great mistake to make the attempt – or indeed have any dealings with them'.[34] The other factor that weighed against military intervention was that 'people in England seem to imagine that fighting can be carried on without people being killed'.[35] By the twenty-first century Western dis-approval of any form of battlefield casualties had become even more entrenched.

Churchill regarded casualties as a factor of military life, subscribing to Bindon Blood's view that 'it is what soldiers are made for'. But Churchill's experience on the North-West Frontier, and his later adventures in the Sudan and South Africa, gave him a deep awareness of the human cost of conflict. As a political leader during both the First and Second World Wars, Churchill made a point of keeping in close contact with soldiers fighting on the front line to make sure he kept its horror clear before his eyes.

*

The time had come for Churchill to bring the curtain down on his Afghan adventure, and he set sail for England on 18 June, boarding the SS *Oriental* at Bombay to 'proceed without further delay to the centre of the Empire'.[36] Churchill would return to India one more time as a serving soldier in December 1898 to help his regiment win the All-India Regimental Polo Tournament, the only cavalry regiment from southern India to achieve the feat. The regiment had trained hard for the event for three years, but on the eve of the tournament Winston slipped on some stone stairs and dislocated his shoulder. It was touch and go whether he would play, but the team captain decided to include him because of his experience, and Churchill took the field with his elbow strapped tight to his side. The team won with Winston scoring the winning goal, and the victory was celebrated with 'prolonged rejoicings, intense inward satisfaction, and nocturnal festivities from which the use of wine was not excluded'.[37]

The tournament won, Churchill proceeded with his plan to leave the army and earn his living through writing while biding his time for a chance to enter Parliament. 'Had the army been a source of income to me instead of a channel of expenditure, I might have felt compelled to stick at it,' he told his grandmother. The cost of maintaining two horses, though, together with the expensive uniforms, meant he was always in debt. 'I can live cheaper and earn more as a writer, special correspondent or journalist: and this work is moreover more congenial and more likely to assist me in pursuing the larger ends of life.' Even so, he left the army with a heavy heart, 'very sorry to leave all my friends and put on my uniform and medals for the last time'.[38] Before he left Bangalore, the regiment threw a dinner in his honour, 'and paid me the rare compliment of drinking my health for the last time I dined with them'.[39]

In the spring of 1899, Churchill took advantage of his last ever visit to India to stay with Lord Curzon, the Viceroy, at his official residence in Calcutta. By this point Churchill's exploits on the North-West Frontier in 1897 and in the Sudan the following year had made him a household name in Britain, one that even featured in music-hall variety shows:

> You've heard of Winston Churchill;
> This is all I have to say –
> He's the latest and the greatest
> Correspondent of the day.[40]

Curzon was in the process of drawing up his plans to settle the frontier issue, in which Churchill still took an interest, telling his mother that 'there is no doubt they will realise what a wretched position we are in on the Frontier'.[41] During the week that Churchill stayed with the Curzons, he talked so much that the Viceroy gave him a lecture on the dangers of garrulity.[42] For his part, Churchill appears to have overcome the animosity he had felt towards Curzon when they had met two years previously, and he had mocked him as 'the spoiled darling of politics'. The Viceroy, he told his grandmother, was a remarkable man with great charm of manner, and the two of them had enjoyed several long and delightful conversations.[43]

Churchill's dedication to India would remain with him for the rest of his life, and in the 1930s he became a vehement opponent of Mahatma Gandhi's campaign for independence,

founding the Indian Defence Committee to oppose the government's proposals to grant India self-rule. Churchill often
denounced Gandhi as a 'fakir' and 'fanatic', terms he had no
doubt learned while on active service on the North-West
Frontier. He believed that if Britain lost India, she would lose
her empire, and he argued that India was totally unsuited for
democracy, because 'instead of conflicting opinions you have
bitter theological hatreds'.[44] Leo Amery, the Secretary of State
for India during the Second World War and a contemporary of
Churchill's at Harrow, believed Churchill's views on India were
so intemperate that he wondered if 'on the subject of India
he is really sane'. On another occasion Amery quipped that
'Churchill knew as much of the Indian problem as George III
did of the American colonies'. Churchill had never paid much
attention to Indian issues per se during his polo-playing days
in the 1890s, and it showed. His lack of knowledge on the
subject was 'most painfully exposed' when he appeared before
the joint parliamentary select committee in 1933 to debate the
issue, forcing him to resort to repetitive rhetoric.[45] Churchill
maintained his opposition to independence, even encouraging
Mohammed Jinnah, the founder of Pakistan, to campaign for
an independent Muslim state. Churchill hoped that the prospect
of partition would make independence less likely, but in the
event India split in two, and the new state of West Pakistan,
including the troubled tribal belt, was born.

Returning to London from India on 2 July 1898, Churchill
immediately threw himself into achieving his twin goals of
furthering his political career and getting himself attached to
Kitchener's army in the Sudan. On 14 July he spoke at a
political meeting at Bradford, where he received a warm reception. 'I was listened to with the greatest attention for fifty-five
minutes,' he told Jennie, 'at the end of which time there were
loud and general cries of "Go on". Five or six times they
applauded for about two minutes without stopping.'[46]

But his greatest coup was to be invited to meet Lord

Salisbury, the prime minister, who had just read *The Story of the Malakand Field Force* and was keen to meet the author, who also happened to be the son of his former colleague. As Martin Gilbert, the distinguished biographer of Churchill, has memorably noted, 'Thus it was that Churchill entered 10 Downing Street for the first time.'[47] In *My Early Life* Churchill recalls how the man who had helped to destroy his father's political career greeted him 'with a charming gesture of welcome and salute' before conducting him to a small sofa in his vast office, one that Churchill himself would occupy forty-two years later. 'I entered for the first time that spacious room overlooking Horse Guards Parade in which I was afterwards for many years from time to time to see much grave business done in Peace and War.'[48] The distinguished elder statesman told Winston that his book had helped him to form a 'truer picture' of the Indian frontier issue than any of the other documents he had been obliged to read. At the end of the meeting, which overran by a good ten minutes, Salisbury remarked to Winston 'how much you remind me of your father, with whom such important days of my political life were lived'. And he drew the meeting to a close with the kind offer, 'If there is anything at any time that I can do which would be of assistance to you, pray do not fail to let me know.'[49]

After meeting with the most patrician of prime ministers, Churchill's ticket to Egypt was virtually guaranteed, and he wasted no time making sure he followed up on Salisbury's offer. The prime minister agreed to write to Kitchener requesting him to consider Churchill for the Expeditionary Force, and when Kitchener's reply was non-committal, Churchill continued to lobby a number of close family friends to intercede on his behalf, including Lady Jeune, a friend of his mother's, who sent Kitchener a telegram stating bluntly: 'Hope you will take Churchill. Guarantee he won't write.'[50] Churchill was well aware that his literary endeavours were his biggest handicap. But his lobbying efforts eventually paid off, and towards the end of July he received a telegram informing him that he was to go to Egypt at once, where he was to be stationed with the 21st Lancers.

Churchill was about to embark upon the next great adventure, one that would ultimately take him to the southern end of the African continent, where his daring escape from captivity by the Boers would make him a national hero in England, and guarantee him the career in politics he so badly wanted. Before leaving London Winston contacted another family friend, Oliver Borthwick, the owner of the Conservative-leaning *Morning Post*, who commissioned him to write 'as opportunity served' a series of letters for the newspaper at £15 a column – three times the fee he had received for his *Telegraph* dispatches. His journalistic commission secured, he set sail for Egypt on the morning of 27 July 1898, the memories of his recent escapades on the Afghan frontier already fading. That September Churchill experienced the most thrilling moment of his entire military career, when he took part, with the 21st Lancers, in one of the last full-scale cavalry charges of the British army at the Battle of Omdurman.

Churchill's participation in the Malakand Field Force had launched his military career, and he hoped further success in Egypt would lead to the fulfilment of his political ambitions. The North-West Frontier and its 'fierce hill men' had served their purpose. As for the terrible carnage he had witnessed in the seemingly endless war on the Afghan border, Churchill was not so sure. 'Whether it was worth it I cannot tell,' he remarked in *My Early Life*.[51] The modern generation of soldiers who have more recently found themselves fighting in the Pashtun badlands would no doubt voice similar sentiments as, for all the enormous technological advances that have been made in the hundred or so years since Churchill came to Malakand, there is little to suggest the conflict will not end in comparable stalemate.

On the civilian side, the construction of motorways, airports and a wide range of social amenities has made the tribal belt far more integrated with the outside world. But, as I discovered during my visits to the frontier, the dramatic increase in the West's military capabilities has not been successful in persuading the Pashtun tribesmen to lay down their arms and abandon their cherished desire for independence. These days computer operators located in Nevada – some 7,000 miles from the Afghan border – can launch deadly drone strikes against the Taliban with the click of a mouse.[52] But the Taliban, using basic weaponry such as rocket-propelled grenades and home-made roadside bombs, have proved more than a match for NATO's finest.

Indeed, more than a decade after Western forces first arrived to do battle on the frontier, the prospects for a lasting peace for the region, whether in Afghanistan or Pakistan, seem as remote now as they did in Churchill's day. In the meantime, thousands more young soldiers have lost their lives or suffered appalling injury in the violent campaign to impose order on a part of the world that has never tolerated outside interference. As for the tribes, their losses have been catastrophic, both in terms of the numbers of lives lost – many of them civilians – and the devastation wrought to property and land. Even so, as Churchill discovered for himself, they show little inclination to surrender themselves to foreign control. I have spent many years as a foreign correspondent covering wars. And looking at the forbidding, snow-capped mountain peaks as I prepared to take my leave of Malakand, it seemed to me that Churchill's riddle of the frontier was as far from being solved as it has ever been, and that the cemeteries of the North-West Frontier will continue to be filled with its victims for many years to come. As Churchill himself later remarked, 'Ah, horrible war, amazing medley of the glorious and squalid, the pitiful and the sublime, if modern men of light and learning saw your face closer, simple folk would see it hardly ever.'[53]

Acknowledgements

Any work concerning the life of Winston Churchill draws on the excellent Churchill Archives Centre at Churchill College, Cambridge, where Allen Packwood and his staff were welcoming and most helpful in getting me started on the young Winston Churchill's adventures on the North-West Frontier. I am similarly indebted to the staff at the National Army Museum in Chelsea and the British Library for their help in locating contemporaneous reports and memoirs from the period Churchill spent fighting on the North-West Frontier. At the *Telegraph* I am grateful to Gavin Fuller for digging out the relevant articles from the newspaper's archive. Professor Lloyd Clark gave me a most informative tour of the Royal Military Academy at Sandhurst, which is where the great military historian Sir John Keegan, to whom this book is dedicated, taught for many years. Over many years of covering the contemporary conflict in Afghanistan I have benefitted from the insights provided by a number of senior officers in the British Armed Forces, in particular General Sir Mike Jackson and General Sir David Richards. I have received similar help from the US military, where General David Petraeus was especially generous with his time.

Further afield, I would like to thank Tony White and Chris Riley at NATO HQ in Brussels for arranging a most informative visit to the International Security and Assistance Force in Afghanistan. For my visit to Pakistan and the tribal areas, Wajid Shamsul Hasan and his staff at the Pakistan High Commission were most helpful in enabling me to acquire the necessary permissions, while in Pakistan itself Shoiab Sultan Khan and Shandana Khan of the Aga Khan's Rural Support Programmes Network provided me with a once-in-a-lifetime visit to the Hindu Kush, during which I was grateful for the company of Brooks Newmark MP and my *Telegraph* colleague Peter

Oborne, who also helped me with research relating to Chitral. Dr Hamayun Khan gave me a masterful exposition on the politics and history of the frontier tribes, as did Asif Durrani, while I am indebted to the Pakistani military's Inter-Services Public Relations department for organizing a memorable visit to Malakand and the surrounding region. I would like to thank Peter Bergen and his wife Tresha Mabile for sharing their valuable insights on the dynamics of the modern conflict in Pakistan.

My thanks are also due to Peter Robinson, my literary agent, for enthusiastically backing this project from its inception, and to Georgina Morley and her editorial team at Pan Macmillan for handling the manuscript with their customary professionalism and diligence. My greatest debt, though, is to my beloved wife Katherine who not only tolerated my constant absences, but provided valuable assistance with the research, took a keen interest in reading the early drafts, and was a constant source of encouragement, support and inspiration.

Notes

The letters referred to in the notes can be found in *The Churchill Documents Volumes 1 and 2*, as well as Randolph S. Churchill's companion volume, *Youth 1874–1900*. For ease of reference I have used the correspondents' initials. The references from *The Story of the Malakand Field Force* are taken from the Colonial Library Edition of 1898, while references from *My Early Life* are taken from the Eland Publishing edition of 2000.

PROLOGUE

1 *The Times*, 1 October 1897.
2 Winston S. Churchill (WSC), *The Story of the Malakand Field Force* (Longmans, 1898), p. 246.
3 WSC to Jennie Randolph Churchill (JRC), 16 May 1898.
4 WSC to JRC, 22 December 1897.
5 WSC to JRC, 17 November 1897.
6 *Young Winston*, Columbia Pictures, 1972.
7 Author's interview, 6 November 2012.
8 *Guardian*, 8 August 2009.
9 'Counterinsurgency', U.S. Army Field Manual No. 3–24, Headquarters, Department of the Army, Washington DC, 2006.
10 Author's interview, London, 21 July 2011.
11 WSC to JRC, 21 October 1897.

One: Passing Out

1 WSC, *Malakand Field Force*, p. 8.
2 Ibid., p. 10.
3 WSC, *Daily Telegraph*, 6 November 1897.
4 WSC, *Malakand Field Force*, p. 4.
5 Randolph S. Churchill, *Winston S. Churchill: Youth, 1874–1900* (Heinemann, 1966), p. 346.
6 WSC to JRC, 5 September 1895, quoted in Randolph S. Churchill, *The Churchill Documents*, vol. 2: *Young Soldier, 1896–1901* (Hillsdale College Press, 2006), p. 785.
7 John Keegan, *Churchill* (Weidenfeld and Nicolson, 2002), p. 20.
8 Anne Sebba, *Jennie Churchill, Winston's American Mother* (John Murray, 2007), p. 15.
9 R. F. Foster, *Lord Randolph Churchill, A Political Life* (Oxford University Press, 1981), p. 24.
10 Cited in Winston S. Churchill, *My Early Life* (Macmillan, 1930), p. 19.
11 Ibid.
12 Sebba, *Jennie Churchill*, p. 114.
13 Foster, *Lord Randolph Churchill*, p. 127.
14 Robert Rhodes James, *Lord Randolph Churchill* (Weidenfeld and Nicolson, 1939), p. 249.
15 Martin Gilbert, *Churchill* (Heinemann, 1991), p. 13.
16 Ibid., pp. 11–12.
17 WSC, *My Early Life*, p. 19.
18 Ibid., pp. 19–20.
19 Quoted in Gilbert, *Churchill*, p. 32.
20 R. S. Churchill, *Winston S. Churchill: Youth*, p. 184.
21 Ibid., p. 196.
22 Ibid., p. 212.
23 WSC, *My Early Life*, p. 59.
24 Ibid., p. 45.
25 Ibid.

26 Keegan, *Churchill*, p. 27.

27 R. S. Churchill, *Winston S. Churchill: Youth*, p. 214.

28 Gilbert, *Churchill*, p. 48.

29 WSC, *My Early Life*, p. 62.

30 Randolph S. Churchill, *Winston S. Churchill: Companion*, Volume 1, Part I (Heinemann, 1967), p. 554.

31 Ibid., p. 578.

Two: The Wild Frontier

1 Captain W. R. Robertson, *An Official Account of the Chitral Expedition, 1895* (Calcutta, 1898), p. 27.

2 Quoted in T. A. Heathcote, *The Afghan Wars, 1839–1919* (Osprey Publishing, 1980), p. 2.

3 Quoted in Stephen Tanner, *Afghanistan* (Da Capo Press, 2009), p. 134.

4 David Loyn, *Butcher and Bolt* (Windmill Books, 2009), p. 20.

5 WSC, *Malakand Field Force*, p. 5.

6 Quoted in T. A. Heathcote, *The Afghan Wars*, pp. 16–17.

7 Tanner, *Afghanistan*, p. 136.

8 WSC, *Malakand Field Force*, p. 40.

9 Tanner, *Afghanistan*, p. 141.

10 Cited in Peter Hopkirk, *The Great Game: On Secret Service in High Asia* (Oxford University Press, 1990), p. 238.

11 Tanner, *Afghanistan*, p. 153.

12 WSC, *Malakand Field Force*, p. 314.

13 Hopkirk, *The Great Game*, p. 238.

14 Charles Allen, *God's Terrorists* (Little, Brown, 2006), p. 41.

15 Ibid., p. 55.

16 Tanner, *Afghanistan*, p. 190.

17 Quoted ibid., p. 199.

18 Quoted in Allen, *God's Terrorists*, p. 52.

19 Private interview with author, March 2012.

20 Quoted in Loyn, *Butcher and Bolt*, p. 83.

21 Loyn, *Butcher and Bolt*, p. 75.

22 WSC, *Malakand Field Force*, p. 294.

23 Ibid., p. 313

24 Tanner, *Afghanistan*, p. 209.

25 Loyn, *Butcher and Bolt*, p. 120.

26 Ibid., p. 121.

27 Heathcote, *The Afghan Wars*, p. 138e.

28 Loyn, *Butcher and Bolt*, p. 130.

29 Cited in Heathcote, *The Afghan Wars*, p. 133.

30 Loyn, *Butcher and Bolt*, p. 131.

31 Robertson, *Official Account*, p. 2.

32 WSC, *Malakand Field Force*, p. 29.

33 Robertson, *Official Account*, p. 10.

34 WSC, *Malakand Field Force*, p. 32.

35 Robertson, *Official Account*, p. 25.

36 Ibid., p. 30.

37 Ibid., p. 34.

THREE: A SUBALTERN AND A GENTLEMAN

1 WSC to JRC, 1 May 1894.

2 WSC, *My Early Life*, p. 61.

3 Ibid., p. 67.

4 David Scott Daniell, *4th Hussar: The Story of the 4th Queen's Own Hussars, 1685–1958* (Gale and Polden, 1951), p. 197.

5 WSC, *My Early Life*, p. 62.

6 Ibid.

7 Duke of Cambridge to JRC, 6 February 1895.

8 WSC to JRC, 31 August 1895.

9 WSC, *My Early Life*, p. 62.

10 WSC to JRC, 3 July 1895.

11 WSC, *My Early Life*, p. 64.

12 Scott Daniell, *4th Hussar*, p. 223.

13 Richard Harding Davis, *Real Soldiers of Fortune* (Charles Scribner's Sons, 1906), p. 81.

14 WSC to JRC, 23 May 1895.

15 Sebba, *Jennie Churchill*, p. 146.

16 WSC to JRC, 16 August 1895.

17 'A Cornet of Horse', 'The Royal Military College, Sandhurst', *Pall Mall Magazine*, December 1896.

18 WSC to JRC, 2 May 1895.

19 WSC to JRC, 6 June 1895.

20 WSC to JRC, 3 August 1895.

21 Sabba, *Jennie Churchill*, p. 88.

22 WSC, *My Early Life*, p. 77.

23 George N. Curzon, *Leaves from a Viceroy's Notebook* (Macmillan, 1926), p. 130.

24 George N. Curzon, *Tales of Travel* (Hodder and Stoughton, 1923), pp. 48–54.

25 Ibid.

26 Captain John Nixon, 'The Value of Chitral', 20 May 1895.

27 Robertson, *Official Account*, p. 93.

28 WSC, *My Early Life*, pp. 76–7.

29 WSC to JRC, 4 October 1895.

30 JRC to WSC, 11 October 1895.

31 WSC, *My Early Life*, pp. 59–60.

32 WSC to JRC, 21 October 1895.

33 Sebba, *Jennie Churchill*, p. 205.

34 WSC to JRC, 10 November 1895.

35 WSC to Jack Churchill, 15 November 1895.

36 Ibid.

37 Sebba, *Jennie Churchill*, p. 210.

38 R. S. Churchill, *Winston S. Churchill: Youth*, pp. 282–3.

39 WSC, *My Early Life*, p. 77.

40 *Daily Graphic*, 13 December 1895.

41 WSC, *My Early Life*, p. 79.

42 Ibid.

43 *Daily Graphic*, 17 December 1895.

44 WSC, *My Early Life*, pp. 83–4.

45 *Daily Graphic*, 27 December 1895.

46 Ibid.

47 *Daily Graphic*, 13 January 1896.

48 *New York Times*, 20 November, 1895.

49 *Vanity Fair*, 6 March 1846.

50 *New York World*, 15 December 1895.

51 *New York Herald*, 19 December 1895.

52 Ibid.

53 Gilbert, *Churchill*, p. 62.

Four: Passage to India

1 WSC to JRC, 4 August 1896.

2 Ibid.

3 W. L. Thomas to WSC, 14 January 1896.

4 The station is now called Hounslow West.

5 *Sun*, 27 December 2011.

6 WSC, *My Early Life*, p. 89.

7 Ibid., p. 90.

8 Ibid., p. 91.

9 Lord Lansdowne to JRC, 3 July 1896.

10 WSC to JRC, 4 August 1896.

11 WSC to Frances, Duchess of Marlborough, 8 September 1896.

12 Field Marshal Lord Roberts, *Forty-One Years in India* (Macmillan, 1900), p. 334.

13 Lawrence James, *Raj: The Making of British India* (Little, Brown, 1997), p. 227.

14 Ibid., p. 343.

15 Ibid., p. 356.

16 Albert Hervey, *A Soldier of the Company: The Life of an Indian Ensign, 1833–43* (Charles Allen, 1988), p. 136.

17 WSC to Frances, Duchess of Marlborough, 8 September 1896.

18 Francis Yeates-Brown, *The Life of a Bengal Lancer* (Gollancz, 1930), pp. 16–17.

19 Richard Holmes, *In the Footsteps of Churchill* (BBC Books, 2005), p. 166.

20 Sebba, *Jennie Churchill*, p. 215.

21 WSC to JRC, 18 September 1896.

22 WSC, *My Early Life*, p. 99.

23 Ibid., p. 100.

24 WSC to JRC, 14 October 1896.

25 WSC, *My Early Life*, p. 106.

26 WSC to Jack Churchill, 15 October 1896.

27 WSC, *My Early Life*, p. 103.

28 WSC to JRC, 12 November 1896.

29 WSC to JRC, 4 October 1896.

30 WSC to JRC, 4 November 1896.

31 WSC to JRC, 12 November 1896.

32 WSC to JRC, 6 June 1899.

33 *Observer*, 9 November 2003.

34 Gilbert, *Churchill*, p. 174.

35 WSC to JRC, 4 November 1896.

36 WSC to JRC, 23 December 1896.

37 Ibid.

38 JRC to WSC, 24 December 1896.

39 WSC to JRC, 14 April 1897.

40 WSC to Jack Churchill, 15 October 1896.

41 WSC, *My Early Life*, p. 107.

42 J. E. C. Welldon to WSC, 28 September 1896.

43 WSC to JRC, 4 February 1897.

44 WSC, *My Early Life*, p. 109.

45 Virginia Cowles, *Winston Churchill the Era and the Man* (Hamish Hamilton, 1953), p. 55.

46 Keegan, *Churchill*, p. 35.

47 WSC to JRC, 18 November 1896.

48 Michael Paterson, *Winston Churchill: Personal Accounts of the Great Leader at War* (David and Charles, 2005), p. 104.

49 Scott Daniell, *4th Hussar*, p. 229.

50 Ibid.

51 Sir Herbert Kitchener to JRC, 30 December 1896.

FIVE: THE SEAT OF WAR

1 WSC, *My Early Life*, p. 120.

2 WSC to JRC, 17 March 1897.

3 WSC to JRC, 6 April 1897.

4 *The Times*, 3 July 1897.

5 R. S. Churchill, *Winston S. Churchill: Youth*, p. 343.

6 *The Lady*, 5 August 1897.

7 *Eastern Morning News*, 3 August 1897.

8 WSC to JRC, 1 January 1897.

9 WSC, *My Early Life*, p. 120.

10 WSC to Jack Churchill, 29 July 1897.

11 WSC to JRC, 7 August 1897.

12 WSC to JRC, 17 August 1897.

13 WSC to JRC, 24 August 1897.

14 Sir Bindon Blood to WSC, 22 August 1897.

15 G. E. Buckle to JRC, 10 September 1897.

16 WSC to JRC, 12 November 1896.

17 Sebba, *Jennie Churchill*, p. 220.

18 WSC, *My Early Life*, p. 121.

19 WSC to JRC, 24 August 1897.

20 WSC to JRC, 29 August 1897.

21 WSC, *My Early Life*, p. 122.

22 Captain R. Kincaid-Smith to JRC, 30 August 1897.

23 Robertson, *Official Account*, p. 82.

24 Ibid., p. 83.

25 WSC, *Malakand Field Force*, p. 37.

26 Loyn, *Butcher and Bolt*, pp. 152–3.

27 Hopkirk, *The Great Game*, p. 500.

28 WSC, *Malakand Field Force*, p. 38.

29 Ibid., p. 41.

30 Ibid., p. 10.

31 Allen, *God's Terrorists*, p. 215.

32 Viscount Fincastle and P. C Elliott-Lockhart, *A Frontier Campaign: A Narrative of the Operations of the Malakand and Buner Field Forces, 1897–1898* (Methuen, 1898), p. 20.

33 Loyn, *Butcher and Bolt*, pp. 92–3.

34 Fincastle and Elliott-Lockhart, *A Frontier Campaign*, p. 52.

35 WSC, *Malakand Field Force*, p. 43.

36 Ibid., p. 45.

37 Ibid., p. 97.

38 Ibid., p. 98.

39 Ibid., p. 105.

40 Fincastle and Elliott-Lockhart, *A Frontier Campaign*, pp. 62–3.

41 WSC, *Malakand Field Force*, p. 105.

42 Hilaire Belloc, *The Modern Traveller* (Edward Arnold, 1898).

43 Fincastle and Elliott-Lockhart, *A Frontier Campaign*, p. 46.

44 H. F. Walters, *The Operations of the Malakand Field Force and the Buner Field Force, 1897–98* (Government Central Printing Office, Simla, 1900), Appendix A (1).

45 WSC, *Malakand Field Force*, p. 74.

Six: Knight of Pen and Sword

1 WSC to Jack Churchill, 31 August 1897.

2 WSC to Jack Churchill, 7 January 1897.

3 Cowles, *Winston Churchill*, p. 55.

4 WSC to JRC, 28 January 1897.

5 WSC to JRC, 12 February 1897.

6 Ibid.

7 Scott Daniell, *4th Hussar*, pp. 228–9.

8 Ibid., p. 229.

9 WSC, *Daily Telegraph*, 6 October 1897.

10 WSC, *My Early Life*, p. 124.

11 R. S. Churchill, *Winston S. Churchill: Youth*, p. 352.

12 WSC, *Malakand Field Force*, p. 117.

13 WSC, *My Early Life*, p. 128.

14 Fincastle and Elliott-Lockhart, *A Frontier Campaign*, p. 79.

15 General Sir Bindon Blood, *Four Score Years and Ten, Sir Bindon Blood's Reminiscences* (G. Bell and Sons, 1933), p. 295.

16 Fincastle and Elliott-Lockhart, *A Frontier Campaign*, p. 89.

17 Blood, *Four Score Years and Ten*, p. 297.

18 Ibid.

19 Fincastle and Elliott-Lockhart, *A Frontier Campaign*, p. 93.

20 WSC, *Malakand Field Force*, p. 92.

21 Ibid., p. 89.

22 G. J. Younghusband, *The Story of the Guides* (Macmillan, 1909), p. 184.

23 WSC, *Malakand Field Force*, p. 117.

24 *Daily Telegraph*, 12 September 1897.

25 Interview with Sir Angus Stirling, 12 November 2012.

26 WSC to JRC, 5 September 1897.

27 Ibid.

28 WSC, *Malakand Field Force*, p. 119.

29 WSC to JRC, 30 August 1897.

30 WSC, *Daily Telegraph*, 6 October 1897.

31 WSC, *My Early Life*, pp. 124–5.

32 Ibid., p. 126.

33 Ibid., p. 128.

34 George Crile, *Charlie Wilson's War* (Grove/Atlantic, 2002).

35 Fincastle and Elliott-Lockhart, *A Frontier Campaign*, p. 78.

36 WSC, *My Early Life*, pp. 129–30.

37 WSC, *Malakand Field Force*, pp. 125–6.

38 WSC, *My Early Life*, p. 129.

39 Blood, *Four Score Years and Ten*, p. 303.

40 WSC, *Malakand Field Force*, p. 102.

41 WSC to JRC, 5 September 1897.

42 Paterson, *Personal Accounts*, p. 111.

43 WSC, *Daily Telegraph*, 9 October 1897.

44 WSC, *Daily Telegraph*, 7 October 1897.

45 WSC, *Malakand Field Force*, pp. 161–2, 123.

SEVEN: HIGH STAKES

1 WSC, *Malakand Field Force*, p. 134.

2 Ibid., p. 140.

3 Ibid., p. 142.

4 Ibid., p. 147.

5 Ibid., p. 149.

6 Ibid., p. 150.

7 Ibid., p. 153.

8 WSC to Lieutenant R. Barnes, 14 September 1897.

9 Fincastle and Elliott-Lockhart, *A Frontier Campaign*, p. 115.

10 WSC to Lieutenant R. Barnes, 14 September 1897.

11 WSC, *Malakand Field Force*, p. 172.

12 WSC, *Daily Telegraph*, 7 October 1897.

13 WSC, *Daily Telegraph*, 8 October 1897.

14 WSC, *Daily Telegraph*, 9 October 1897.

15 Ibid.

16 Blood, *Four Score Years and Ten*, p. 303.

17 WSC, *Malakand Field Force*, p. 178.

18 Ibid.

19 Ibid., p. 180.

20 Walters, *Operations*, p. 51.

21 Ibid., p. 52.

22 Ibid.

23 WSC, *Malakand Field Force*, pp. 181–2.

24 Ibid., pp. 287–8.

25 Ibid., p. 183.

26 Walters, *Operations*, p. 53.

27 WSC, *My Early Life*, p. 138.

28 Ibid., pp. 138–9.

29 Ibid., p. 139.

30 Ibid.

31 WSC, *Malakand Field Force*, p. 188.

32 WSC, *My Early Life*, p. 140.

33 WSC, *Malakand Field Force*, p. 189.

34 WSC, *My Early Life*, pp. 141–2.

35 WSC, *Malakand Field Force*, p. 144.

36 Ibid.

37 C. R. B. Knight, *Historical Records of The Buffs (East Kent Regiment) 3rd Foot, Part Two: 1704–1914* (Medici Society, 1935), p. 567.

38 WSC to JRC, 19 September 1897.

39 Ibid.

40 Fincastle and Elliott-Lockhart, *A Frontier Campaign*, pp. 126–7.

41 Walters, *Operations*, pp. 54–6.

42 WSC, *Malakand Field Force*, p. 201.

43 WSC, *My Early Life*, p. 145.

44 *London Gazette*, 11 January 1898, p. 151.

45 Blood, *Four Score Years and Ten*, p. 303.

46 WSC to JRC, 2 December 1897.

47 R. S. Churchill, *Winston Churchill: Youth*, p. 361.

48 WSC, *Malakand Field Force*, p. 206.

EIGHT: A SPLENDID EPISODE

1 WSC, *My Early Life*, p. 146.

2 WSC, *Malakand Field Force*, p. 208.

3 Ibid., p. 209.

4 Ibid., p. 210.

5 *Daily Telegraph*, 3 December 2009.

6 WSC, *Malakand Field Force*, pp. 219–20.

7 Blood, *Four Score Years and Ten*, p. 303.

8 WSC, *My Early Life*, pp. 147–8.

9 E. W. S. K. Maconchy, 'Memoirs' (unpublished, typewritten manuscript in the collection of the National Army Museum, London, ACC No. 7908–62–1).
10 Douglas S. Russell, *Winston Churchill, Soldier* (Brassey's, 2005), p. 172.
11 *Daily Telegraph*, 2 November 1897.
12 *Daily Telegraph*, 6 November 1897.
13 *Daily Telegraph*, 9 November 1897.
14 WSC, *Malakand Field Force*, pp. 241–2.
15 Walters, *Operations*, p. 66.
16 Ibid.
17 WSC, *Malakand Field Force*, pp. 187–9.
18 Ibid., p. 190.
19 WSC to JRC, 16 May 1898.
20 WSC to JRC, 2 October 1897.
21 WSC, *Malakand Field Force*, p. 192.
22 Walters, *Operations*, p. 60.
23 Blood, *Four Score Years and Ten*, p. 305.
24 WSC, *Malakand Field Force*, pp. 243–4.
25 Walters, *Operations*, p. 63.
26 Ibid., p. 68.
27 Ibid., p. 69.
28 WSC, *Malakand Field Force*, p. 261.
29 *Daily Telegraph*, 26 October 1897.
30 *Daily Telegraph*, 13 November 1897.
31 WSC to JRC, 2 October 1897.
32 Sir Bindon Blood to Colonel J. P. Brabazon, 4 October 1897.
33 Colonel J. P. Brabazon to JRC, 1 November 1897.
34 Walters, *Operations*, p. 71.
35 Author's interview, Chitral, September 2012.
36 WSC to JRC, 12 October 1897.
37 *Daily Telegraph*, 3 December 1897.
38 *Daily Telegraph*, 6 December 1897.
39 WSC to JRC, 21 October 1897.
40 WSC, *My Early Life*, p. 149.

41 WSC to JRC, 2 November 1897.

42 Winston S. Churchill, *Savrola* (Longman, 1900), p. 30.

43 WSC to JRC, 10 November 1897.

44 WSC to JRC, 2 December 1897.

45 Russell, *Winston Churchill, Soldier*, p. 178.

46 WSC to JRC, 31 December 1897.

47 WSC to JRC, 25 February 1897.

48 WSC to JRC, 5 January 1898.

49 WSC to JRC, 19 January 1898.

50 *The Churchill Documents*, Vol. 2, p. 913; *The Times*, 7 April 1898.

51 Prince of Wales to WSC, 22 April 1898.

52 WSC to JRC, 25 April 1898.

NINE: A ROUGH HARD JOB

1 *Daily Telegraph*, 6 December 1897.

2 WSC, *Malakand Field Force*, p. 312.

3 David Gilmour, *Curzon* (John Murray, 1994), pp. 195–6.

4 Author's interview, Islamabad, 20 September 2012.

5 Author's interview, Islamabad, September 2012.

6 Author's interview, Malakand, September 2012.

7 www.qingqi.com.pk/home.php.

8 Author's interview with Pakistani officer, September 2012.

9 Author's interview Pakistani intelligence official, August 2012.

10 Author's interview, Bajaur, April 2010.

11 Peter Bergen, *Manhunt* (Crown Publishers, 2012), p. 69.

12 Author's visit, April 2010.

13 *Reuters*, 20 May 2011.

14 Author's interview with Pakistani military officer, Malakand, September 2012.

15 Author's visit, 21 February 2009.

16 Author's interview, 7 November 2012.

17 Author's interview with Afghan education official, Kabul, April 2012.
18 Author's interview with General David Petraeus, London, 21 July 2011.
19 WSC, *Malakand Field Force*, p. 312.
20 Bruce Riedel interview for Council on Foreign Relations, 24 January 2012.
21 Author's interview with Ryan Crocker, Kabul, 29 March 2012.
22 *The Churchill Documents*, Vol. 2, pp. 948–9, Sir E. Wood to Sir H. Kitchener, 10 July 1898.
23 WSC to JRC, 2 December 1897.
24 WSC to Jack Churchill, 2 December 1897.
25 WSC to JRC, 22 December 1897.
26 WSC, *My Early Life*, p. 161.
27 WSC, *Malakand Field Force*, p. 290.
28 WSC, *My Early Life*, p. 356.
29 WSC to JRC, 26 August 1898.
30 WSC to JRC, 18 March 1898.
31 WSC to JRC, 13 April 1898.
32 Aylmer Haldane, *A Soldier's Saga* (William Blackwood and Sons, 1948), p. 119.
33 *The Times*, 3 May 1898.
34 WSC to JRC, 19 January 1898.
35 WSC to JRC, 17 November 1897.
36 WSC, *My Early Life*, p. 177.
37 Ibid., p. 207.
38 WSC to Frances, Duchess of Marlborough, 26 March 1899.
39 WSC, *My Early Life*, p. 208.
40 Sung by T. E. Dunville, Lancashire music-hall comedian; cited in Carlo D'Este, *Warlord: A Life of Winston Churchill at War, 1874–1945* (HarperPerennial, 2009), p. 132.
41 WSC to JRC, 2 March 1899.
42 Gilmour, *Curzon*, p. 144.

43 WSC to Frances, Duchess of Marlborough, 26 March 1899.

44 Speech to Indian Empire Society, 25 May 1932.

45 Robert Rhodes James, *Churchill: A Study in Failure, 1900–1939* (Penguin, 1970), p. 299.

46 WSC to JRC, 15 July 1899.

47 Gilbert, *Churchill*, p. 90.

48 WSC, *My Early Life*, p. 163.

49 Ibid.

50 *The Churchill Documents*, Vol. 2, p. 949, Lady Jeune to Sir H. Kitchener, July 1898.

51 WSC, *My Early Life*, p. 147.

52 *Daily Telegraph*, 24 September 2012.

53 Gilbert, *Churchill*, p. 122.

Bibliography

Allen, Charles, *God's Terrorists* (Little, Brown, 2006)

Allen, Charles, *Soldier Sahibs: The Men Who Made the North-West Frontier* (John Murray, 2000)

Azoy, G. Whitney, *Buzkashi, Game and Power in Afghanistan* (The University of Pennsylvania Press, 1982)

Belloc, Hilaire, *The Modern Traveller* (Edward Arnold, 1898).

Bennett Jones, Owen, *Pakistan: Eye of the Storm* (Yale University Press, 2002)

Bergen, Peter, *Manhunt* (Crown Publishers, 2012)

Blood, General Sir Bindon, *Four Score Years and Ten: Sir Bindon Blood's Reminiscences* (G. Bell and Sons, 1933)

Bonham Carter, Violet, *Winston Churchill as I Knew Him* (Eyre & Spottiswoode and Collins, 1965)

Bowling, A. H., *British Hussar Regiments, 1805–1914* (Almark Publishing Co., Ltd., 1972)

Braithwaite, Rodric, *Afghansty: The Russians in Afghanistan 1979–89* (Profile Books, 2011)

Brake, Laurel and Demoor, Marysa, *Dictionary of Nineteenth Century Journalism in Great Britain and Ireland* (Academia Press and the British Library, 2009)

Brendon, Piers, *Winston Churchill: A Brief Life* (Secker and Warburg, 1984)

Caroe, Olaf, *The Pathans* (Oxford University Press, 1958)

Churchill, Randolph S., *The Churchill Documents*, vol. 1: *Youth, 1874–1896* (Hillsdale College Press, 2006)

Churchill, Randolph S., *The Churchill Documents*, vol. 2: *Young Soldier, 1896–1901* (Hillsdale College Press, 2006)

Churchill, Randolph S., *Winston S. Churchill: Companion*, vols. 1 and 2, part I (Heinemann, 1967)

Churchill, Randolph S., *Winston S. Churchill: Youth, 1874–1900* (Heinemann, 1966)

Churchill, Winston S., *My Early Life* (Eland Publishing, 2000)

Churchill, Winston S., *Savrola* (Longman, 1900)

Churchill, Winston S., *The Story of the Malakand Field Force: An Episode of Frontier War* (Longmans, 1898)

Cooper, Leo, *Young Winston's Wars: The Original War Despatches of Winston S. Churchill War Correspondent 1897–1900* (Leo Cooper, 1972)

Cowles, Virginia, *Winston Churchill the Era and the Man* (Hamish Hamilton, 1953)

Cowper-Coles, Sherard, *Cables From Kabul* (Harper Press, 2011)

Crile, George, *Charlie Wilson's War* (Grove/Atlantic, 2002)

Curzon, George N., *Leaves from a Viceroy's Notebook* (Macmillan, 1926)

Curzon, George N., *Tales of Travel* (Hodder and Stoughton, 1923)

D'Este, Carlo, *Warlord: A Life of Winston Churchill at War, 1874–1945* (HarperPerennial, 2009)

Eade, Charles (editor), *Churchill By His Contemporaries* (Simon and Schuster, Inc., 1954)

Fergusson, James, *Taliban: The True Story of the World's Most Feared Fighters* (Bantam Press, 2010)

Fincastle, Viscount, and P. C. Elliott-Lockhart, *A Frontier Campaign: A Narrative of the Operations of the Malakand and Buner Field Forces, 1897–1898* (Methuen, 1898)

Foster, R. F., *Lord Randolph Churchill, A Political Life* (Oxford University Press, 1981)

Gall, Sandy, *War Against the Taliban: Why It All Went Wrong in Afghanistan* (Bloomsbury, 2012)

Gilbert, Martin, *Churchill* (Heinemann, 1991)

Gilbert, Martin, *Churchill and America* (The Free Press, 2005)

Gilmour, David, *Curzon* (John Murray, 1994)

Haldane, Aylmer, *A Soldier's Saga* (William Blackwood and Sons, 1948)

Harding Davis, Richard, *Real Soldiers of Fortune* (Charles Scribner's Sons, 1906)

Hasan, M. Fazlul, *Bangalore Through the Centuries* (India Historical Publications, 1970)

Heathcote, T. A., *The Afghan Wars, 1839–1919* (Osprey Publishing, 1980)

Hervey, Albert, *A Soldier of the Company: The Life of an Indian Ensign, 1833–43* (Charles Allen, 1988)

Holmes, Richard *Sahib: The British Soldier in India* (Harper Press, 2006)

Hopkirk, Peter, *The Great Game: On Secret Service in High Asia* (Oxford University Press, 1990)

James, Lawrence, *Raj: The Making of British India* (Little, Brown, 1997)

Johnson, Rob, *The Afghan Way of War* (Hurst and Company, 2011)

Keay, John, *The Gilgit Game* (John Murray, 1979)

Keegan, John, *Churchill* (Weidenfeld and Nicolson, 2002)

Kilcullen, David, *The Accidental Guerrilla: Fighting Small Wars in the Midst of a Big One* (Hurst and Company, 2009)

Knight, C. R. B., *Historical Records of The Buffs (East Kent Regiment) 3rd Foot, Part Two: 1704–1914* (Medici Society, 1935)

Lieven, Anatol, *Pakistan: A Hard Country* (Allen Lane, 2011)

Loyn, David, *Butcher and Bolt* (Windmill Books, 2009)

Maconchy, E. W. S. K., 'Memoirs' (unpublished, typewritten manuscript in the collection of the National Army Museum, London, ACC No. 7908–62–1)

Magnus, Philip, *Gladstone: A Biography* (John Murray, 1954)

Manchester, William, *The Last Lion: Visions of Glory 1874–1918* (Little, Brown, 1983)

Munshi, Mir and Khan, Sultan Mahomed, *The Life of Abdur Rahman, Amir of Afghanistan*, 2 vols (John Murray, 1900)

Newby, Eric, *A Short Walk in the Hindu Kush* (Secker and Warburg, 1958)

Paterson, Michael, *Winston Churchill: Personal Accounts of the Great Leader at War* (David and Charles, 2005)

Pilpel, Robert, *Churchill in America 1865–1961: An Affectionate Portrait* (Harcourt Brace Jovanovich, 1976)

Rashid, Ahmed, *Taliban: The Story of the Afghan Warlords* (Pan Books, 2001)

Roberts, Andrew, *Salisbury: Victorian Titan* (Weidenfield and Nicolson, 1999)

Roberts, Field Marshal Lord, *Forty-One Years in India* (Macmillan, 1900)

Robertson, Captain W. R., *An Official Account of the Chitral Expedition, 1895* (Calcutta, 1898)

Rowse, A. L., *The Early Churchills* (Macmillan, 1956)

Russell, Douglas S., *Winston Churchill, Soldier* (Brassey's, 2005)

Sale, Lady, *A Journal of the Disasters in Afghanistan, 1841–2* (John Murray, 1843)

Sandys, Celia, *Chasing Churchill: The Travels of Winston Churchill* (Carroll and Graf, 2003)

Schofield, Victoria, *Afghan Frontier* (Buchan and Enright, 1984)

Scott Daniell, David, *4th Hussar: The Story of the 4th Queen's Own Hussars, 1685–1958* (Gale and Polden, 1951)

Sebba, Anne, *Jennie Churchill, Winston's American Mother* (John Murray, 2007)

Soames, Mary, *A Daughter's Tale* (Doubleday, 2011)

Steward, Rory, *The Places in Between* (Picador, 2004)

Tanner, Stephen, *Afghanistan* (Da Capo Press, 2009)

U.S. Army Field Manual No. 3–24, *Counterinsurgency* (Headquarters, Department of the Army, Washington DC, 2006)

Walters, H. F., *The Operations of the Malakand Field Force and the Buner Field Force, 1897–98* (Government Central Printing Office, Simla, 1900)

Wheeler, Stephen, *The Ameer Abdur Rahman* (Bliss, Sands and Foster, 1895)

Yeates-Brown, Francis, *The Life of a Bengal Lancer* (Gollancz, 1930)

Younghusband, G. J., *The Story of the Guides* (Macmillan, 1909)

Younghusband, G. J. and Younghusband, Francis, *The Relief of Chitral* (Macmillan, 1895)

Index